# MEDIA, EDUCATION, AND AMERICA'S COUNTER-CULTURE REVOLUTION

# MEDIA, EDUCATION, AND AMERICA'S COUNTER-CULTURE REVOLUTION

*Lost and Found Opportunities for Media Impact on Education, Gender, Race, and the Arts*

Robert L. Hilliard

**ABLEX PUBLISHING**
Westport, Connecticut • London

**Library of Congress Cataloging-in-Publication Data**

Hilliard, Robert L., 1925–
   Media, education, and America's counter-culture revolution : lost and found
   opportunities for media impact on education, gender, race, and the arts / by
   Robert L. Hilliard.
      p.  cm.
   Includes bibliographical references and index.
   ISBN 1–56750–512–0—ISBN 1–56750–513–9 (pbk.)
   1. Mass media and culture—United States—History—20th century.  2. Mass
media—Social aspects—United States—History—20th century.  3. United States—
Social conditions—1960–1980.  I. Title.
P94.65.U6H55  2001
302.23'0973'09046—dc21      00–021980

British Library Cataloguing in Publication Data is available.

Library of Congress Catalog Card Number: 00–021980
ISBN: 1–56750–512–0
    1–56750–513–9 (pbk.)

First published in 2001

Ablex Publishing, 88 Post Road West, Westport, CT 06881
An imprint of Greenwood Publishing Group, Inc.
www.ablexbooks.com

Printed in the United States of America

The paper used in this book complies with the
Permanent Paper Standard issued by the National
Information Standards Organization (Z39.48–1984).

10 9 8 7 6 5 4 3 2 1

# Contents

# Preface

The 1960s and 1970s were exciting years to be living in Washington, D.C., especially if one was working in the federal government. It was a time of repression and a time of freedom. It was a time of conservatism and a time of change. Part of the political establishment attempted to maintain the status quo of civil rights and civil liberties. Another part listened to the will of the people and attempted to reflect, in Congressional legislation and executive branch orders, the demands for more democracy.

Most politicians pursued a war and most of the public opposed it—and the latter succeeded in stopping it. The will of the people persuaded one President not to run for reelection and forced another President to resign.

People marched-in, sat-in, taught-in, and loved-in. It was a time of nonviolent ferment that had rarely been seen before in this country or, for that matter, in almost any other country in the world. It resulted in profound, albeit mostly transitory, cultural and social change. Remarkably, it was a revolt without guns, a revolution without bloodshed. The slogan was, "peace, man, peace." In fact, what violence there was came not from those who stormed the hypothetical Bastilles of America with words and music, but from the police and military establishments that were ordered to oppose them.

Through it all another revolution was reaching its peak, providing both the platform and the reflection of this social and cultural one. It was one that had been growing since the turn of the century: mass communications. Of the three great revolutions of the 20th century—energy, transportation, and communications—many experts believe that communications will in the long run have the strongest and longest-lasting effects.

It was the media—indeed, if the now apocryphal story is even partially true, it was principally one media personality, Walter Cronkite—that played a key role in persuading President Lyndon Johnson not to seek another term. It was the media, especially television, that helped the public understand what was really happening in Vietnam and helped the White House and Congress to finally understand the mood of the public. When the media finally began to show people, sitting in their living rooms in front of their TV sets, body bags filled with dead American soldiers, and when the media finally interrupted people's dinners with pictures of civilian men and women and children being burned to death by American flame-throwers, uneasiness and anger about America's role in Southeast Asia intensified. The possibility that the media could have helped turn the tide of opinion toward ending the war much sooner, and perhaps saved the lives of tens of thousands of American soldiers and hundreds of thousands of Vietnamese, was punctuated by *Variety* (a pro-industry journal) magazine's subsequent characterization of the media's early coverage of the Vietnam war as "no guts journalism."

It was the media that revealed the White House cover-up of Watergate and forced Congress to take action that, in turn, forced the resignation of President Richard Nixon. It was the media that let the public know about civil rights rallies and women's equal rights marches in Washington and elsewhere. The media told the nation about local and state governments' brutality against and even accessory to the murder of African-Americans and others who sought fair treatment and democratic rights in America's south. The media showed the public the brutal police beatings of protesters at political conventions—Republican and Democratic—in Miami and Chicago in 1968. It was the media coverage of the killing of anti-war students at Kent State and Jackson State that graphically revealed the barbarism of official government attempts to stop criticism of America's Vietnam venture.

While the media revealed the need for equal opportunity for the politically, socially, and economically dispossessed, the media didn't fully take advantage of the opportunity to do something significant about it. Conversely, the media often regulated and even altered its reporting to avoid fanning any flames that might actually alter the status quo and result in meaningful, lasting change.

The effective use of media held the promise of generating new opportunities for understanding, learning, and participation in education and the arts as well as the social and political spheres. But the media took precious little advantage of opportunities to do so, and even where it tried, the educational and arts establishments were frequently so intent on protecting their own status quos that the opportunities were lost.

I was fortunate to be in Washington, D.C., at that time, from the middle 1960s through the 1970s. And I was saddened to watch, after 1973, the gradual fading of the ferment and the dream, and—more than two decades later—to see what many considered remarkable social, economic, and political progress virtually wiped out by new attitudes and political action that began in the early 1980s and repressed and reversed democratic change instead of encouraging it.

As Chief of the Federal Communication Commission's Educational (Public) Broadcasting Branch from 1964–1980, I had the opportunity to help develop noncommercial television and radio to serve the country's cultural and social interests and to help educate the educational and cultural establishment to use the media. (One of my favorite mementos of that time, given to me by President Lyndon Johnson, is one of the pens he used to sign the Public Broadcasting Act of 1967.)

As Chair of the Federal Interagency Media Committee (FIMC) from 1965–1978, reporting to the White House (under Johnson, Nixon, Ford, and Carter), I had the opportunity to influence the government's role—through the FIMC's membership of 30–plus federal departments and agencies with media responsibilities—in using and affecting the development of the mass media. Among the FIMC's successes, for example, was the institution of an affirmative action policy in the government's hiring of performers and production personnel and in the issuing of contracts for instructional and public information films, videos and audio programs. This occurred, ironically to some, during the Nixon administration.

As Chair of the Educational Technology Subcommittee of the Federal Interagency Committee on Education (FICE) from 1975–1980—which was under the Secretary of the Department of Health, Education, and Welfare, and later under the Secretary of the Department of Education—I was able to help develop awareness on the part of the federal government, private associations and organizations, and the nation's educational establishment to the emerging technologies and their potential value for teaching and learning. I remember one highly controversial FIMC recommendation to Congress and the White House: that legislation (and funding) be developed to permit every student to eventually have a personal computer. Even many of those relatively few people who knew what a personal computer was back in the 1970s weren't sure why that was necessary.

Throughout the country, conferences, conventions, and other meetings of educators, media practitioners, and industry executives provided me with excellent forums. In my 16 years in Washington I delivered literally hundreds of speeches and papers. I unabashedly used those opportunities to advocate as well as to inform. My advocacies reflected, to the best of my ability, my beliefs in the need for a media-literate society, the need for wise and effective use of media to advance the cultural, social, educational, and artistic agendas of the country, and the need for the media to promote and assist change in those areas toward equal rights and opportunities.

I have selected here, from hundreds of my speeches and papers, compilations from a few that I believe best reflect the issues in America's counter-culture revolution of that period and that—I hope—had some influence on the progress of that revolution. Hopefully, these documents now provide not only an historical perspective, albeit a personal one, but still serve as a goad and perhaps even a catalyst for the continuing and future use of the media for change. In large part, unfortunately, the problems and needs discussed in this book continue to exist.

# Acknowledgments

Media, Education and America's Counter-Culture Revolution is an adaptation and amalgamation of some of my speeches, papers, and essays during my service in several federal government communication and education posts during the 1960s and 1970s. The book deals with the use and misuse of media and their impact—or lack of it—on our country's political, cultural, and educational development. It shows how we fell far short of what we might have done with the media, and suggests what we still might do. It covers a number of areas impacted by the media, including university education, elementary and secondary schooling, children and visual literacy, television and the inner city, the media and racial and ethnic groups, the media and women, commercial and public television, and media and the arts.

All of these issues are discussed in the context of the political and social changes that occurred in this country during the 1960s through the late 1970s, such as student protests, alternative lifestyles, the civil rights revolution, anti-Vietnam war demonstrations, civil liberties actions, and the women's movement.

It was not easy in those years to take an anti-establishment stand, as these chapters will reveal I frequently did, especially if one was working for the establishment. It made it easier knowing I was not alone—buoyed and encouraged at the FCC by the uncompromising pro–public-interest stands of Commissioner Nicholas Johnson, and aided and frequently abetted by my principal assistants, Allen Myers and Beverly Taylor, and my secretary, Minnie Rainey. The FCC's first African-American Commissioner, Benjamin Hooks, was supportive of my efforts to inject affirmative action concerns into the public broadcasting establishment. Friends in Congress such as Democrat John Dow, and Republican Orval Hansen, who sometimes broke with their parties to do the right thing for the public, were personal role models for my doing and saying what I felt was the right thing. Praise for my papers and speeches from another friend, Chief Justice of the New York State Supreme Court Appellate Division Harold A. Stevens, provided strong encouragement. Public interest group heads like Nolan Bowie, Pluria Marshall and Domingo Nick Reyes, media executives like Charles Benton of Films, Inc., broadcasters, administrators and researchers such as Carroll Newsom, Harold Taylor, Howard Myrick, Sandy Bennett, Bob Lincoln, Cecil Hale, Jerry Sandler, Bernarr Cooper, Barbara Allen, George Hall, Gertrude Barnstone, Ralph Jennings, Hallock Hoffman, Betty Jo Mayeske, John Schwarzwalder, Vicki O'Donnell, Mary Umolu, Emil Greenberg, Morrie Novik and Bert Cowlan, government colleagues like FCC Chair Bill Henry, Hy Goldin, George Smith, Elizabeth Duncan Koontz, George Daoust, Chester Higgins, Bob Main, Rick Jerue, Art Stambler, Ted Harris, Alex Korn, Wilson Dizard, Dave Berkman, Eileen McClay, Connie Holleran and Bernie Michael, IUC colleagues such as Dorothy Davies and Jean Leva, activist friends such as John Randolph, Shaf Nader and Caesar Chavez, writer and teacher Erik Barnouw and critic-educator Robert Lewis Shayon inspirited me. Commissioners and Chairs of the FCC Rosel Hyde, Bob Lee and Jim Quello, who may have disagreed with some or most of my stands, supported my right to make them. Magazine publisher Chuck Tepfer was more than generous with his support of my efforts. Others whose names belong above I ask to forgive my temporary lapse of memory.

Mary Ellen Verheyden-Hilliard and my children, Mark and Mara, gave me encouragement, ideas, critiques—and patience—during the years the speeches and papers in this book were developed and presented, for which I am most grateful.

William Cody and Louise Jacob, Ablex acquisitions editor and production editor respectively, Greenwood production editor Linda Ellis-Stiewing and copy editor Nina Sheldon have my thanks for their good work in seeing this book through to publication. I appreciate Christina Braidotti's proofreading. I thank Carla Brooks Johnston for her reinforcement and special help with this book.

# CHAPTER 1

# Motive, Myth, and Media

As in most countries of the world, whether in Europe, Asia, Africa, or the Americas, counter-culture protests usually begin in educational institutions, with the protesters finding fault with one or more aspects of their education. Students have traditionally been in the forefront of efforts to change society, perhaps because of greater awareness than the general public of ideas and issues; perhaps because youth's perceptions of self-immortality create delusions of personal safety; perhaps because inexperience in the real world of labor and management strife, of oppressed and oppressor, over-simplifies the problems and consequences of protest; and perhaps yet-to-be-tested responsibility for others creates naïvete. Whatever the reasons, students have created change.

Sometimes, protests begin over little things: the quality of food in the college dining hall, the crowded conditions of dormitory rooms, harsh disciplinary rules, or the length or difficulty of term papers and examinations. Sometimes, larger issues of life and death motivate the protesters. War. Dictatorship. Pollution. Freedom. It is the latter that fuels the strongest protests. Although the counter-culture revolution in the United States in the 1960s and 1970s developed out of a number of different concerns, it was the U.S. role in the war in Vietnam that became the focal point. Because the protesters were in large part university students, educational institutions became substitute targets for a government and military considerably less vulnerable to protest than university buildings and administrators.

A combination of lifestyle and political issues prompted the student movements in the United States. Disillusionment with the establishment was fueled by the assassination of President John F. Kennedy and what appeared to many to be the cover-up of his killers and a likely conspiracy. The initiation of a draft, which principally affected college-age males, spurred protests against the Selective Service System, including public burning of draft cards. So concerned was the government with these protests, that it caused the arrest and prosecution of a student who wore a jacket emblazoned with the words, "Fuck the Draft." The Supreme Court subsequently upheld the student's First Amendment rights to such freedom of expression. Ronald Reagan's early political successes were based in part on his opposition to student protests when he was governor of California. But the students persisted, with the development in 1964 at the University of California at Berkeley of what came to be called the Free Speech Movement.

Social conditions as well as the Vietnam War spurred protests. At UCLA, students marched with Cesar Chavez as he sought decent working and living conditions for his United Farm Workers and helped Chavez gain national support for the migrant workers that culminated in a nationwide grape boycott that resulted in recognition of the United Farm Workers by the farm owners. Students began to demand that universities recognize the needs of so-called minority groups, provide previously denied opportunities to members of those groups to obtain higher education, add faculty members from those groups who could serve as role models for students, develop courses designed to serve the special needs of those students, and offer a wider, more democratic multicultural understanding to all students.

Unlike the apathetic, status-quo oriented students of the post–Reagan era, who as children were highly influenced by the Reagan yuppie "me-me-me" philosophy, the so-called "sixties" generation expressed concern for other people, in what they considered an oppressive, unfair, insensitive society. Their concerns were reflected in their participation in the civil rights movement in the southern United States in the early 1960s, risking—and encountering—not only bodily harm and incarceration, but even death. A few years later, in the early 1970s, the burgeoning women's movement for equal rights attracted many university students to its efforts.

Some protests were directed at university administrations that appeared to ignore the issues by not committing their institutions to action on the specified topic. Students who felt that the universities were abandoning their educational responsibilities by concentrating on amorphous theory and ignoring direct application of theory to attempt to solve society's ills gained both publicity and notoriety by taking over some key offices and buildings of their institutions, principally through sit-ins in presidents' offices. Such a takeover at Columbia University in 1968 sparked similar student action elsewhere. Sympathetic faculty, while rarely participating in physical actions, held teach-ins.

Not only were there protests, but student organizations dedicated to continuing the protests were formed. Some organizations, such as The

Weathermen, espoused violence as the only way to make the general public aware of the seriousness of a problem. Violence directed at the perceived enemy—in this case, the U.S. military—occurred on a number of campuses, such as the burning of ROTC buildings at Rice University and other schools. Other groups, such as the Students for a Democratic Society (SDS), were committed to action of a less violent kind, but were painted with the same brush by the media.

The media played key roles. At first ignoring the protests in the belief that lack of publicity would force the protesters to give up their campaigns, the media could eventually no longer ignore the swelling tide or the critical news nature of these events and began to cover the student protests, albeit in large part slighting the substance and emphasizing the sensational. The protesters, aware that they needed media coverage to reach the public with their messages, were not deterred by an unsympathetic press. Instead, they increased their efforts to break through the media censorship. In part, it was the media's reluctance to provide a forum for the protesters, as they did for the students' antagonists, that prompted some students to resort to violence as a means of obtaining reportage of their concerns.

The media concentrated on the bizarre in representing counter-culture revolutionists. Even now, more than a generation after, people who discuss the protesters of the 1960s and 1970s tend to describe them as long-haired, unwashed, funkily dressed, dope-taking, alcoholic, violent, foul-mouthed, and amoral. While there were many counter-culturists who fit into one or more of those categories—as would be true for any group of young people at any time—the overwhelming majority were average middle-class people, reflecting the average middle-class American in their behavior and dress. The counter-culture revolution was not so much about politics, although it was sparked by concerns about war and civil rights, but about the quality of life. The counter-culturists sought peaceful, cooperative existences for whatever lifestyle they chose. They did not, as the establishment did, attempt to impose their concepts of proper behavior on others, but principally withdrew from those aspects of the world they found oppressive. Music became both a foundation and an outlet. Woodstock was both the medium and message, reflecting the communal, love-thy-neighbor lifestyle as well as the mental and emotional stimulation of the lyrics and the music. In fact, the hippies of the '60s were considerably less bizarre than the spiked-haired, lip-ringed, tattooed youth of the turn of the new century.

The height of the protests was in the late 1960s and early 1970s. The anti-Vietnam war movement dominated, replacing the civil rights movement of the early 1960s in intensity. The women's rights movement did not emerge as a significant factor until the early 1970s. Media coverage of the brutal government treatment of nonviolent protesters at the 1968 major party political conventions in Chicago and Miami, and of the killing of protesters by the armed forces at Jackson State University and Kent State University in 1970, were instrumental in turning the tide of public opinion against government policy and the war, and toward a peaceful end to the Vietnam venture.

Although the anti-war efforts were successful, forcing the government to pull out of what many called "the big muddy," many in the so-called peace movement saw society as immobile and unresponsive in accommodating new lifestyles based on human need and insistent on maintaining what movement members viewed as an oppressive culture. They saw educators strengthening rather than altering what counter-culturists believed was a stifling educational system. They were further disillusioned by the 1968 assassinations of two more leaders who appeared to understand more than most the need to change society, and who had given them some hope for the future: Martin Luther King, Jr. and Robert Kennedy. The Democratic party's refusal to give credence and support to Eugene McCarthy, the one politician the '60s generation felt best represented their ideals and goals, increased their cynicism.

The media did little to support their concerns and, in fact, denigrated their beliefs and behavior, creating an even bigger chasm between them and the general public. They were not to be accommodated in the world in which they lived. Many dropped out of school and out of society itself, and established counter-culture mini-societies. These freer lifestyles were most often reflected in communes, in both urban and rural settings. Some of these communes, with the '60s generation now the fathers and mothers of a new generation and a still newer generation emerging, continue to exist.

One of the things that America and the counter-culture revolutionists did learn from that period—and what will be a recurring theme throughout this book—is that the media are the most powerful forces in the world for affecting and manipulating people's thoughts and feelings and are almost universally dedicated to maintaining a nation's political and cultural status quo.

Although this chapter reflects speeches given in the 1960s and the 1970s, the problems discussed in it still remain flagrantly unsolved. It has therefore been updated, reflecting in several places not only the 1970s, but the first decade of the 2000s as well. Thus, it provides a base for "looking backward." The remaining chapters of this book may thus be seen not only from the historical perspective of the media's role in America's counter-culture revolution of the 1960s and 1970s, but also in the context of the media's continuing relationship to societal issues at the beginning of the new millennium.

The following is an adaptation of material from an address, "The Requirements for Progress," to the American Management Association Second International Conference on Education and Training, August 9, 1966, New York City; an address, "Television in Education: For Which Century?" to the 17th annual convention of the Audio-Visual Department of the National Education Association, April 3, 1967, Atlantic City, NJ; and an address, "Telecommunications and the Future of Education," to the World Future Society Conference on Education, October 20, 1978, Houston, TX.

In the early 1970s college students were figuratively if not literally burning down college buildings because they were frustrated with trying to change a system that was so amorphous that it slipped in and out of their hands like quicksilver. They decided that the only way to make education in this country—or in any other country, for that matter—relevant to society and ideas, rather than to administrators and mortar, was to burn down the existing system and start from scratch with at least some of the vistas of what the 20th century could have been.

Most people reading this are dissatisfied in one way or another with the educational system as it now stands, both the formal one and the informal one that reaches the mass of the people through the media. But, like virtually all people who are dissatisfied with anything in the world, most of us would rather talk about it than do anything about it. Even at the point of outrage, unless we are so affected by something that it becomes virtually a matter of life or death, we will rarely take any overt action to change it.

Most of the time we pretend that what is happening is not so. We—sometimes unconsciously—search for almost any reason to shift our attention from a reality that would either require our action or would give us feelings of guilt. For example, all of us ostensibly are against war, yet for years many of us who were able to at the time refused to participate in or even recognize the unprecedented public protest against United States activities in Southeast Asia; we shifted our concern to being more shocked at the appearance of some of the protesters than at the government's actions in Vietnam.

We do the same thing with our children's education. We spend five years helping infants grow, helping them develop independent minds and bodies. Then shortly after they turn five years of age we abruptly lock them up for five hours a day, five days a week in a regimen designed to prevent them from further physical and mental exploration and growth as individual, unique human beings. We put them in schools that, under the guise of cultural solidification, strive for cultural conformity.

Virtually every school system, every school, and every classroom is still doing, today, what was done before that radical technologist Gutenberg invented movable type, before the printing press made ideas and information available from many sources, before the monks and scholars could no longer force exclusive dependence on a teacher-spewed, student-swallowed-and-regurgitated system of education. Despite the fact that today we have film, television, radio, computers and the Internet, satellites, and many other ways to open up the world and to provide opportunity for individualized learning for every student, the educational system has not changed essentially. Its focal point still is the teacher, not the learner.

Educators, by and large, resist change and too many of them continue to categorize as a frill, as something peripheral, as educational nonsense, and even as harmful that which offers the greatest opportunity we have today to lead and strengthen education in the new millennium, to pull education, educational institutions, and educators out of the 19th century and into the 21st century: mass communications.

Of the three great revolutions of the past one hundred years—energy, transportation and communications—communications has given us the tools, the necessity and the content for change, all in one and all at once, which we have only barely begun to use and—only vaguely—to comprehend. To use communications effectively—that is, to use communications to directly solve critical social, political, economic, environmental, health and educational problems of the world—requires the creation and the implementation of unprecedented change.

The term communications, as used here, refers to all forms of interpersonal and intergroup contact: the so-called mass media, such as cyberspace, radio, television, film, and print; the performing arts, including theater, dance, and music, not as entertainment, but in their roles as communicators of thought, feeling and motivation; the graphic and plastic arts, including painting, sculpture, and calligraphy; architecture, not as a box to hold people, but as a process to intellectually and emotionally move and free people; electronic systems such as computers; satellites; the still developing lasers and holographs; and, of critical importance, person-to-person communications. Too often these forms have been ill-used, misused, or not used at all. Only accidentally or with tentative sporadicity have they been applied to directly solve critical human problems.

Because the contents of this book deal with the counter-culture revolution of the 1960s and 1970s, the emphasis is on those media most accessible and most used for mass interchange during that period, especially television, and on the uses of the media available at that time to solve problems in our society. Several decades later, as this is being written, television remains the most popular medium. At the beginning of the year 2000, 92% of adults over 18 watched television, 84% listened to the radio, 81% read newspapers, and 23% used the Internet, although the latter figure is expected to continue to increase dramatically during the next decade.

As noted earlier, much of the material here is based on my speeches and papers during 16 years in several federal positions. It addresses a variety of audiences on a variety of communications subjects: educational systems and institutions devoted to the needs of the learner and not to the convenience of the teacher and administrator; government responsibility to provide media access for all citizens; media ownership by minorities; communications within the inner city and for suburbia; use of the media to make the arts and museums as available to the masses as to the elite; public broadcasting as a legitimate alternative to commercial broadcasting; and, basic to all, television literacy to enable us to control the media rather than, as continues to happen, the media controlling us.

People and communications have become so interdependent that sometimes we do not differentiate between what is conveyed and the means by which it is being conveyed, by whom and to whom. Have we lost sight of what we are saying, in our efforts to find better and more efficient ways of saying it?

Is the medium the message? Hasn't this slogan become an entity unto itself apart from what it says, proving its own point? Is anything changed if we say, instead, the conveyor is the content? The name Marshall McLuhan, for example, carries more than just the designation of a person or the description of an idea: it carries a combined intellectual and emotional reaction that means more than content alone.

When McLuhan said, "The medium is the message," it was a startling idea. It still is. Think about it. It removes from our individual conscious control the effect of the communications input that reaches us. It is a revolutionary statement, as controversial as if Freud had said it—which, of course, in effect, he did.

It is still a surprise to learn that some people are still surprised to learn that media are more than means of transmission, that in themselves they can affect thought and feeling, that amorphous, nonsubstantial, a-human electronic communications have profound impact as substance as well as process. It started neither with Freud nor with McLuhan. We have known the nature of communications ever since the first human uttered the first sound and danced the first dance and painted the first picture on the wall of a cave to communicate something to another human. Hasn't music always been communicated as substance as well as process? Isn't the medium of music also the message? Beethoven didn't write those opening four notes of the Fifth for a flute! Artists, as the perceptors and the preceptors of the philosophical myth of the age in which they live, have long recognized the interactive relationship of media to people.

The term myth, as used here, refers to that which we live by, that which explains our customs, institutions, rites and social phenomena. It is the *raison d'être* of life, it is why one feels about things the way one does. It is manifest in everyone's life. It is the invisible gestalt of society and the world at a given time.

In ancient Greek times, for example, people believed that they had no free will. They believed that they had no determination of what life could be. Everything ostensibly was predetermined and left in the laps of the gods. Later on, two thousand years ago, a new myth stressed the concept of free will, of individuals determining, up to a point, the patterns of their lives, although final judgment was not yet in their hands. The developers and interpreters of this Christian myth established people's boundaries of behavior within the confines of the societal institutions that they, the former, created and governed. With the growth of technology, particularly the developments in energy, transportation and communications, we have in the last century begun to see the emergence of another myth. Philosophically and in practice we are a society of interaction, a world in which people cannot act in isolation. Because of the many-sided contiguities between individual and mass, in physical actuality and in visual and aural experiences, we live in a mutual relationship with all other persons, things, ideas and experiences. Communications and transportation have made this possible; the destructive potentials of energy—such as nuclear eradication and contamination—have made universal group interdependence necessary for individual survival.

Artists have always reflected and interpreted the philosophical myths of their age. They have used the arts not only as entertainment, but as communication. Moliere's plays, for example, give us far deeper insights into the people, attitudes and practices of seventeenth-century France than do history books. This is because Moliere's plays communicate not only overt information, but through his use of the theater medium as an affective force in itself, tie our emotions to the people and events of his plays and enable us to feel as well as understand his time.

Throughout the centuries the use of the arts in the dual roles of content and conveyor of philosophical myth has become more deliberate and more clear. One of the greatest innovators was Pablo Picasso. In the 1940s, in an article in the *American Magazine,* Paul LaPorte wrote how, because of the new developments in transportation and communications, we no longer were limited to seeing the world through a limited fixed single-plane viewpoint. We could now see any given object from many viewpoints and from many sides virtually at once. The concepts of space and time are radically altered. Picasso not only perceived but presented this compression of time and space through his cubism. Through Picasso's art we experience a significant aspect of the myth of our time. The means of presentation prominent in the second half of the twentieth century—including multi-media and electronic arts—represented a continuity of Picasso's innovative leadership, and strengthened the affective role of art as medium, sometimes even without consciously discernible content.

The automobile is a prime illustration of conveyor as content. Over and above its use to transport us places, the automobile significantly changed our cultural patterns and our personal and public behavior as individuals and as a group. For example, until the availability of the contraceptive pill, the automobile probably had the greatest effect on our patterns of sexual behavior, relationships and growth throughout most of the twentieth century.

Television coverage of the events at Birmingham, Oxford, and other sites of the civil rights struggle of the 1960s did as much as anything else to effect the passage of federal civil rights legislation. Many people who tried to ignore what was going on could no longer pretend that they didn't know about it (as the Germans during the Third Reich pretended not to know about the concentration camps). Even many racially prejudiced people in the United States began to question their convictions when the consequences of their beliefs were brought before their eyes. Reading or hearing about riots and brutality in the streets is one thing. It is quite another when you see it happening right in front of you in your own living room.

A medium does not replace the content of the message; it adds to it. It provides complementary and supplementary stimuli, which make the content more effective and clear.

We have been thrust, in spite of our fears, our lassitude, and our immaturity as humans when measured against the evolutionary potential within us, into a revolutionary world. Each age, each era, has its own revolution, to a greater or lesser degree, and in this respect we and our times are not unique. Perhaps, through the exponential growth of technology, ours is moving a little faster and is a little more identifiable as well as a little more confusing than others—making our own roles and responsibilities harder to ignore.

Communications have potentially revolutionized thought, feeling, and behavior by enabling any man, woman or child anywhere in the world to exchange visual and aural experiences with any man, woman or child any other place in the world, and to do it in the same instantaneous time frame. Communications have opened our horizons and provided us with many-sided views, knowledge, and understanding that we did not previously have. We even react to new stimuli differently than our parents did. Our children—that is, the younger generation—do the same. Prepared for and requiring new and different educational processes and content, including the use of the computer and cyberspace, they react even more differently than we did and do. Yet, even though we continue to learn more every day about the impact already made by communications, we have not yet begun to consciously utilize the real potential of communications for the impact that could be made.

One of the country's most respected educators made the following suggestion for "improving" the education of students. "There's no reason why in a history course a faculty member cannot give a class five lectures at the beginning, say, and then tell them to read a number of books and come back in a month's time." As a step forward in the learning process this suggestion moves us from approximately the eighteenth century to the nineteenth. Too many educators are trapped in the educational myth of the middle ages. To them, lectures and books are the limits of the educational horizon, and even slight variations in their use, like the one above, seem to them quite innovative, even if centuries out of date. Education, whether it likes it or not, is part of the world myth. It cannot divorce itself—although it frequently tries—from the world in which it exists. Few educators would disagree with this belief. Unfortunately, verbal, platitudinous agreement too often is as far as they go. Look at the educational institutions and systems in this country and note to what degree education functions—or, rather, doesn't function—in concrete interrelationships with the other elements in society.

When one considers that education is the core of all world happenings—developments, progress, failures, and successes—it is all the more tragic that education is so deeply mired in a cultural lag so that, by and large, it still functions as if there had been no technological revolution. Just because educators (those who create, control and implement the functions of education) as a whole appear to be satisfied with a system still rooted in the eighteenth and nineteenth centuries does not make the system right. Technology has provided the opportunity and means to bring education out of the past. Yet, the public, as well as the educational establishment, is content to let it remain there by reinforcing its status quo and remaining there with it.

It should be noted that in the 1990s some governing elements of society made strong efforts to provide comprehensive technology to education and to teach and motivate educators to use it. President Bill Clinton and congressional members of his Democratic party attempted on several occasions to pass legislation that would accomplish this goal; the more conservative Republican-controlled Congress, matching in its philosophy the status-quo conservatism of many educators, rejected such education reform.

Communications—television especially and, increasingly, the Internet—have an inestimable effect upon people, molding our orientation to the world, our psychological and physiological approach to thinking, seeing, feeling, and learning. Education has not reflected this impact as effectively. At its greatest use, only about 20% of the school systems in the United States used television as an integral, ongoing part of the learning process and even in those institutions it has been used primarily to transmit traditional curricula and to reinforce equally outmoded administrative and teaching philosophies. As the new century dawned, 50 years had passed since computer-assisted instruction first was proven to be potentially beneficial to education. How much progress have we made in a half-century to make computers a part of every child's learning environment? By and large, only those students whose parents or guardians can afford to buy them personal computers or who live in affluent school districts have that educational advantage. Perpetuating the unequal opportunities that continue to be imposed by other factors, poor children are with few exceptions deprived of this relatively new learning tool. It is significant to note that even in some situations where students do have computers available, educators are reluctant and/or unable to use them to full advantage.

We continue to support a formal education system that tries to motivate the student towards automaton learning, toward memorizing more and more materials to spit back as a machine out of fear and pressure of not doing as well as the next student on those standardized mechanical storage and retrieval systems of robot-like teacher-fed and robot-like student-swallowed-and-regurgitated information measurements we call examinations. This insulting disrespect to the capacity and potentials of human beings to learn and teach reflects the ancient myth when people were thought to have no independent determination over the course of their lives, but were part of a philosophically systematized predetermination.

It is ironic that it would be considered blasphemous by most of American education if one were to suggest that our capacity is not to memorize, but to create; that our minds are not to store information, but to apply it; that we are living things with feelings and imaginations that can and should take the mundane and make it beautiful and meaningful for ourselves and for all the world.

What are the ideal goals of education? Combining the instrumentalist, rationalist and eclecticist philosophies, they are, or should be, the following: to educate the human being to achieve effective participation as a citizen in the affairs of the world, to achieve self-realization, to acquire some degree of vocational efficiency, and to attain ethical and aesthetic growth. Education has largely ignored the potentials of modern technology to facilitate the achievement of these goals.

Children presumably are getting a formal education in order to live more fully and effectively in the present and future real world of their lifetimes. Yet, by and large, we are educating them in a way that can be said to be analogous to tilting at the windmills of the industrial revolution. The education establishment seems to forget that today's students are going to spend most of their lives in an increasingly complex interactive society, with pressures to make instant choices from a plethora of options. Traditional methods of teaching and learning are of dubious value. Not only must communications be used to make us aware of and understand the new knowledge of the world, but its composition and application must reflect its function as message as well as conveyor.

Our schools continue to stress information-learning as a student's most important goal. Measurement of achievement is based principally on the memorization of data. Not only has such memorization become irrelevant, but with each passing decade it becomes more and more impossible. At the exponential rate at which new knowledge is discovered, by the time the child born today graduates from college the amount of knowledge in the world will be four times as great. By the time that same child is fifty years old, it will be 32 times as great, and 97% of everything known in the world will have been learned since the time that child was born. Memorizing all the information of even a small part of a given field is impractical. With all the world's information available at the click of a computer mouse, learning should concentrate on where to locate such information and, most importantly, how to evaluate and apply it. As Albert Einstein reportedly said, "why should I clutter up my mind with something I can look up someplace?"

Many of the brightest, most creative students continue to either rebel against or drop out of our educational system. Too many teachers and administrators continue to pretend that education takes place only in a classroom, solely from a teacher; they do not recognize either the degree to which education has already taken place and is taking place through the media, or that education is a process of learning, not teaching.

Education and its learning and teaching resources should reflect and be part of the total society. All experiences of and relationships among human beings, particularly in the early stages of growth, should at least be acknowledged if not integrated into the process of formal education. For example, there are today many college presidents, administrators and faculty who purport to teach students in the classroom to understand and respect the principles of American democracy, but the moment the class is over permit and even encourage the students to hurry off to fraternities, sororities or similar organizations to actively practice anti-democratic discrimination and segregation against other students for reasons of race, religion, economic status or similar factors. Look at the economics, sociology, psychology, political science, and other curricula of colleges and universities. How many courses—if any—require students to actually go out into the community and work with the homeless, with welfare mothers, with ethnic and racial groups, with political campaigns, and in other situations where they not only learn how to apply the classroom theory to the real world, but make a difference in helping people change society for the better? Most educators prefer to assume responsibility for only part of the learning of their students, abandoning their obligations in matters that may be controversial or difficult to administer.

One reason many educators reject the media as integral parts of the educational process is their embarrassment that the media's view of the world is broader than that of the classroom, therefore frequently calling attention to those areas in which educators are derelict. Television and the Internet, more than formal education, have stimulated student concern with the conditions of the world in which they live, and have given them greater insight than has the formal educational process into their personal critical areas of learning during their school and college years, including dating, drugs, sex, violence, making money, preparation for war, concern for peace, environmental survival, and alternative systems, styles, and methods of living. Considering the paucity of really controversial and significant material on television, the pertinence of our school and college curricula to the real world is bleak, indeed.

Education must not hide behind the noncontroversial platitudes and safe fictional rationalizations of Dick and Jane. Otherwise it becomes a philosophical collaborator with the people of Dachau going about their daily business in pretended ignorance of genocide while the smell of hundreds of burning bodies each day permeated their city; with the Chinese armed forces at Tiananmen Square in Beijing, indiscriminately shooting protesting students and condoning such action on ideological grounds; with the citizens of some cities in the United States stoning and beating small children going to school in buses and excusing the brutality as a defense of a way of life; with the representatives of right-wing extremist hate groups in the United States who shoot and murder people and bomb buildings such as the federal building in Oklahoma City, justifying their actions as a means of calling public attention to their frustrations and ideologies. Who taught these people that their bigoted, violent way of life is defensible—or, more significantly, who did not take the responsibility to teach them otherwise? The schools in which the child-beaters and bombers received their education were accredited by the citizens of their respective states and were supported in part by the citizens of the United States through federal tax monies. Education should be judged by what it does to people and not by quantitative yardsticks of physical plants, the size of curricula, and the scores on examinations.

Remember that it was television, by showing the excesses of opposition to the civil rights movement of the 1960s, that probably was more responsible for the democratic progress of that decade than were the schools. Television forced many people to see themselves as they were, even conveying to them a sense of ill in their own actions, and opened up new horizons of human behavior that should have long before been instilled through the formal education process. Technology makes it easier to extend education's responsibilities to the student beyond the classroom. Educators theoretically are not against progress and, indeed, are constantly conferencing and conventioning in efforts to raise the quality of education. Unfortunately, few are willing to go beyond discussion and to risk experiments that might really change the status quo. It sometimes seems that if American education is to move on time into the twenty-first century, we may first have to pull it kicking and screaming into the twentieth century.

In 1887 Edward Bellamy said that "there are three main grounds on which our educational system must rest; first, the right of every man to the completest education the nation can give him on his own account, as necessary to his enjoyment of himself; second, the right of his fellow-citizens to have him educated, as necessary for their enjoyment of his society; third, the right of the unborn to be guaranteed an intelligent and refined parentage." He wrote this in *Looking Backward*, referring to the year 2000. We are now there, and through the application of communications, we can, if we wish, achieve Bellamy's goals.

The question is whether we want to. By creating and maintaining the pretense of a child-centered society, we ease our consciences. We don't have to acknowledge our responsibility for the inadequate and frequently harmful educational system we permit our children to grow up in.

Parents who have traditionally had the position and the power to change schools are those of the middle and upper classes, educated and affluent, who have the time and the resources to participate in the process of education. They drive car pools, they conduct school fairs and auctions, they bake cookies, they invite teachers to dinner, they contribute for the principal's office rug and the teachers' lounge coffee pot; they are the pillars of the PTA. But in the last decades of the twentieth century we have seen a gradual change in parent power. Spurred by the civil rights revolution and women's movement, and made aware through the media that they are not only entitled to but capable of exercising their prerogatives to affect their children's education, lower income and racial minority parents, previously denied in fact or fancy equal opportunity to direct education in their communities, have increasingly led the way for change in their schools.

One of Bertrand Russell's comments on conscience during World War I is analogous to most parents' and PTAs' relationships to the schools. He wanted to encourage a pacifist to take a public stand on his beliefs, despite the arguments of some of Lord Russell's friends that it was unfair to make the young man suffer the indignities and horrors of incarceration. Lord Russell stated that when you stop a person from carrying out the dictates of their conscience, then you are creating a liberal.

The PTAs are full of liberals. That is what has made it possible for education to maintain the status quo. Extremists and right-wing conservatives are willing to act on their beliefs, as opposed to the reluctance of liberals to do so, thus giving the former more and more control of school systems out of proportion to their numbers.

In inner cities most parents have neither the time, resources or influence to participate meaningfully in activities affecting the education of their children. In too many instances the teachers and principals in urban schools don't even live in the areas where they teach, but are in nearby suburbs or other neighborhoods of the city where they won't be exposed to the environment of the students who they are supposed to understand and help.

In most outer-city or suburban schools, where parents do have the time and resources to participate in the educational process, these parents tend to consider it rude and improper to question the decisions and actions of the principals and teachers, whose major efforts frequently are to maintain the comparatively nondisruptive, acquiescent nature of the student body within a framework of a traditional, easy-to-administer curriculum. The needs of the children become, at best, secondary.

Educators who protect the status quo sooner or later become indifferent and even antagonistic to the needs of the child. Parents who are afraid to challenge the educators and the educational system are contributing to the miseducation of their children. Many of us tend to dismiss the action—or non-action—of those administrators and teachers we find incompetent or inflexible, by shrugging the word, "Philistines," and going about our business in the blissful certainty that some day these Neanderthal men and women of education will suddenly discover fire or be struck by lightning and our warnings and cajolings and pleadings will then be justified. As Pogo said, we have met the enemy and they are us.

We need to recreate a system whereby education is child-centered in deed and not only in interoffice memos. We need to instill in parents enough courage and responsibility to take action on behalf of their children. Risking confrontation with a principal or teacher, and isolation from other parents, is difficult. It is easier to continue to assure ourselves that we are child-centered by pointing to the things that we contribute to our children's education, such as money and meetings and car pools and cookie-baking. This relieves our guilt feelings for abandoning our children in the matters that really count.

# CHAPTER 2

# Tuning In and Turning On:
# The Trouble with Education
# Is Education

The '60s counter-culturists turned around the adage, "like father, like son," influencing the previous generation by one hardly a score of years younger. The ferment on college campuses prompted parents with children still in elementary and secondary schools to take a harder look at the education their offspring were getting, and they, too, began to protest and seek change in an educational system they suddenly realized was seriously flawed.

A key area of controversy in the late 1960s and the early 1970s was the emergence of technology as a teaching tool. Radio had been used to enhance classroom learning since the early 1920s. Television, still in its teen years as a regularly available service, had been experimented with in the classroom in the 1950s and over the airwaves through dedicated educational channels, including what are now called public broadcasting stations. A new service available only for education in the classroom, the Instructional Television Fixed Service, was made available to every school system, every school, and every classroom—if they wanted to use it. Personal computers, still some years away, had already demonstrated their potential value through experiments with what was called CAI—Computer Assisted Instruction. The experiments showed that students using CAI could move ahead in their formal learning at their own pace, rather than be held back by the pace of the class as a whole, or, conversely, the students could continue to learn specified subject matter until they understood it, not being forced to move ahead at the class pace without having adequately learned the material. All the media—most significantly television because of its immediate and wide availability—were found through research to be at least as effective in student learning progress as was the standardized traditional classroom approach, and in some cases much more effective, as measured by standardized testing.

In the 1950s and early 1960s a number of projects testing the use of television in education had already taken place—enough, in fact, to have verified the medium's benefit (remarkable in some instances) to the student's learning progress. One of the most dramatic examples was in American Samoa, where television opened an entirely new world to a society struggling to break into the twentieth century. The government-backed experiment in Samoa emerged as a model for the rest of the world. Television was used not to replace teachers, but to strengthen the classroom resources by enabling teachers to build learning activities around the materials presented on television. This and other television-in-education applications in various parts of the world prompted Rene Maheu, director-general of UNESCO, to state in 1967 that, with the availability of television, education must undergo a "radical mutation" . . . inasmuch as "education and communication are inseparable and complement each other."

Using new technology required new ways of teaching and learning. The educational establishment was not prepared to accommodate change. In many instances school systems actually purchased television sets for the classrooms, but did not reeducate teachers to enable them to use the sets. An article in the *School Library Journal* in 1967 noted that in many schools television sets sit in classrooms unused because teachers do not know how to use them. When television sets were placed in the traditional educational environment without changing that environment, the article noted, they were used badly when they were used. "The content of the television had been the televised lecture, and the content of the program a pasted-up workbook."

Although many parents, educators, experts and others made strong efforts to improve the educational process through the use of technology, education as a whole strongly resisted. Students throughout the country were being deprived of enhanced learning opportunities. The counter-culture revolution had not yet penetrated the sacred ivy-protected walls of education.

The following is an adaptation and amalgamation of an address, "Educational Realities: the Requirements for Progress," to the American Management Association's Second International Conference on Education and Training, August 9, 1966, New York City; an address, "Are You Ten Feet Tall?" to the Fifth Annual Instructional Television Conference of the National Association of Educational Broadcasters, the Electronic Industries Association, and the Educational Media Council, April 19, 1967, New York City; an address, "How're You Going to Keep Them Down on the Farm after They've Seen TV?" to the American Management Association Sixth Annual Conference on Education and Training, August 3, 1970, New York City; keynote address, "Communication: the Key," to the Human Factors Society annual symposium, May 25, 1976, Washington, D.C.; and an address, "Curriculum's Technology Lag," to the Third National Conference on Education and Technology, January 28, 1981, Washington, D.C. As you read it, note that what is said about the values of and need for television in education may be said today about the values of and need for computers and the Internet in education.

Early one morning some years ago I found my son, then four years old, busily pasting strips of cellophane tape across the dials of our television set. When he had finished, he stepped back, looked at what he had done, and in a pleased, confident tone, announced: "Now I control the world!" And he did.

For the first time in history, every child everywhere could learn what exists in the world outside of his or her fishing village or desert or mountaintop or jungle or farm or city. For the first time, millions of children whose abilities are wasted generation after generation could learn what is attainable for all humankind.

Television could do what John Dewey wanted education to do at the beginning of the twentieth century: bring the classroom to the world and the world to the classroom. He couldn't do this 68 years ago [in 1900]. He couldn't have done it 18 years ago [in 1950]. Not long ago I read a review of a new edition of Dewey's *Lectures on the Philosophy of Education*, originally written in 1899. The reviewer stated that Dewey's philosophy "has only a limited relevance to the problems in our schools and colleges that perplex us most." The implication of the review seemed to be that Dewey's stress on the socialization of the child—that is, the education that could put the child into an effective relationship with, including control over, the environment—was not entirely desirable or successful, as related to the potentials and needs of education.

The reviewer seemed to be considerably further away from the realities of education today than Dewey was at the beginning of the twentieth century. Not only would the implementation of Dewey's goals reverse the growing student-teacher gap, but finally we would have the means to implement those goals.

Most educators, administrators and teachers, some reviewers of Dewey's books, large numbers of parents, and too many legislators are not ready for twentieth-century education, no less twenty-first-century education, only a few decades away. One of the country's largest cities has for years refused to use television as an integral part of its instructional process. When the deputy superintendent was asked to consider the use of television in the schools, he stated that he had never seen anything good on television and that, therefore, television had no value for education. One must question not only his and his colleagues' TV program selectivity, but their awareness of research showing television's contributions in the classroom and their knowledge of the educational practices of the other largest cities in the country, all of which were using television as a formal part of instruction.

Parents, students, and educators are caught in a Sartre-like concentric circle which seems to offer no apparent exit. Citizens elect school boards, which appoint principals and teachers, all of whom have likely been through the same schooling process that perpetuates itself through the people it has schooled. Unless they have been exposed to alternative methods of education or have been sensitized to the unmet needs of the people, and understand that the present methods of education are inadequate, they maintain the fiction that the educational system that educated them is the best of all possible systems.

Even where television has been used, however, it mostly has been peripheral, a barely-suffered adjunct to traditional processes. Many of us have been influenced by the cry from the Parent Teachers Association (PTA) of South Conserve that it tried television in its classroom and didn't like it and that therefore TV was of no use in education. That it may have been used incorrectly was not even conjectured. We have heard the concern of the teacher who doesn't want television because it is inanimate and can't wipe the noses of the children when they sniffle. That books don't wipe noses either is not considered germane. Perhaps most revealing about such concern, other than the insecurity of many teachers at the prospect of being compared to more competent teachers on television, is what some apparently consider to be their main classroom function.

Education's resistance to innovation sometimes seems all-important, even to the point of ignoring research which can show educators how to do their jobs more effectively. So completely and thoroughly did over 20 years of research indicate that television is at least as effective as traditional classroom methods in the learning of standardized information materials that the Ford Foundation, after tens of millions of dollars of grants for such research, switched its funding to implementation projects.

It is ironic that what research proves television can do at least as well as the classroom is what some of us consider to be the least desirable function of education, but what most educators consider to be education's principal purpose: information learning. Whenever anyone mentions standardized tests as a means of measuring either ability or knowledge, they should be reminded of the group of economically poor Black children in one of the elementary schools in New York City whose Intelligence Quotient (IQ) scores went up an average of 20 points not long after a Black Panther group began giving them hot breakfasts before school, whereas they previously had had nothing at all to eat in the morning.

The principle use to which we have put television in education is not laudable: to fill the student with information. The fact that the outstandingly successful proponent of this approach is "Sesame Street" does not change the fundamental failure. We need to be concerned with the use of television to reach the potentials we have not yet nearly begun to tap: ego, self-motivation, and the relationship of learning to the humanistic needs of society.

Children are ready for media. In the United States, television has become the most important source of education for children. Probably more learning takes place today, in 1968, within the four feet in front of the television set than within the four walls of the classroom. I suggest that the same thing will be true for decades to come. By the time the average child has graduated from high school, he or she has spent about 10,800 hours in the classroom and about 15,000 hours watching television. The child who enters the first grade already has watched about 4,000 hours of television—more time than would be spent in the classroom for both a bachelor's and a master's degree.

Yet we continue to conduct our educational institutions as if the twentieth century and television never happened. Look at your—or your neighbor's—child's classroom. (Wouldn't it be interesting to be able to just walk in, without giving the principal and teacher a chance to set up the special presentation of "open house" or "parent's day"!) What you'll find will more than likely remind you of that song Pete Seeger sang in the early 1960s, "Ticky-tacky Boxes." That's where your kids are, with all the others, in the same ticky-tacky box, watching the same ticky-tacky teacher, looking at the same ticky-tacky material on the same ticky-tacky blackboard, sitting at the same ticky-tacky desks, reading from the same ticky-tacky textbooks, and even doing the some ticky-tacky problems and other so-called educational "work." All the children doing exactly the same things, as if they were all exactly alike, out of the same mold.

That's why it has been so easy to fool so many people for so long about such things as Watergate, Vietnam, Iran, and oil shortages. That's why, despite history's lessons of what the Goebbels of the world have done, there are so many Americans who really believe that we should not question the authorities' right to suppress information and to deprive individuals of their rights to openly question officials and official actions on matters affecting people. The schools are doing little to counter such unthinking conformity. They certainly discourage any questioning of their own philosophies, processes, and techniques, no matter how irrelevant or potentially harmful to the needs of their students. They tend to create a nation of sheep.

Whatever happened to old-fashioned conservative individualism? The so-called conservatives are no longer conservative. They are, in fact, radicals who are afraid of individual independence and want to return to monarchial or dictatorial suppression of minority, controversial, or dissenting attitudes or ideas.

Except for the comparatively few classrooms where the individualized learning of the so-called open classroom has been put into practice, schools are lock-step institutions. By the time they are halfway through elementary school, most children are already an uncritical part of the information-memorization-process that passes for education. We continue to let education make our children into machines rather than using machines—including television—to free our children to learn as individuals and become thinking, creative human beings.

For example, information and skills—including language memorization, arithmetic drill, history facts, and grammar, among other things—are still being taught by a live teacher when they can be taught at least as effectively through currently available technology.

Ideally, we should be able to have enough respect for our teachers to acknowledge that they are more valuable than machines and we should stop using them as though they were machines. Unfortunately, too many teachers do not have enough respect for themselves to stand up for their rights to be more and do more than machines. That is because they are not emotionally able to free themselves from machine-like teaching. They do not have enough confidence in their own abilities to face the challenge of a give-and-take learning situation. They are unable to say to a child: "I don't know." Most teachers are unable to deal with the fact that since the communications revolution any given child, from kindergarten on up, may know as much or more than the teacher in any given area. (The teacher who attempted to humiliate the student who insisted over the teacher's objections that there were no tigers in Africa was just uninformed. But the teacher who became angry at the student who presented a contradictory theory about the formation of the continents simply hadn't seen the television documentary the student saw the night before. Both teachers, by their actions more than by their lack of knowledge, are incompetent.)

The seemingly precocious child came along only rarely in the past: the one who was a prolific reader before the teacher began teaching him or her the alphabet; the one who knew the arithmetic table even before the teacher wrote 2 plus 2 on the blackboard; the one who had personally experienced many foreign cultures through travel with his or her parents before entering school. Since television, however, almost all children have learned considerably more than the syllabi even begin to imagine they have. Through television they have learned history, have been exposed to the fine lines of differences and similarities between countries, have experienced art and architecture, have observed scientific experiments, have learned from commercials how to read and count, and have even begun to develop a sophisticated understanding—as well as a distorted one from situation comedies—of family relations.

Those teachers who are incapable of the self-respect and self-confidence required to face openly the intellectual challenge and knowledge of the television generation invariably maintain their last refuge—authority. The corollary is conformity.

Television's purpose is not to replace teachers, but to provide them with resources and techniques that will reorient their roles into more important and effective ones in helping students learn. Through the use of media we can free teachers to spend more time on individualized work with students, and free students from the excess time needed for factual feeding so that they may devote that time to their fulfillment as nonmechanized human beings (even if it means destroying the teacher-beget-the-pupil-in-his/her-own-image syndrome): not memorizing, but creating; not storing information, but applying it.

For years, one of the most perceptive publications in the field of education has been *The News Letter*, published by Dr. Edgar Dale at Ohio State University. In 1967 Dr. Dale wrote that a teacher must be an "effective communicator." He stated that "to communicate is to share ideas and feelings in a mood of maturity. There is both the problem of values—the willingness to share—and a problem of means—the ability to share. New tools can sharply increase the power of the teacher to provide students with access to excellence. . . . Much of the excellence in the past has been recorded in books." Dr. Dale stated that access to books requires libraries, librarians, and the ability to read, all of which need to be increased. "But knowledge, ideas, methods of work, are increasingly communicated in forms other than those requiring high-level reading skills. . . ."

Teachers should not do what the mediated instructor can do as well or better. The teacher's task is to perform the unique human activities which media cannot perform.

The irony is that those teachers who cannot or will not adapt to a system of education where the child is the focal point can indeed be replaced by television or by any other tool or method that makes learning rather than teaching the key. These are the teachers who are unable to help people learn. They can only teach. They know their personal survival depends on their continuing to make children behave as computers rather than as human beings. It is not entirely facetious to suggest that if teachers spent their time helping people learn, entire schools of education as now constituted would disappear. One showing of the Soviet film "War and Peace" would eliminate the current class contributions of many teachers of European history for at least a week.

Students need teachers in the classroom who can help them discover what they do not know and what they need to know, help them find out where to learn, and help them interpret and understand what they have learned. But as long as the educational system remains the way it is now, that won't happen, and teachers will continue to be police officers and lecturers. In a high school in Maryland, an experimental combination of television and open classroom resulted in the experimental classes effectively covering six weeks of the planned curriculum in two weeks. The classroom teachers were at a loss. That high school went back to the traditional system of education within two years. What would the fourth grade teacher do if the third grade pupil were permitted to learn in terms of his or her capabilities and went beyond the fourth grade planned curriculum before reaching the fourth grade? This is, in fact, what has happened in many instances because of the head start with television. Many teachers, as presently practicing their profession, are eminently replaceable.

Progress does not simply mean using new techniques. What counts is how they are used in relation to the learner. For example, consider the experience of one child who was in the class of a teacher who put in learning stations. This was a new technique, an innovation for that elementary school, but innovations alone do not make a good teacher. The child was given a question on measurement on an exam. The exam paper showed a straight line two inches long. The student was asked to draw a stick three inches long. He drew a stick—with the knots in it, and even a leaf or two along the way. The ends were three-dimensional. Measured with a ruler, it had absolute perfect measurement, but the teacher marked it wrong, pointing out that it was obviously incorrect because the picture of the sample stick that she had drawn on the exam question was a straight line. Although the directions did not say anything about copying the original drawing style, the child had committed the unpardonable educational sin of thinking for himself, of being creative, of doing something relating to the real world around him. That classroom teacher, for all her attempts at innovation, hardly assured that student of the value of the educational system.

No wonder so many students are dissatisfied with their formal education. The child entering school who has watched TV—both the good and the bad—is much more knowledgeable, other things being equal, than the child who hasn't watched TV. But factual knowledge or information acquisition is the least important part of it. Most important is the impact television has made on the learning process. Today's students, from nursery school through college, are of a television generation. Television has given them a special awareness of visual observation and learning and has created the ability to relate nonimmediate, mediated experiences to live experiences. They have acquired a special awareness that enables them to learn more quickly and effectively through visual means than through the traditional print means. Yet, paradoxically, these students are also more capable with print means, having learned control over media in general through the more natural visual medium. They even read better than previous generations, having learned print techniques through television.

For many children, particularly those who are disadvantaged or with nonmajority-culture backgrounds, the visual medium is the principal orientation to concept and skill learning, and these children continue to be deliberately and effectively discriminated against by schools that continue to stress print as the principal medium of learning.

It is ironic that on one hand the schools stress reading as a goal, and on the other hand turn off children from reading by using those methods which make reading a chore rather than a pleasure. Children who have begun to read and who would continue to do so if they were provided the kind of motivation they find, for example, on "Sesame Street," are early on subjected in school to nonentertaining, authoritarian, print- and grammar-oriented materials and methods that make reading unattractive work rather than enjoyment.

We find too many schools and school systems demonically possessed with quantitative number measurements as an indication of reading ability. School boards have been known to have equated with Armageddon test scores that show high school classes reading at what is termed a fourth grade level. Accepting the quantitative skills associated with a fourth grade reading level, a fourth grader does know how to read. Reading, like everything else, takes practice. Those who enjoy reading in the fourth grade or at the fourth grade level keep on reading, and the more they read the easier it gets. But if the school emphasizes quantitative scores and makes reading, like every other subject, a competition in which there is one winner and all the rest losers—if the school makes reading a chore in which the goal is not to achieve personal satisfaction but to reach a quantitative level on a test—how can anyone be expected to want to learn to read? How many parents have had confrontations with the school librarian because their third grade child was refused the privilege of taking out a "sixth grade" book! How many times have parents had to complain to the public library because their seventh grade child was refused permission to check out a book from the "adult" (not pornographic) section!

Johnny and Jenny can read. The schools are doing their best to prevent them from doing so on terms most conducive and motivating for Johnny and Jenny.

The educational log has become a seesaw with a horde of children at one end and an artificially inflated teacher at the other end, with every child hanging on for dear life.

The mass media not only can provide motivation through visual and aural action rather than through nonmeaningful (to many children) print symbols, but can provide a socializing situation for the student, can make the outside world a part of the classroom, can make the real problems of the outside world the learning problems; the solutions learned—or at least the understanding obtained—is what constitutes education.

All students have seen war, seen assassination, seen civil revolt, seen the moon. Live. Close up. Why should we expect any of them to sit still while we try to teach them these things from a blackboard and out of a book? Why should they sit still when we try to tell them that a stick is nothing more than a thin straight line?

Marshall McLuhan recognized this when he wrote that "discrepancies between the riches of the TV feast and the poverty of the school experience [are] creating a great ferment, friction and psychic violence. . . . When children go to school they are filled with rage at the puny curriculum. . . . Why should they go to school to interrupt [their] education?"

Nevertheless, every day, we still conduct our educational institutions as if sitting on one's rear end within the confines of four walls for a certain number of hours per day for a certain number of weeks per year has something to do with learning.

There are three places in society where human beings are held irrevocably against their wills: jails, insane asylums and schools.

Yet, educational administrators still question why some of the brightest, most capable students, in Timothy Leary's words, drop out or turn on. The tragedy is that most administrators and teachers still place the blame on virtually everyone and everything except the most compelling factors: themselves and their inadequate educational techniques and processes.

Too many educators are living in the myth of the American past—the teacher as separate from the main fabric of society, a loner who was fed, clothed and sheltered by townspeople in exchange for teaching their children the three Rs, who was considered successful if the children achieved a fourth grade level of skills. The educator served a short-term purpose, not to help children learn to think and create, but to make them minimally suitable for some vocational employment.

There were also the rare, dedicated teachers, the ones who realized they were pioneers and who did more than just teach the three Rs, and who helped countless youngsters break from the poverty of the backwoods and the city slums and become the leaders of the new nation.

It was only when adults began to need the jobs that children were holding that child labor laws and education laws were passed and more and more children were kept in schools for longer and longer periods of time. Although the motivation was hardly laudable, the results were, for many children. For some children who were already in school or would have been under any circumstances, the long-term results were not necessarily beneficial. Teaching became a profession and educators began to be assimilated into the economic fabric of society. Where once many teachers may have been loners—the radicals, the revolutionaries by the very nature of their out-group status in society—they now became tightly bound to the economic and, to an increasing degree, the social and political status quo. Newspaper and magazine stories during recent presidential campaigns have noted that political experts were surprised to discover a trend toward conservatism among college professors during the past two decades. Just as the doctors, the lawyers, the assembly line workers, the union members had gradually become more and more assimilated into society and thus more accepting of the status quo, so have educators. Most do not want change. Change is no longer considered necessary to a teacher's self-interest.

Most parents are similarly satisfied and don't want change. Helen Keller once told about her cousin who didn't like Lake Normandy because her child came home from there "so full of herself." Consider that even some of the people who would most benefit from change don't want change, but want only to fit into the status quo. Many Blacks want their children to catch up, to fit in, and therefore they support traditional educational approaches so that their kids can be like the white kids—not realizing that a change in the educational system could give their children at least a chance at equal progress compared to the currently white-oriented educational tradition and curricula, which are hardly bastions of equal opportunity. A change in the educational system could give minority children opportunity in a new system oriented to no one but each individual child.

Both the success and failure of America is that it assimilates. At the same time that assimilation moves toward equality, it co-opts rebellion and change. Just when the majority of a minority begins to say to hell with this system, we've played your game and it hasn't paid off, the system begins to pay off. Just enough for enough people so that the desire for real change reverts to a minority of the minority.

Children are a minority. Change is not deemed necessary any longer for the teacher. It is discarded as unnecessary for the learner, for the child. The acknowledged minorities today—African-Americans, Latinos, Asian-Americans, Native Americans, women, the handicapped, the aged, and others—all have spokespersons to make their wishes known. But who speaks for the children? The children have no voice. They have, however, two strong supports: television and the legacy of the students of America's counter-culture revolution, who have been willing to act as the conscience of a nation when economic and political security make cowards out of most of the rest of us.

Students no longer are going to stay down on the figurative farm. There have been critical issues before in history, but they did not arouse student reaction and action as did the events of the 1960s and 1970s. The significant difference is that today's students grew up with television, having spent 40% more time in front of the television set than in the classroom by the time they graduated or will graduate from high school. They have seen the realities of the outside world and they are not willing to accept the insular, isolationist, esoteric irrelevance rampant in formal education, as did many of us from a previous generation, who did not have the advantage of TV. Television has made students today more aware and intolerant of an educational system and practice which force them to go out of the classroom and the school whenever they want to deal with the critical issues of the world in which they live.

Even presidents who filled the Department of Health, Education and Welfare and the Office of Education with too many people who were more interested in economic management than humanistic services were perceptive enough about the sources of power to understand the importance of media in education. In his Education Reform address to Congress on March 3, 1970, President Nixon stated that "American education is in urgent need of reform. We must stop thinking of primary and secondary education as the school system alone. . . . Most education takes place outside the school. Although we often mistakenly equate 'schooling' with 'learning,' we should begin to pay far greater attention to what youngsters learn during the more than three-quarters of their time they spend elsewhere. In the last twenty years there has been a revolution in the way most boys and girls—and their parents—occupy themselves. . . . Our goal must be to increase the use of the television medium and other technological advances to stimulate the desire to learn and to help teach."

Television is not a panacea for all ills. Too much of television in the schools reminds one of the classic cartoon that shows the school superintendent walking into a classroom where a teacher is writing $2 + 2 = 4$ on the blackboard. The superintendent says that what the school needs is television to make learning more exciting. The next frame shows the same classroom, but with a large television receiver up front. And what are the children watching on the TV screen? A teacher standing at a blackboard writing $2 + 2 = 4$!

Many of the better programs and materials are too often used incorrectly or not at all. But when television is used well it can be very successful. It can make learning exciting by bringing in experiments, live events, master teachers, dramatic sketches, practical situations and other visual experiences that are impossible or too expensive for each individual teacher to make available otherwise to his or her students. Unfortunately, even when these resources are used, they are too frequently teacher-oriented rather than learner-oriented and result in passive rather than participatory student experiences. It doesn't have to be that way.

In December, 1968, one of the landmark opportunities for learning in this century took place: the first manned flight around the moon sent back live television coverage. Every student in every classroom had the chance to see and discuss with the teacher one of the great events in history as it was actually happening. Yet, in the vast majority of classrooms and schools, including those where television sets were available, the students did not see it as it occurred. Many teachers arranged for students to read about it, to bring in newspaper clippings and discuss it the next day. Did one single principal or dean reprimand one single teacher for abdicating responsibility for their students' most effective learning opportunity?

Through television we can show the student the world: every event, every crisis, every procession, every problem. Through television, the student can see and hear construction workers building the city, men and women working on the farms, doctors in hospitals, lawyers in courtrooms, subway conductors, airline pilots, bakers baking bread, and even teachers teaching. They can find out from these workers what they think and feel about their jobs and how they relate to the rest of the world. They can learn first hand what is going on in Washington and Teheran, in Tel Aviv and Cairo, in Grosse Point and Appalachia. The 1972 live TV satellite coverage of President Nixon's trip to China opened a new world to many people. Right now any high official can hold two-way radio conversations with citizens throughout the country. [*President Carter did so in 1977, as did President Clinton on numerous occasions in the 1990s.*]

A television set is, in the minds of many, only a substitute for an in-person field trip. Yet, how many field trips offer the opportunity for close-up views and detailed explanations for every visitor of the most important aspects of whatever is being visited? Think of the last time you went to a power plant or a hydroelectric dam. How much of the intricacies of the machinery and its effects did you see? How much did you understand? How much of the details of play did you see the last time you were in the upper grandstand or the bleachers in a ball park? Of course, the excitement and glamour of in-person total participation is not possible through the mediated experience. The live medium is always better than the inanimate one. However, given the optimum experience from a field trip as compared to the second-hand one from television, how many field trips did the students you know take last year? One hundred? Fifty? Ten? To Washington? The U.N.? San Francisco? China? Iran? Moscow? The Middle East? Uganda? Afghanistan? Under the oceans? Up to the moon? They were in all those places through television.

Television instruction has thus far stressed the teaching of skills and information. "Sesame Street" has demonstrated how effectively this can be done. But television can do considerably more. It can motivate. Commercial TV has done that successfully. It has motivated children—and their parents—to buy dangerous toys, teeth-rotting candy, sugared cereals, and a plethora of other Madison Avenue inducements harmful to the user. Television has virtually ignored, however, another kind of motivation, that which relates to the ego, self-understanding, and pride—what psychologists call self-concept.

There are many ways a child's self-concept can be strengthened through careful and deliberate television programming. The child can relate his or her own experiences, thoughts and feelings to those of people he or she sees in documentaries, news stories and features. The child can be helped directly to understand herself or himself through specially prepared and presented guidance materials.

Learning through thinking rather than memorizing can be enhanced through television. Among the many kinds of noninformation learning the student can receive in the classroom through television is the simulation or game experience in which two or more individuals or groups are presented with a real situation—for example, finding the solution to the drug problem in their neighborhood or school. One group might be put in the position of addicts, another in the role of social workers, another as law enforcement authorities, and still another as parents. The format may include several videotapes of alternate solutions prepared in advance, and when a solution is chosen that tape is played to show the consequences of the choice. Each group of participants may be at a different site: classroom, school, city, even region. They are brought together by television so that even groups that might otherwise never meet or relate in any way are able to communicate with each other aurally and visually.

Simulations through television can be programmed for people who in real life are actually involved in the problem being simulated. Large business and industry organizations employ this approach frequently when they are faced with diverse attitudes or recommendations from different sources. Just as sociodrama, or therapy through role-playing, has proven effective, TV game simulation, with no real chips on the table, might motivate countries in conflict to begin to find solutions to their problems.

I have designed something I call Participatory or Interactive Television, to bring the viewer into subjective as well as objective relationships with the television medium. Its purpose is to create additional dimensions to both the medium and the learning experience. Television has been used thus far principally in a one-dimensional mode: as a conveyor, carrying stimuli from the television studio (or tape) to the viewer at home or in the classroom. The viewer has generally been passive, only rarely (and then incidentally and largely accidentally) physically participating in the television presentation-reception process. "Sesame Street" and "The Electric Company," as exciting as their techniques have been in gaining and holding attention and in motivating memorization, have not involved the viewer in active participation. In 1959 I experimented with viewer participation in a creative dramatics demonstration developed by Grace Stanistreet, director of the Adelphi University Children's Center for Creative Arts, for a commercial television children's program—the Shari Lewis program. The child at home viewing the program was involved briefly as a participant in the creative dramatics presentation in a way I will explain in a moment.

Careful structuring of materials and preparing the child in advance can provide the child at home and especially in the classroom with the opportunity to directly participate in virtually any artistic experience, even with a professional ensemble. For example, a performer does not literally and objectively see himself or herself on the stage. The viewer-participant can enact a role left unfilled in a play presented over television, with the director blocking the movements of the performers in the televised presentation so that the participant at home or in the classroom fits into the physical action. The camera can serve as the viewer-performer's eyes and moving body. The participant can see and relate to the other performers on television in much the same way he or she might do so if working with them on a stage.

The viewer-musician, similarly, can play an instrument as part of a musical performance with an orchestra or band, the participant's instrument included in the score, but not present in the studio ensemble.

The same approach is applicable to all of the performing arts, but not limited to them. Participatory/Interactive Television can include professional endeavors such as editing a newspaper in a newsroom, the classroom providing the reporters' and editor's tools, and the demonstration newsroom on television prearranging with the classroom the specific jobs the student-participants will fill. Participatory television may be applied to the architectural planning of a building, an office sales conference, preparing a restaurant menu—to virtually any profession or trade.

Participatory Television is especially adaptable to those activities of a democratic society in which citizens take an active role. For example, the viewer can be a member of a jury. The jury might consist solely of viewers, the case taking place on television as it would take place before a jury's eyes in a courtroom. An actual case can be used, with the cameras placed near the jury box, the participant-viewer ostensibly a juror seated at the rear of the box, watching and hearing the events just as the real jury is doing. Simulated jury room deliberation by the classroom (or home) participants would provide an otherwise unobtainable decision-making learning experience.

While we don't yet have the technology for true interactive visual communication, we will some day have it—perhaps through the development of the fledgling computer through experiments taking place at the National Science Foundation—and we should begin to prepare for it.

Instructional TV programs are experimenting with combinations of resources, including visual effects, live performers, dramatic sketches, animation, sculpture and art, music, inanimate objects, both ordinary and extraordinary live people, and even critical and not-so-critical world events as they are happening. Works of art and drama can be used not only to help the student understand aesthetics, but to explain the history of the times in which they were created or, as in Shakespeare's historical plays, to which they relate.

The artists at work as well as their works of art can be explored. Through objective camera technique, viewers can learn to understand the artist's intellectual motives and perhaps even identify with the emotional ones. They can observe the reactions of others to the art works and compare them with their own. They can judge these works with others in a historical perspective and analyze their relevance to their own current and immediate worlds.

Perhaps the most important contribution the media can make to a student's healthy academic growth is to provide an opportunity for self-esteem through individualized progress in terms of one's own ability and efforts and not in terms of those of other students. Computer-assisted instruction, for example, can remove the student from education's current system in which only one person—the one with the highest grade—is the winner and all the rest are losers. By making a student a loser often enough, the schools are pushing that person into a pattern of predictability—the self-fulfilling prophecy of failure—for the rest of his or her life. Most schools and colleges not only seem to be in the business of creating losers, but they organize their administrative resources to perpetuate the losers' lack of confidence by telling them publicly, privately and in every way the educational institutions can conceive—through tests, posted grades, report cards, promotions, awards—that they are losers, are being punished for being losers, and are incompetent and inadequate as human beings. If this seems to be an exaggeration, you need only recall your own experiences in school or college—unless you happened always to be the one winner per classroom—or you can talk candidly now with your children, their friends, or other students about what's happening to them in school today.

If the media do nothing more than provide opportunities for noncompetitive individualized learning, they will be worth every bit of support we can give them.

There is no question that television already has had a great impact on children, and there is no question that television can have an even greater effect. What is in question is whether we, as citizens, parents, and students, are going to take an active interest and role to make certain that television and other media are used in humanistic and positive ways.

# CHAPTER 3

# School Work and Homework

Whatever progress was made in local systems in the 1960s and 1970s in the use of media, specifically television, to raise the level of teaching and learning was due largely to the federal government. While the government resisted the changes in the political sphere demanded by the counter-culturists, it was not as threatened by the proposed educational reforms. In general, the government allied itself with those progressive educators throughout the country who recognized the potential value of media in education. Even administrations that were conservative in other areas were supportive of proposals designed to strengthen education through media use.

President Richard Nixon, for example, endorsed a number of federal projects to bring the media into the schools and advocated their adoption. (Although the reader of this book easily deduces that the author strongly disagreed with most of Nixon's policies, it is significant that the author, then Chief of the Educational (Public) Broadcasting Branch of the Federal Communication Commission (FCC), was asked to contribute material for the President's speeches; I did so, working with the White House speech writers on such material as Nixon's education reform address to Congress in 1970, which is quoted in part, below. Lyndon Johnson was a forceful advocate of educational broadcasting, and under his aegis the Public Broadcasting Act of 1967 was signed.)

Beginning in the early 1960s under President John F. Kennedy, a series of bills was passed by Congress establishing offices and appropriating funds for the development throughout the country of educational television and radio. The Educational Broadcasting Facilities Program (later the word "broadcasting" was changed to "telecommunications" and "educational" was changed to "public") was administered by the Office of Education (later the Department of Education) in the Department of Health, Education, and Welfare for many years. It finally faded away as aid programs were slashed in the 1980s by the Reagan administration. One significant program in the 1970s supported the development and acquisition by schools of media materials designed to foster students' greater understanding of the special cultural, political, and social contributions and needs of America's diverse ethnic and racial groups. Another program supported research projects using media that enhanced student learning and progress and that could be replicated on a national level. In 1963 the FCC recognized the need for television channels dedicated principally to in-school use and authorized the Instructional Television Fixed Service (ITFS), a microwave frequency system. When with the FCC I developed—with the strong support of FCC Commissioner (later FCC Chair) Robert E. Lee—the National Committee for the Full Development of the ITFS, which included regional and local committees that involved hundreds of educators throughout the country. These committees succeeded in helping the development of hundreds of ITFS channels, although, as it turned out, the ITFS service never received any dedicated funding from Congress, and after less than a decade the committees were disbanded through the lobbying efforts of the public broadcasting establishment, which became more and more concerned with potential competition to its stations from ITFS.

Nevertheless, throughout the 1960s and 1970s government support for media in the classroom was there. The problem was getting educators to use it.

The following is an adaptation and amalgamation of an address, "Television in Education: For Which Century?" to the 17th annual convention of the Department of Audio-visual Instruction of the National Education Association, April 3, 1967, Atlantic City, N.J.; an address, "Educational/Public Broadcasting: Universal, Unique, University," to the 7th annual College Conference of the International Radio and Television Society, April 19, 1968, New York City; and an address, "Alternatives for Education: To Improve Learning," to the 22nd annual convention of the Association for Educational Communications and Technology of the National Education Association, April 18, 1972, Minneapolis.

How can our schools take advantage of the visual orientation of today's student? How can we tune in to education a media generation that has been tuned out in many schools and colleges by outmoded curricula and techniques? How do we prepare children for the twenty-first century, where learning knowledge will be secondary to understanding its effects? How do we motivate children to recognize, develop and apply their individual unique abilities through pride and self-confidence? How do we prepare future generations to deal with the impact of the mass media on their lives?

Although little was done to implement his recommendations, President Richard Nixon's education reform address to Congress in 1970 included support for television and other technology as a solution to achieving more effective learning and teaching. "The technology is here," he said, "but we have not yet learned how to employ it to our full advantage. How can local school systems extend and support their curricula by working with local television stations? How can new techniques of programmed learning be applied so as to make each television set an effective teaching aid? How can television, audio-visual aids, the telephone and the availability of computer libraries be combined to form a learning unit in the home, revolutionizing homework by turning a chore into an adventure in learning?"

As citizens, parents and students there are some things we can do, individually and cooperatively, if we wish to see some of these potentials realized.

1. Through our PTAs, school boards, citizen organizations and student groups, we can insist that the media, including television, become important, integral parts of the educational process, not just reinforcing traditional curricula and techniques, but providing the student with new, stimulating bases for learning. This requires a reevaluation of teaching philosophies, methods of teaching, and training of teachers. It requires schools to reorient their priorities from serving the administrative ease of the teachers to serving the learning needs of the students. It requires PTAs to shift their primary efforts from tea parties, white elephant fairs, and rubber-stamping principal and teacher pronouncements, to direct and concrete concerns about what goes on in the classroom.

2. We can make certain that television is not used as a frill, but that it literally brings to the student the best teachers, experiments, events and other resources available from every place in the world. We don't even need ETV [educational television] stations. We can do this through closed-circuit use of films, videotapes and videodisks. We can do this through the newly developing Instructional Television Fixed Service. And we can even do this on a worldwide basis, if we wish. The development of satellite communications during the past few years of this '60s decade means that we technically can link every schoolroom in the world with every other schoolroom in the world.

3. We can see to it that schools recognize the effects of TV on the learning abilities of children. Because of the knowledge that children bring with them from television to their beginning formal school experience, we can begin to teach them much sooner not only how to develop their reading, writing and arithmetic skills, but also how to relate their awareness of events and people—through news, documentaries and plays—to themselves and to their understanding of the world. In addition, we must con-

vince teachers to recognize and utilize the visual orientation that virtually all children bring with them when they start school. For example, to teach them to read by using books as the sole or principal base is to work against their learning orientation and abilities, not with them. Through the use of television, a medium they are tuned in to, they could learn reading and other skills relatively easily and quickly. Programs such as "Sesame Street" have shown how this can be done. What percent of the schools are using books? One hundred percent, and rightly so. Books have been and should be a principal source of learning. The question is whether the print medium should continue to be the sole or primary method for conveying information and ideas to children who have grown up in a world where their principal stimuli have been visual and aural, and who much more quickly, easily and effectively have learned and can learn through non-print media. If the television camera, antenna and receiver had been invented first, would education today be looking askance at an interloping printing press and book?

4. We must be certain that the schools use television for more than conveying just information and skills. Television is an excellent means for motivating children, especially those who are disadvantaged or who have been the victims of discrimination or prejudice. The importance of confidence and pride cannot be overemphasized. Professor Jack Frymier of Ohio State University wrote in *Motivation Quarterly* that "positively motivated students tend to have a more positive concept of self." He states that "no person is born hating himself. No person is born feeling good about himself. An individual's concept of self is learned, and it is learned in part on the basis of feedback he receives at home . . . at the playground . . . and at school." When we consider that the teaching approach in most classrooms destroys the child's ego—if not through overt verbal abuse, then through tests, grades and other competitive comparisons with other children, which are unrelated to the student's individual worth—we can understand why so many children feel badly about school and, concomitantly, badly about themselves. Where we may be unwilling or unable to do something directly about the destructive effects of most classrooms, we can try to counterbalance these effects through positive media use. As noted earlier, this would require going beyond the scope of programs such as "Sesame Street," which, despite its excellent techniques, is limited principally to information and skills learning.

5. We must be sure that television is used in education to bring in the real world. It should give the student in the classroom the intellectual experiences that many of them are now forced to seek in the streets. It should provide full views of critical, controversial issues, and it should not limit them to the usual two moderate and generally similar opposing sides, but should include the many sides of any given issue. Television can reveal a great di-

versity of ideas and attitudes that most of us rarely have a chance to see or hear.

6. Similarly, television can provide each student with the opportunity to have his or her points of view made known. Student views are usually stifled or condescended to in the classroom, especially on the elementary and secondary levels. Many students believe that there is no way of getting their ideas and feelings across to the adult world, and therefore too frequently turn to an alternate, alienating world of alcohol and drugs. Others transform their frustrations into violence. Interactive television provides a way for the student to transcend the conformity imposed by insecure individual teachers, and permits the student to express himself or herself not only to a teacher in a distant television classroom, but to a larger number of adults and peers, to the extent that the television system reaches out to other classrooms and schools. The development of satellite, cable and microwave technology, and the availability of cartridge and disc recorders and playback units for personal use, permit the use of television not only in the school and in the home, but to and from the school and home, as well. *Technologically, we can interconnect virtually any place in the country and in the world for an exchange of ideas and materials, giving us all an opportunity to participate in the educational process, for the first time since the one-room schoolhouse, in an open, free atmosphere as close as education probably can get to participatory democracy.*

7. Once we have convinced the schools and colleges to use television, we must prevent them from limiting their educational communications to that medium alone. Multi-media learning carrels, for example, can utilize a multitude and mixture of communications resources from computers to talking typewriters, which enable the learner to obtain material on virtually any subject from many different sources on demand. The individualized carrel enables the student to learn at his or her own pace, not held back in a subject in which she or he is strong, not pulled ahead without fully understanding a subject in which she or he is weak. A student no longer has to be chained to the group pace of the class he or she happens to be in. A multi-media learning carrel can include video, audio, facsimile, print, reproduction and programmed learning machines—all computerized to permit the student to select, from one or more central multi-media library points, that particular learning resource material which is of greatest value to him or her at that moment of learning. Through computerized interface with programmed material and with similar easy access, electronically and live, to expert personnel (teachers), any student anywhere can have literally at his or her fingertips the best educational resources from any place in the world. [*In the year 2000, the Internet greatly facilitates this process; yet, the same argument made 35 years before for the increased school use of multi-media carrels may be made for increased use of the Internet in the school rooms of the new century.*]

A dramatic example of what machines can do is the experience in the early 1960s with a ten-year-old girl in Mississippi who had been promoted routinely from grade to grade by school officials although they were certain that she was retarded. She had thus far gone through elementary school seemingly incapable of understanding or participating in even the simplest classroom lessons, exercises and homework. She sat through each class as if in an uncomprehending stupor. Her school was one chosen to participate in a computer assisted-instruction (CAI) experiment, in which each student could learn at his or her own pace with a computer that provided the level and speed of materials as individually needed. The girl was permitted, more as a matter of condescending kindness than with any expectation of positive learning results, to participate. Computer results soon indicated that she was learning at much greater speed than, and far in advance of, the others in her class. Computers can be programmed into educational infinity as far as the human mind or capability is concerned. It was discovered that the girl was not retarded, but a genius. She had been so bored by the level of teaching that she had retreated into a cocoon, verbally and socially. How many thousands, perhaps tens of thousands, of youngsters like her sit silently in classrooms today, passing time in an educational atmosphere that does not permit them to learn according to their individual capacities? Technologically-facilitated individualized learning should be directed and heightened by tutorial assistance from the teacher, who can be freed through the use of technology from the traditional, time-consuming information lectures and testing and can devote more attention to individual students.

8. We can encourage schools to use machines to teach those materials that are mechanically learned (grammar, spelling, arithmetic, history, reading, languages, science and similar skills). This will permit greater concentration on and incorporation of teaching approaches that encourage the creative and evaluative abilities of the student—including advanced learning in the subjects noted above. These approaches include: flexibility in classroom schedules; curricular freedom for students in terms of their individual learning needs rather than the imposed needs of a large group; individually oriented curricula; development of evaluation procedures geared to the individual student, including the abolition of standardized tests; emphasis on tutorial work as opposed to lectures; educational environments consistent with the physical and psychological freedom necessary for the most productive individualized learning.

9. We can help the schools investigate the alternative means of transmitting television and other media for optimum learning and economic efficiency. Television alone can be received in various ways: through the cooperation of a local PTV station; via low-power, multi-channel Instructional Television Fixed Service systems, which provide up to four channels for simultaneous use and which can be installed and operated at relatively

low cost; through cable systems that can serve both homes and schools with the same channels; by closed-circuit, point-to-point wired connections at schools or campuses which can be operated live or in conjunction with videotape, cartridge or disc units; through satellites, which in another decade, the 1980s, will surely be linking educational centers in various parts of the United States and in other countries. Other newly developing techniques, such as laser and fiberoptic communications and world-wide computer interconnection, should soon reach economic as well as technological feasibility.

10. We can urge the schools to recognize the importance of media, particularly television, in the lives of young people and persuade educators to reorient curricula to reflect this importance. The need and urgency are discussed in this book in the chapter on "Television and Political Control." Most people in school today will spend most of their adult lives with aural and visual rather than with print communications. They will spend more time watching television than doing anything but sleeping and, possibly, working. At least three times as many hours each week will be devoted to being communicated to by television than by books, newspapers and magazines. With few exceptions, formal education requires 12 years—kindergarten through high school—of courses in English composition and literature designed to make the student intelligent and critical when dealing with print. Few school systems, however, require even one comparable course in the visual media. In order that we may have a nation of intelligent and critical viewers—as well as readers—who will be able to understand and evaluate the powerful mass media and not be manipulated by them, it is necessary to institute visual and aural literacy courses for all students from elementary through graduate school. Unless we learn to control our reactions and responses to television, television most certainly will control us.

11. We can encourage the classroom teacher to learn how to use television and other media in the classroom successfully. Many teachers are so insecure that they do not use television at all. Many others who do use it do so badly, guaranteeing its failure as a teaching and learning tool. In too many classrooms a teacher switches on a television set, sits in the back of the room for the half-hour the televised lesson in on, then switches off the set and goes on to a different subject. Yet, that same teacher is not likely to assign a book to be read without preparing the students or discussing it with them afterwards. The classroom teacher needs to learn, similarly, how to prepare the students beforehand for the TV materials, work with the students individually during the TV presentation, and follow up the televised lesson with discussions, projects and evaluation. Inasmuch as one purpose of television is to bring to the classroom materials (experiments, site visits, master teachers, news personalities, among other resources) that the teacher and school are not ordinarily or otherwise able to provide, the televised lessons must be integrated carefully into the day-to-day curriculum.

A teacher, to use television correctly and effectively, has to fully under-stand its potentials and know the techniques of utilizing it in the classroom. Through PTAs and other educational and civic associations, we can help the teacher obtain the necessary skills by convincing our school boards, teacher training institutions, and individual principals to require and pro-vide pre-service and in-service courses and workshops. Even these are available via television. It is pertinent to note that teacher training institu-tions in the Soviet Union, where educational television began in the mid-1960s (compared to the early 1950s in the United States) require every potential teacher to have at least six months of study in the use of technol-ogy in the classroom, including television. In the United States not more than one or two states at any given time have required formal preparation in the use of instructional television for teacher certification. Another Sput-nik gap?

Let's suppose that you are now convinced that the use of television and other media provides at least one of the answers to education's problems, and suppose you are prepared to make your beliefs known to the teachers or principal of your child's school, to your professors or dean, or to your community's school board or your college's board of trustees. It is easier said than done. Few college-age youth can cope with the angry tirades or sulks of their parents if their university reprimands them for challenging the status quo. As for parents challenging teachers or principals, I remem-ber the woman in the PTA of my children's elementary school who op-posed the establishment of an ombuds-office for the school. "I never have any problem talking with our principal or teachers," she said. "I just put on my coat, take a tranquilizer, and go."

Many people who might otherwise be supportive of new approaches in education turn away from them because their participation in achieving change may result in situations that not only are unpleasant but are fright-ening for them. One thing one learns from participation in a PTA is that even the most outspoken political liberals are more than likely to be educa-tional conservatives.

Some people, when it comes to educational innovation through media, justify their noninvolvement through what has become a classic example of super-sophistication: their self-proclaimed intellectual pretensions would be denigrated by permitting intercourse with the alleged low-level stimuli of television. That there is a higher percentage of junk produced in print ev-ery day than on television seems to be irrelevant to them. They do not trust themselves to use the same selectivity and self-control in choosing televi-sion programs that they presumably use in choosing print materials. We have now had television for several decades and still there are people—in-cluding educators and other habitués of ivory towers—who continue to in-sist that under no circumstances would they have a television set in their home. Indeed, a number of my colleagues in the Federal Communications

Commission who regulate the television industry admit that they rarely or never watch television.

Some people are against television because they believe it encourages sex, profanity and subversive controversy. They want TV abolished or, at the very least, placed under strict censorship controls. Others criticize television for its violence, exploitation of children, prejudicial characterizations of minority groups and women, saccharine pictures of society, censorship of controversy, responsiveness to corporate vested interests, and irresponsible hawking of goods and services. Most of these people, however, recognize television's potentials as well as its problems; they would not abolish it, but improve it.

One might ask those who advocate the abolition of television whether they believe we should also burn all our library cards. As noted earlier, a higher percentage of material put into print is worse, from aesthetic, psychological, intellectual and other standards, than that put on television. Should we prevent people from reading magazines because some of the articles and many of the advertisements are not worthwhile and may even be harmful? The answer, of course, is not to destroy either the television studio or the publishing house, the TV camera or the printing press, the television set or the book. The answer is to try to make all media, including television, more relevant and meaningful.

The question of relevance has been a difficult one for commercial television to deal with and, to an extent, for public television as well. Things that are relevant are also frequently controversial. Fear of criticism from commercial advertisers and noncommercial political or educational funding sources often results in stations censoring material that may be deemed controversial. The list is legion. It includes the infamous "blacklist" and subsequent "graylist" for 15 years in the 1950s and 1960s in which the broadcasting industry refused to hire anyone who was accused—not necessarily indicted or convicted, even assuming that artistic merit and freedom should in any way be dependent on political conformity—of being a communist, a subversive or even sympathetic to any left-wing ideologies. It includes the 1970s censorship of and ultimate demise of the Smothers Brothers show—which had refused to delete anti-Vietnam war comments by some of its guest performers. How often do we see on television a real live Ku Klux Klanner or a John Bircher? On how many programs dealing with communism do we see a real live Communist Party member?

One of the most comprehensive accounts of censorship in television was presented in the 1970s by David W. Rintels, television writer and chair of the Committee on Censorship of the Writers Guild of America, to the Senate Subcommittee on Constitutional Rights. Rintels revealed that a poll of Guild writers showed that 86% had found from personal experience that censorship exists in television, and that 81% believe that television is presenting a distorted picture of the political, economic and racial events in the

United States. Some of Rintels' examples of censorship are so disturbing that one is tempted to react with protective laughter. In one script he and a collaborator dealt with a soldier in Vietnam who is killed in a moment of foolish pride. But Vietnam is controversial. The network wanted the locale changed to Spain, the war to a bullring, and the soldier to a matador.

Rintels described the art of writing for "The FBI" television series, and stated categorically that the program's implication that its stories are based on official FBI cases is false. He cited one instance in which he proposed to write an FBI story based on the church-bombing murder of the four Black children in Birmingham by anti-civil rights forces. The producer checked with the sponsor, with the FBI, with the producing company, and with ABC. Rintels was told that they would be happy to have him write such a story, as long as the church was in the North, that no Blacks were involved, and the bombing had nothing to do with civil rights. In another instance he was told that he could write a program he had proposed on police brutality provided the charge was trumped up, the policeman vindicated, and the man who brought the charge prosecuted.

Rintels noted that at the time of his testimony no FBI program had been done on civil rights, had shown the FBI bugging, wiretapping or using a paid informant, or had dealt with establishment organizations breaking the law, such as anti-trust violations.

Television writer Robert Collins told of his being asked three times to write episodes for "The Bold Ones," one of the more courageous and relevant series on television. His first theme was about possible amnesty for draft evaders. This was turned down on the ground that advocacy of amnesty was not the consensus of the country and therefore was unacceptable. The second theme was turned down, not because it dealt with whether a government employee was necessarily a security risk because he was homosexual, but because the homosexual character was portrayed as sympathetic and not psychopathic. His third story dealt with the Pentagon's storage of nerve gas near an urban area and was turned down without explanation.

Broadcasting frequently has done a superb job of facing the issues. "Naked City," "The Defenders," "East Side, West Side" [later, "Lou Grant," which was subsequently discontinued by CBS after lead actor Ed Asner was attacked by the right-wing and was deemed to be controversial] have been programs willing to deal with controversy, at least on occasion, and sometimes boldly and clearly. It is significant, however, that while there are seemingly endless reruns of "I Love Lucy," "Gilligan's Island," "Hogan's Heroes" and similar programs on television, there are rarely, if ever, reruns of any politically relevant ones.

In the 1970s it seems as if commercial television is beginning to be more forthright with controversial subjects, either as the theme for a given episode, as a subplot, or as part of a discussion among characters. This may be due to a sudden onrush of altruistic socio-political responsibility. On the other hand, keeping in mind television's propensity to replicate success, one of the most successful programs in television has been "All In the Family," which openly deals with controversial issues through the characterizations of Archie Bunker and his son-in-law. Additional Norman Lear programs have contributed to a greater freedom on the airwaves, with controversy an integral part of programs such as "Maude" and a peripheral part of programs such as "One Day At a Time." Finally, with "Mary Hartman, Mary Hartman" and "All That Glitters," Lear opened doors for other producers to move—albeit with trepidation and on tiptoe—away from the bland and noncontroversial show designed not to antagonize any sponsor, potential viewer, or product buyer anywhere. Some producers and network executives believe they act as a matter of courage or political principle. It should be noted that "All in the Family" made money, "Maude" made money, "One Day At a Time" made money. Even "Mary Hartman, Mary Hartman," independently syndicated and mostly carried in non-prime time periods, made money. If the successful money-making formula included controversy, so be it. In retrospect, considering programs like "Mary Hartman, Mary Hartman," Lear was probably ahead of his time. As one looks at a TV program guide even shortly after the counter-culture revolution that ended in the mid-1970s, one sees some "relevant" programs, but compared to the overwhelming fare of the "Mork and Mindy"" and "Happy Days" genre, they are few and far between.

Broadcasting's leading historian, Erik Barnouw, has observed that "when a story editor says, 'we can't use anything controversial,' and says it with a tone of conscious virtue, then there is danger." Fear of controversy is not limited to commercial television. Although most public television stations seem to carry programs that tend to be more relevant to the issues and ideologies of the day than do commercial stations, they also tend to be more self-censoring. In 1971 public television joined its commercial counterpart in refusing live coverage of a significant event in American history: the largest gathering of citizens ever to come to Washington to make known their grievances against their government—the April "March on Washington" opposing U.S. actions in Vietnam. Throughout the years public television has censored programs on both the national and local levels, ranging from an award-winning program which was critical of American banks' business dealings with the poor to a political satire of a U.S. president.

In 1972 the President of the Public Broadcasting System (PBS), Hartford Gunn, attacked the attempts of "those in positions of real power to attempt to influence a public medium on the basis of their own personal bias." He decried attempts to apply pressure to censor programs as "alien to the basic purposes for which public broadcasting was established." He stated that "public affairs programming deals with contemporary issues, politics and events. These are the very ingredients of tomorrow's history books as well as today's political and social science." He added that the American system was built on the philosophy of a free exchange of ideas. But just a few weeks before that speech, PBS initiated the withdrawal of a scheduled program, "The Politics and Humor of Woody Allen," which contained a satire on President Nixon and his administration and which was objected to by people in high places. A few months prior to that, PBS was responsible for the deletion of a segment of "The American Dream Machine" that dealt with the practices and procedures of the FBI, as described by a former member of the FBI, and which was objected to by J. Edgar Hoover. (A subsequent chapter in this book, "A Public Television Alternative to Public Television," analyzes the problems of self-censorship inherent in public broadcasting, and offers a solution.)

Because of the general content of television over the years, many of us tend to express special gratitude to those stations and sponsors that provide us with programs dealing with the critical affairs of the world in which we live, as if we were getting some special favor. We forget that the airwaves belong to us, not to the stations or to the advertisers. The frequencies used for broadcasting are public property, loaned free to the stations for three-year periods [*later extended to five years for radio and seven for television, and subsequently to eight years for both*], and at all times, according to law, are supposed to be serving the public interest, convenience and necessity.

Yet, with all its faults, television probably has provided us with more education and information on controversial issues more often than have most schools and colleges. A Jules Feiffer cartoon expresses it perfectly. Two college students are standing and talking: a short coed with a long pony tail and a tall boy with an athletic letter on his sweater. The girl is saying, "so I was watching 'Sam Benedict' and everybody was attacking him because in court he was defending a Nazi and a Communist." The boy looks down at her and says "The rat." The girl leans back and says "Not Sam Benedict. Why, did you know that in this country the Fifth Amendment says that everyone no matter who they are has the right to a fair trial?" The boy, with an incredulous look on his face, says "No kidding." The girl says, "Then I was watching 'The Defenders' and everybody was attacking them because in court they were defending an atheist." The boy sneers and says, "The finks." But the girl says, "Well, not exactly. Did you know that in this country the Supreme Court has said that it is not actually against the law to not have a religion." The boy, unbelievingly, says, "Come on." The girl then says, "Then on 'Naked City' a couple of days later they had this case where the police tapped these telephone calls but the case got thrown out of court." The boy, puzzled, says "You mean wire tapping is illegal?" Then the girl says, "You really have to watch television if you want to find something out about this country." And the boy says, "Well, where else they gonna teach you? In school?" That cartoon was published in 1963. Has anything changed?

With many wealthy and influential commercial broadcasting stations and academically protected public TV stations frequently fearful of becoming involved on behalf of public interest needs, how can we—parents, adults, children—be expected to take stands and perform actions that these more powerful entities shy away from? Involvement can take place on two levels, outside the home and in the home.

First, we can get involved in the needs of our own children with our own time and energies. In the home, if we are dissatisfied with a particular television program we can switch off the set, just as when we are dissatisfied with a particular book the child is reading we can return that book to the library. We can help the child select the best possible television programs available just as we guide the child in selecting a book. If nothing is available that we think is of value or at least not harmful to the child, we have the option of turning the child's interests and energies in other directions. We should try not to allow a child to sit at a television set without a trustworthy interpreter unless we are first satisfied that what is being watched can be absorbed and understood in a positive manner, just as we do—or should do—with books and magazines.

For the child, the television set is overwhelmingly powerful. Nothing else takes the child so consistently and so diversely into a wider world, and brings the world—its experiences, thoughts, events, objects, ideas, feelings, actions—to the child. We too often forget that the imaginations of children are broad, exciting and stimulating. It is only as we go through the formal educational system as it is now constituted that we begin to conform, to restrict our minds and thoughts and feelings. We quickly dry up our most precious of creative potentials and base our learning principally on the irrelevancies of information examinations and IQ tests. Contrary to what adults generally believe, children's imaginations—particularly those of younger children—are sometimes more critical than those of adults. Children frequently do let themselves be led into, and are able to create, almost any fantasy. Yet, unless they are psychologically disturbed, their imaginations demand a valid, believable base for the fantasy. It is the degree to which television actions are made believable to the child and the extent to which the child's imagination is stimulated toward positive or negative behavior that have created difficulty for parents as well as for sociologists and psychologists concerned with children's transference of television stimuli into societal behavior. For example, a continuing area of concern is violence on television. In early 1972 the Surgeon General of the United States released a report of a study by his Scientific Advisory Committee on Television and Social Behavior. The report was entitled "Television and Growing Up: The Impact of Televised Violence." It should be noted that the television industry was given veto power over the proposed membership of the advisory committee. The Committee report stated "that there is a modest relationship between exposure to television violence and aggressive behavior or tendencies." It further stated: "It must be emphasized that the causal sequence is very likely applicable only to some children who are predisposed in this direction." Nevertheless, concerns about the negative impact of violence on television exist. The possible relationship of the conclusions in the Advisory Committee report to political rather than to scientific motivations was raised by some of the staff members who worked on the report. One research coordinator, at the National Institutes of Mental Health, stated: "There's no question . . . that normal children watching a large amount of TV violence will become more aggressive." Another researcher said, "watching violence in a television context can instigate aggressive behavior in children."

Further concerns of the public and of many citizen groups are relevant to the kinds of character images children may be encouraged to relate to or believe in. Female children, especially, see themselves rarely represented in the programs they watch and, when they are represented, it is most always in positions subservient to, weaker than, and not as capable or intelligent as the male characters. Male children, concomitantly, have virtually no alternative but to identify with insensitivity, egotism, violence and omniscience, creating for them, as for the female children, identification stereotypes that are self-fulfilling and therefore insidiously harmful to the child's future psychological, intellectual and physical health.

Another concern, frequently voiced by parents as well as other adult critics of television, relates to the commercials on children's programs and the sense of values that such commercials tend to suggest for children. Children are vulnerable, too, to political, social, and economic attitudes on TV that may influence their formative years without offering them alternative views. Child viewers tend to adopt the value judgments of their television heroes, even cartoon characters, without the critical ability to differentiate what is good or bad for them and for the world they live in. Some years ago a member of a youth gang who shot to death a member of another gang told the court that he was merely proving to himself his power to act like his television cartoon hero, Mighty Mouse.

Some programs seemingly have no impact on the child, but are simply dull and tasteless, wasteful of the child's time, of no value to the development of the child's moral or ethical tastes, and of no enrichment to a child's otherwise unceasing growth and learning. Who is to say that even programs such as these are not harmful?

This is not to say that television per se, as an inanimate medium, is either good or bad for children. The point is that television has affected and does affect children and that we must alter, or compensate for, the negative effects, and exploit and encourage the positive ones. What we cannot do is to ignore television, just as we cannot ignore any of the facets of the world around us that have the greatest bearing on our thoughts, feelings, and actions.

What is the adult's role in relation to what the child watches on television? First, we must differentiate between audience ratings and value. The child may "love" the program. But that alone is not a criterion of its value. The child may "love" candy, too—but the responsible parent (and, we hope, responsible station manager, agency account executive, network vice-president, producer, director or writer) will not allow him or her to subsist on it.

Grace Stanistreet, one of the country's leading teachers of creative arts for children, has written about some of the responsibilities of children's theater that may be applied just as validly to television. "Many people with the responsibility of selecting programs for the young," Stanistreet states, "watch the child at a children's play and take his or her reaction to it as the best recommendation. Would they take a child's word about what to include in the week's menu? Or what the family should wear, or when they should go to the dentist? But these things are fundamental to good living, they may protest. Is theater or television different? Isn't exposure to cultural experience fundamental to good living? A child has no built-in standards for judgment and evaluation. He or she is in the process of acquiring good habits, appetites, tastes, standards by association, example, influence. Wise parents know the parts they must play in developing these in their children. A parent must select the exposures, the images, the experiences out of greater knowledge of the child's needs and what will serve those needs. A parent does not impose his or her will, desires, purpose, taste, but refers and defers at times to the child's purpose, desires and abilities. A parent makes decisions based on both, not solely on one or the other."

To what degree have we, the parents, become involved in the choice of our children's television experiences in the place where it is easy for us to do so, in our own homes? One recent study revealed that 45% of the mothers surveyed could not identify what shows their children aged 6–11 watched. The survey did not include fathers, but it is likely that even fewer fathers know what their children's television viewing habits are. The survey turned up some significant information on parent attitudes. Forty-three percent of the mothers considered reruns of programs in the vein of "The Brady Bunch" and "The Waltons" just as educational as the programs on public television. Is this because of a lack of knowledge of the content of the programs or because of a judgment that any dramatic presentation even vaguely resembling real life is a more valuable learning experience than most of the other programs usually seen? Twenty-five percent thought "Sesame Street" was meant to be entertaining rather than educational, and while 68% knew their children watched "Sesame Street," 80% knew their children watched programs along the lines of "Mork and Mindy" and "Laverne and Shirley." Most significant is that only 9% of the mothers stated that they have tried to get their children to tune in to a specific program.

To what degree is parent abandonment of responsibility for the child's television experience responsible for some of the negative effects parents complain about? If there is so little involvement in the home, how can we expect any serious effort outside of the home? We have all grown up being told that "you can't fight City Hall," and certainly the broadcast industry and its advertisers are among the most powerful "City Halls" in the world. How ludicrous it would be, for example, if three mothers—let's say in Boston—who were unhappy about the commercials and programs their children watched decided to try to do something about it. Think how unrealistic it would be for them to actually form an organization—they might call it something like Action for Children's Television—oriented toward citizen action. Think how impractical it would be if they went so far as to file petitions with the Federal Communications Commission and with the Federal Trade Commission.

What could they accomplish? Stimulate the concern and support of millions of people throughout the country? Generate thousands of pages of documents at the FCC and FTC concerning their petitions? Put so much pressure on the television industry that even before the FCC and FTC ruled on the petitions, the television networks and stations made changes on their own? Receive financial support from foundations and the public to build a strong, nationwide organization?

The three mothers in Boston who started Action for Children's Television (ACT) accomplished this much and more in the space of just a few years. In 1971 ACT petitioned the Federal Communications Commission to (1) require stations to present at least 14 hours per week of programming for children under 12, (2) eliminate commercial practices such as hosts of children's shows promoting products within the program, and (3) eliminate all commercials on children's programs. In 1974, prompted by public concern generated by ACT, the FCC issued a Children's Television Report and Policy Statement which presented the following guideline suggestions to commercial stations:

- provide diversified programming to meet the varied needs and interests of children, particularly educational and informational programming;

- provide age specific programming for both preschool children (ages 2 to 5) and school age (ages 6 to 12) children;

- correct the scheduling imbalance which clustered most of the programming for children on weekend mornings;

- reduce advertising time on children's programs to new amounts established by the broadcasting industry. This limits advertising time to 9 1/2 minutes per hour on weekends and 12 minutes per hour on weekday programs;

- maintain a clear separation between program content and commercials by clustering commercials at the beginning or end of programs, or using visual or aural devices to separate program and commercial;

- eliminate "host selling" or "tie-ins"—methods by which a children's show's character endorses products to the audience.

At the same time, in the early 1970s, ACT filed petitions with the Federal Trade Commission, including requests that the FTC ban all food and toy advertising on children's programs, take action against several specified products deemed harmful by ACT, and prohibit advertising of candy. [*In 1978 the FTC issued a proposal which would eliminate all commercials directed at children too young to understand their selling intent, eliminate advertising of highly sugared foods, require counter-advertising for some food ads, and eliminate advertising of candy. In 1979 and 1980 the FTC found itself in a maelstrom of congressional discontent. Its proposals on children's TV advertising and other investigations into the practices of business and industry as they affect the public resulted in powerful pressures from those being investigated. Although the proposals were watered down by Congressional order, Congress wanted the entire investigation stopped and threatened to close down the FTC by eliminating its appropriations for the fiscal year. The FTC stood firm. Congress did close down the Commission for a day, and the FTC was forced to capitulate and end the investigation. In response to the public pressures generated by the ACT petition to the FCC and by the FCC guidelines, commercial television subsequently eliminated most of its host-selling and tie-in commercials, and reduced by about 20 to 40 percent the commercial time on children's programs. During the 1980s, in the Reagan deregulation period, the federal agencies abandoned their watchdog responsibilities and many of the abuses addressed by ACT and other citizen groups were resumed. Finally, a decade later, Congress passed the Children's Television Act of 1990, in the passage of which ACT played a key role. The Act required a reduction of advertising time on children's TV programs and development by broadcasters of children's programs that were culturally and educationally of value. In the mid-1990s, under the Clinton administration, the FCC strengthened the implementation of the 1990 Act by requiring stations to present at least three hours per week of quality, educational children's shows.*]

The work of ACT shows that it is possible for the individual, ordinary citizen to perform active, significant roles both in and outside of the home in getting the kinds of television materials we believe best for our children and for ourselves. Outside of participating in organizations, you can write to stations and sponsors whenever you have a complaint—or praise—about a program. The sponsor's bottom line is the sales figure for the product or service advertised. As television critic Jay Nelson Tuck once said, four dirty postcards from a vacant lot will make any sponsor do anything. Although he said this during the 1950s McCarthy era when stations, networks and sponsors literally blacklisted people on nothing more substantial than a dirty postcard from a vacant lot, the principle, unfortunately, still applies. Sponsors and networks infrequently act primarily on the basis of the public interest. Their records of service to the community have been questioned frequently purely on ethical grounds. So you may as well pressure them on whatever you deem important.

Working with or supporting one or more of the national or local citizen groups concerned with broadcasting can help make your wishes known and achieve your goals with minimal commitments of time, energy and money on your part.

Communication technology has developed other services, in addition to broadcast stations that reach us with television programming. Already, in the mid-1970s, millions of homes are being served by cable systems, many of these systems originating programs from local studios or carrying pay-TV programming from national or regional distributors. For years the FCC required that most cable systems provide a free instructional channel, a free local government services channel and a free public access channel in each community. These are in danger of being eliminated. [*Cable services and fees were largely deregulated by Congress in 1984, partially reregulated in 1990, almost totally deregulated again in the Telecommunications Act of 1996.*] Sometime in the 1980s we may see a completely new service: direct satellite-to-home programming. Such a system could supersede the local station concept as we now know it. Will all programs originate from one source, with no determination of local need? Other new technologies, including the possibility of a computer-based international exchange of communications, are likely to make public participation in the determination of television content more difficult in the next few decades.

We are presumably a child-oriented society, and yet those things that our children do most—such as watching television—we tend to do the least about. If television's potential is to be used for the advancement of human progress, then most of all it belongs to the children. Television's primary efforts should be oriented toward fulfilling the needs of the children in our attempt to educate them to be the kinds of human beings we want them to be, to be the kinds of individuals in their own personal orientations toward life and ideas that we hope they can be, to be the kinds of people who can achieve and maintain an ever-peaceful, prosperous world for all of humanity—the kinds of people we laud, that we ourselves clearly are not, and that we hope the new generation can somehow become.

One answer is to make all media, including television, more relevant and meaningful for our children. But unless a pattern of public involvement is established now, it may soon be too late. The networks, the stations, the advertising agencies, and the sponsors early on knew what their goals were and have gone full speed ahead in implementing them. The mothers in Boston, some church groups, and a number of citizen communications organizations subsequently established their goals and responsibilities and are doing their part.

Are you doing yours?

# CHAPTER 4

# An Open University and School

The oxymoronic combination of isolationism and cold war mentality that dominated America in the years following the end of World War II was attacked by the college and university students as part of their protest against United States involvement in Vietnam and the establishment's efforts to impose upon all Americans a dual conformity of ideas and behavior. The students had first learned about the world around them in the politically repressive McCarthy era of the 1950s. Much like the young Germans whose parents were Nazis, many young Americans tried to atone for their parents' support of the neofascist principles and practices McCarthyism engendered in the United States from the late 1940s through the 1950s. They saw a wider world with which they wanted to communicate: a world beyond their immediate environment's narrow borders of place and ideas. Music was one means, an international language of feeling. The *idea* of Woodstock became a global phenomenon. It signified a reaching out beyond what they felt was a repressive society's imposed boundaries. It went beyond the arts and provided a base for understanding and helping other human beings achieve their potentials in an otherwise hostile society. Music and Woodstock became symbols for a significant part of the new culture in the counter-cultural revolution. The revival of a Woodstock event in the 1990s was, to some, an attempt to recapture the passion and caring of the 1960s and 1970s. In fact, the Woodstock festivals at the turn of the new century, especially the event held in 1999, reflected the opposite: not a counter-culture revolution, but an affirmation of the Reagan-era "me-me-me" philosophy, ego-centered and self-serving. Whereas their parent's generation at Woodstock 1969 protested against war and for civil rights and liberties, the attendees at Woodstock 1999 protested against nothing except—and this is not written altogether facetiously—the high price of bottles of water and the hot weather. Yet, while they appeared to eschew the responsibilities to other human beings that their parents had embraced a generation earlier, the 1999 Woodstock youth also appeared to have an inner conscience plagued by their lack of commitment to society. One hopes that it is that conscience and not simply mindless immaturity that accounts for their self-mutilation of piercing their noses, cheeks, lips, eyelids and other parts of the body for the insertion of baubles, and the painful etching of permanent tattoos onto their skins.

Formal education in the 1960s and 1970s remained mired in tradition. To break away from their restrictive intellectual as well as emotional environment, many saw no other course than to drop out and turn on. While seeking greater and deeper communication with the world at large, they found themselves separating themselves from it, creating their own small worlds where they could be who they felt they were without pretense or hypocrisy. Some found new facets within themselves and the courage to reenter society and actively change it. Some became a lost generation, unable or unwilling to sell their psyches for a semblance of formalized security. These students called national attention to two controversial opposite propositions: one, that there were problems with America's higher education system and, two, that millions of Americans who were capable of learning on an advanced level did not have the geographic, economic or physical advantages of the student protesters and were being deprived of an education to which they felt they, too, were entitled. It didn't have to be that way. Colleges and universities with commitment and courage could have made it possible for both of these groups to have a higher education. The advocacy for a U.S. "Open University" that follows is not moot, although it was originally presented in the 1960s and 1970s and, more formalized, in 1980, as one solution to the inequitable availability of higher education in America. As this is written, at the close of the twentieth century and the beginning of the twenty-first, the United States still does not have a national open university available to any person who has the desire and ability to pursue a university education. The television-based open university projects that were available were limited in scope and not given the support necessary to reach their potentials. In year 2000 America has a new opportunity through a new medium: the Internet. The Internet's interactive quality makes it more effective than all previous media for teaching and learning on an individual basis. The principles espoused below for a Television Open University are just as applicable—and necessary—today for an Internet Open University.

The following is adapted from an address, "Government Concerns and Policies: Current and Future," to the National Conference on Open Learning and Nontraditional Education, June 19, 1975, Arlington, VA; an address, "Computers and Alternative Learning Systems," to the Conference on Computers and Communications, September 16, 1975, Airlie House, VA; a seminar presentation, "United States Media-based Open Learning Developments," to the U.K. Open University, BBC and ITV staff, September 23, 1975, Milton Keynes, England; from two papers published in *Educational and Industrial Television*, "Media, Education, and the Open University," October 1980, and "A Video Resource Center for the Open University," November 1980.

The first satellite that orbited the earth ushered in for educators an unprecedented opportunity for national and international exchange of teaching and learning resources. Yet, 20 years after the October, 1957 launching of Sputnik, American education had still to obtain its own permanent, full-time domestic satellite transponder, or to share satellite space on a regular, continuing basis with the education agencies of other countries.

Sometimes one wonders not only where education is going, but whether it is willing to go at all. How much has education learned from or been motivated by the satellite education experiments in the 1970s, such as those in Alaska, the Rocky Mountain region and Appalachia in the United States, and in India through U.S. joint Canada-U.S. satellite projects?

If any other endeavor in our society were so derelict in using the technological resources that would permit it to do a more efficient job and produce a better product, you can bet that its foot-dragging practitioners would be turned out as incompetents.

In the early 1970s a comprehensive and exciting development in the use of media technology for education on a mass scale was the establishment of the British "Open University." Designed to provide higher education opportunity for people who, for one reason or another, were either school drop-outs or never began college, the "Open University" in 1980 [*when this was originally written*] has 70,000 enrolled students (54,000 in degree courses) through a combination of print correspondence, radio and television. As the *BBC Radio Times* put it, these are students who are unable to continue their formal education on a college level "through failures in the system, through disadvantages in their environment or upbringing, through mistakes of their judgment or through sheer bad luck."

In its first year, 1971, the "Open University" increased the college enrollment in Britain by almost 50%. More than 75% of the 16,000 students who took examinations for credit passed. By 1980 more than 39,000 had graduated, with the yearly graduating total reaching 5,400. The dropout rate was only 16%. Any one in Britain over 21, whether or not he or she has had any previous educational experience, can earn a Bachelor of Arts degree by completing six one-year courses, including two foundation courses chosen from the arts, mathematics, science, social science or technology. All students receive packets of material to study and assignments to complete. These are integrated with some 37 hours of television and some 50 hours of radio programs each week over BBC, out of which the student watches and listens to the selected programs comprising his or her course areas. Although television and radio are critical bases for the program, only about 10% of a student's total academic time is spent with the media. Study centers throughout the country provide students with individual assistance from counselors and tutors. In addition, all students working for degree credits in foundation courses must attend a one-week intensive residential session, complete 12 major pieces of independent work, and pass a comprehensive examination.

By 1980 a number of countries, including Israel, Pakistan, Saudi Arabia, Japan, Venezuela and Columbia had comparable universities in the process of development or in the planning stage. In the United States there has been talk of an Open University on a nationwide scale since Britain's plan was first announced in the mid-1960s. A principal difference between U.S. and U.K. needs was the greater accessibility of formal college degree programs for more people in the United States, including a nationwide growth of community and junior colleges. However, the need for professional and continuing education in this country has been just as acute, with the concept of "life-long learning" receiving increasing federal government support. This is true particularly for the potential learner isolated by reasons of geography, social or economic disadvantage, physical handicap, or similar factors beyond that individual's control.

Part of the difficulty in implementing innovative programs in the United States to serve these peoples' need has been in getting the potential sponsoring organizations—such as foundations and the U.S. Office of Education (in the spring of 1980 incorporated into the new Department of Education)—to break with tradition. Although extolling programs they fund that give the appearance of creating change in American education, they often are accused of being overly careful in supporting projects that actually do create change. Consider George Bernard Shaw's comment that when Savanarola told the ladies of Florence to give away their jewels and finery in order to create new and better priorities in the world, they hailed him as a saint, but when he actually induced them to do it, they burned him at the stake as a public nuisance.

The principal sources of philanthropy, whether public or private, are, by the very nature of their being in a position to be philanthropists, representative of the controllers and protectors of the existing political, social, and economic establishments in our society. Therefore, their efforts are conscientiously devoted to conserving what they consider to be the best in society, that which they see as most advantageous to the world in which they live. The appearance of change provides a sense of progress, a satisfaction of accomplishment and a denial of elitism. Actual change, even from the most altruistic viewpoint, challenges at the very least the bases that enable the public or private sector philanthropist to be in a position to be philanthropic.

Further difficulties stem from the organizational mode and from the principal programming orientation of noncommercial public/educational television in the United States. Contrary to popular belief, public television is not a unilateral national network operated by PBS. Each station or State system is controlled by a board that is supposed to be appropriately representative of and responsive to its particular state or local community. The principle of local control, which has provided a strength-through-diversity for many national efforts, is not in question here. However, if we were to have the currently licensed 150 different public television entities attempting to determine the directions and operations of a national Open University, a splintering of effort and a lack of effective central coordination would be bound to occur. Further, inasmuch as each local station decides what is to be carried on its station, the availability of Open University programming does not necessarily mean access to it by all people who want it. Because station priorities have already made it clear that cultural-entertainment-public affairs programming is preferred over instructional materials, widespread access to an Open University would require the availability of a second channel of distribution in every community.

One solution is to use a domestic satellite-to-home system, bypassing the individual stations as a principal distribution source and not disturbing or preempting their current programming or system of local control, as discussed in the chapter, "A Public Television Alternative to Public Television." Another solution would be to use non-broadcast technologies, including microwave, cable and other transmission techniques that could be fed into the unused channels on our regular home television receivers. The interactive wired-city concept no longer need be a dream of some distant future. Videotapes and video disks could be important parts of the correspondence aspect of an Open University.

Public television's and public radio's lack of orientation to educational programming is a significant consideration in the development of an Open University, especially since the passage of the Public Broadcasting Act of 1967; under the leadership of CPB, PBS, and NPR, cultural, entertainment, and public affairs programs have received principal attention and support. Instructional programming on public television stations dropped from about 49% of total air time in 1968 to 34% in 1972 to 15% in 1978. No recent studies have been done on noncommercial radio's instructional programming percentages, but it is likely that the overall figure is even lower than that for television.

The perception of the majority of those who control public television is that it should function as a "Fourth Network," providing competition for audiences with ABC, CBS and NBC. The fact is that even under the most propitious circumstances public television is not likely to have anywhere near the funds or the big-name talent resources of commercial television for any realistic competitive challenge. Would public television ultimately be more successful in meeting its responsibilities to the public by increasing its awareness of its "alternative" potentials?

In 1980, PBS, in part responding to internal as well as external recommendations for change, established in place of its single entertainment-cultural-public affairs dominated format, three services: the Blue Service, continuing its principal programming; the Red Service, for specialized and experimental programs; and the Green Service, for children's and instructional programs At first glance, it might seem that the Green Service could provide a media base for an Open University. However, in all communities in the country except 13 there is still only one PTV station in operation, and there is no evidence that stations are likely to preempt their cultural-entertainment-public affairs programming for instructional programming to any greater degree than they do now. For some 20 years, into the mid-1970s, the chief example of a television-based Open University in the United States was Chicago Junior College's program, which offered two-year degrees. Spurred by increased emphasis on "open, independent, lifelong learning," by impending "continuing educational" legislation and appropriations, and by the success of the British Open University, by 1980 some 25 to 30 higher education institutions and consortia in the United States were offering degrees through television. About two-thirds of these are two-year colleges, the remainder four-year institutions. Several are patterned after the British Open University and are using its course materials; they are, however, operating not as a national organization but out of individual institutions on local or limited State levels. Several are part of consortia, the most notable of which is the University of Mid-America, serving as a production network for nine institutions in five Midwestern states. Each of these states handles its own distribution through the stations of its participating institutions, providing about eight courses in each state to a total enrollment of about 2,000. On a more limited geographical but wider course and participation level, the Coastline Community College in California offers a two-year degree to an enrollment of some 10,000. Similar variations mark Open Universities throughout the country.

The fact remains, however, that the United States still does not have a national Open University. The first approximation of one is scheduled to begin in the fall of 1980 through a consortium of seven colleges and universities and eleven television stations, serving students in California, Idaho, Indiana, Maryland, New York, Oregon, Pennsylvania, Tennessee, Vermont and Washington. The National University Consortium (NUC) anticipates that a student could earn a bachelor's degree in six years in subject areas that include the social and behavioral sciences, the humanities, technology and management. In addition to using television, the NUC expects to provide print materials and optional classroom and telephone tutoring.

Another possibility for a national Open University is the exploration in 1980 of the offer by publisher and media owner Walter H. Annenberg of $150 million over a 15-year period to support the production of higher education media course materials. Ten million dollars per year would be donated by the Annenberg School of Communications of the University of Pennsylvania to the Corporation for Public Broadcasting, which in turn would supervise the granting of funds to colleges for the development of television, radio and correspondence course work leading to a degree. The courses would probably be carried by the PBS Green Service, National Public Radio and to some degree by cable, satellites, videocassettes and disks. As noted earlier, this would not guarantee carriage by any given station in any given community. An office of the British Open University interviewed for this paper [1980], while praising the intention of the Annenberg gift, questioned whether $10 million per year could even begin to get a U.S. Open University off the ground, considering that the British Open University spends some $90 million each year for its 140 courses over BBC.

But even if all the economic, political and technological problems were solved, the success of a national Open University in the United States would be dependent on a much more important factor: the educational philosophies and practices that would provide the bases for the Open University. To adapt the Open University to the currently predominant traditional concepts of teaching and learning would doom it from the beginning. We would have to move boldly into new educational approaches, not only fitting the new modes of learning represented by an Open University, but meeting as well the requirements of a twenty-first-century learner and society—now only one generation away.

First, its administration should not be in the hands of traditional institutions such as the existing colleges and universities, which, on the whole, have done little to show that they understand the relationships between media and education. Nor should the Open University be administered by those public/educational broadcasting organizations whose priorities are in other directions. Although maintaining offices dealing with education and praising the importance of educational telecommunication over the years, established enterprises such as the NAEB (National Association of Educational Broadcasters), CPB and PBS undertook or accommodated instructional projects usually as an adjunct to public broadcasting concerns and, sometimes, were apparently prompted principally by financial or political factors. A significant exception is the NAEB's Samoa project in the 1960s. Given the orientation and the record of existing groups, a national Open University should be under the aegis of a new, separate and independent organization whose principal priority and concern are with educational communications.

Second, the Open University concomitantly needs to establish a technological facility that can serve many purposes. The Open University should be more than a University. It should include a "School" serving the needs of the elementary and secondary levels and professional training, with diploma and certificate programs for adults. It should bring education into the practical situations of the home, the job, and the street and provide learning experiences and guidance for people who can apply them immediately in their daily lives. It should go beyond the formal, traditional credit course concept and provide those materials that will serve the many and varied informal learning needs of all ages and interests, with the purpose of improving the quality of life not only for the individual student, but—through that individual's capacity for growth—for the entire community. To do less would be to repeat, in a way, the kind of elitism that public broadcasting is often accused of and to unnecessarily limit the potentials of a system whose basic structure as described above, unlike that of public broadcasting, would permit such a broad service.

The Open University and School should provide learning experiences on all levels in all fields for all persons regardless of preparation, training, or geographical location. The participants in the learning process may be individuals at home, students in formal traditional institutions, or employees who undertake their projects in conjunction with a business, industry or labor organization. They may enroll for credit or non-credit purposes, with a degree optional. Their goal may be to enhance their concrete vocational opportunities or for their personal aesthetic, ethical, or intellectual self-realization.

All appropriate media and communications resources should be used. Although television may very well be the principal carrier, it should not be the only one. In addition to TV, radio and print, as used by the British Open University, computers, satellites, cable, microwave, common carrier, closed-circuit and other electronic means of transmission are available. Other forms of communication, either in combination with the mass media or as direct communication resources on the local level—such as the performing arts and the plastic and graphic arts—should be incorporated into the larger scheme. In England the Open University is carried on the public system, the BBC. In the United States, as previously noted, the public system does not have sufficient multiple outlets or the necessary programming orientation. Although commercial stations could make an important contribution to the public interest by devoting portions of air time to Open University and School programs, there is little likelihood that either Congress or the FCC would require them to give up lucrative commercial time to do so. [*By substituting the Internet for the following 1980 resources, and applying the structure, operations, and goals below in terms of the Internet, a national Open University becomes immediately possible and functional.*]

Personally controlled communications, such as videocassettes and disks, can play important roles. Individual enrollees should have access to such equipment, either through home television recording or, at least, playback units, or at an accessible center. Where the enrollee cannot be reached directly by a medium, programs should be made available in recorded form by mail. Where the enrollee receives the material direct through a medium, such as television at home, the ability to record it and play it back provides unparalleled opportunity for careful and leisurely study not provided in the traditional classroom situation.

Learning sites should be flexible, permitting opportunity for consultation and tutorial assistance from traveling tutors or from tutors-in-residence in particular localities or regions where there is a substantial enrollment. For example, in addition to home reception, a student should be able to go to a physically accessible local site such as a town square, city hall, or library. Libraries in particular can serve as mini-schools where the student can obtain person-to-person learning experiences and exchange ideas with other students, and where the librarian might function as an administrator-faculty member-coordinator of the Open University and School's extension site.

The orientation of both the faculty and students should be toward service to society. Qualifications for teaching and learning should be based on experience, ability, and motivation and not chiefly on academic background or credits. A faculty member, whether tutoring through a medium or coordinating on a local or regional level, should have experience in the subject field and the ability to communicate knowledge and motivate understanding and action, both on a mass basis and in a one-to-one situation. A student should have the motivation and ability to learn and a perception of his or her potential contributions to the needs of society.

Instead of courses or credits per se, each student would orient his or her program to a project designed to prepare him or her to solve a critical problem in the social, political, economic, or environmental sphere of human endeavor. The traditional educational institutions are turning out too many human computers whose learning consists of amassing test grades, courses and credits. The Open University and School has the potential to turn out human beings whose learning of background information, research techniques and implementational theories is oriented toward practical application in meeting the needs of the world in which they live.

The choice of subject matter should therefore be flexible. Students should not be bound by the traditional credit-hour course of study. The new technology makes possible a break from the restrictive four walls of the classroom and the arbitrary credits-per-hour, hours-per-year approach. Student requirements should include a three-phase experience: learning theory and information, development of an applied research plan, and application of the plan in the field. The particular subject matter may be chosen in three principal ways: (1) orientation of the curriculum of the individual student to the needs of a community, large or small—from the student's home town to the entire world; this may include the participation of the community or of a sponsoring industry, social service, or professional organization in determining the student's curriculum needs and specific learning projects and experiences; (2) where the individual is at home and enrolling for the development or upgrading of basic learning skills, as may be the case principally on the elementary and secondary level, the participation of the community in the student's program may be minimal or nonexistent; the student would, of course, play the principal role under any circumstance in the determination of curriculum: the self-evaluation of needs, abilities, and motivation; (3) input from experts—practitioners and academicians—in the development of curricula can be helpful; unfortunately, in traditional institutions curricula is determined almost exclusively by the academicians, with little input from the students, practitioners, or even the community that the learning and the curricula are supposed to serve.

Until such time as the new concepts of learning of this proposed Open University and School are universally adopted, most enrollees' prior learning will have been in traditional institutions that insist on judging ability by quantitative methods alone: that is, grades and credits. In such cases the Open University and School would seek qualitative evaluations from individual teachers at those institutions. Where students are taking work at the Open University and School while retaining basic affiliation with a "parent" institution, the Open University and School would provide qualitative evaluations that might lend themselves into translations for the required credit and grade statistics. The Open University and School could seek accreditation in various regions and States and award its own degrees and diplomas, comparable to the practice in England. There is some question, however, as to whether accrediting organizations in the United States, oriented as they are to non-learning irrelevancies such as numbers of Ph.D.s on a faculty and numbers of books in a library, would be willing to challenge the traditional educational concepts of their controlling institutional members by accrediting an institution oriented to learning rather than to teaching, and whose success might well create serious dissatisfaction on the part of many students with the traditional education of the member institutions.

A student would not have to stay in a fixed geographical place while enrolled in the Open University or School. The flexibility of media learning permits an enrollee to move about anywhere, inasmuch as the materials will always be available and there will be, in whatever locality, a central point such as a library that will have a coordinator-tutor and recording and playback equipment and other supportive resources.

The potentials of a learner-and-society oriented Open University and School reach beyond state and national borders. With the use of satellites, an International Open University and School could link the resources of countries all over the world.

The focal point for an Open University and School should be a Multi-media Resource Center. Some individual educational institutions have developed such centers, providing multi-media materials to students in classrooms, special rooms and dormitory rooms through computerized dial-access devices which permit the students to call up whatever resources are available in all media forms on any given subject. As education—hopefully—makes progress, such centers will grow in more and more institutions and in cities, states and regions. National multi-media resource centers will eventually develop. In the very act of linking together countries of the world through an international Open University and School (as well as national ones), communications can accomplish its purpose of bringing people closer together for mutual understanding and peace. Any given national multi-media resource center could serve as an international center by cataloging, coordinating, and routing materials available from all other centers toward any given destination. Technology obviates the necessity of duplication of materials in many physical centers, as is now the case with traditional libraries. Bulk and quantity for their own sakes create administrative jobs, but are of little value for the learner.

The Multi-media Resource Center is seen by George Hall, a leading designer of technology-based learning systems, as a "technologically facilitated variant" of the learning-tutorial-project system of education, having little or no similarity to the familiar and inefficient classroom-centered schemes employed in virtually all educational institutions today. The learning process would be built essentially around an agreement between the learner and the teacher, in which auto-tutorial techniques, technology based teaching/learning strategies and a humanized form of contingency-management, as Hall states it, puts an individual student's goals and achievement rates into the process as constructive, rather than merely incidental, factors.

The Multi-media Resource Center would not only distribute materials to all sources, but would acquire materials from all sources on a shared basis. Distribution would be oriented not only to educational institutions, but to noninstitutional needs such as professions, organizations, government offices, industry and, as described above in the Open University and School concepts, to the home and to similar reception areas.

The Multi-media Resource Center would provide all the physical modules or packages required by the Open University and School's multi-media approach to transmission and reception: broadcast television and radio, including commercial and educational stations, cable systems, closed-circuit wired systems, common carriers, ITFS microwave systems, microwave, satellites, and other methods. [*Today the Internet encompasses all of these methods of distribution.*]

The Multi-media Resource Center, George Hall stresses, should be flexible, functioning as an interactive mechanism for the use, replication, dissemination, and production of and experimentation with the new technology and with the individualized learning approach in varying physical situations. It must be particularly responsive to the needs and abilities of those participating in the Open University and School, as well as those using the Center's resource through a more traditional institutional connection, to examine problems in relation to the total real-world environment in which the problems exist, and to reach solutions to these problems by considering all relevant factors of that environment. It must, therefore, contain materials that are continually relevant and should be viewed as a series of hardware and facilities modules that will allow the user the flexibility to produce any software, design any hardware, and retrieve any information required by his or her academic research or applied project activities.

The very nature and purpose of the Center suggests a learning approach that clearly reflects the recognition and application of modern technology to education. Goals are set jointly by the student and faculty guide or tutor. The goals and objectives represent skills and practical achievements which the participants and tutors assess as realizable within the resource-time-prerequisite requirements. Both parties must agree that the objective goals represent socially valuable, professionally applicable, and ethically desirable achievements. Once these are agreed upon, then the process of technology use and the required resources are identified. Intermediate, short-range goals are developed in relationship to the available or needed resources, including technologically mediated materials, human mediated resources such as teachers, experts and consultants, and field learning experiences. All of these factors are coordinated toward the achievement of the long-range goals.

The participant must be assured that he or she may move forward at his or her own pace and that the tutor or coordinator, with the backing of other personnel and physical resources, is always ready to provide special guidance and assistance where needed. From that point on the learner can operate his or her own study/application schedule. The learner must have available programmed texts, television programs, audio tape presentations, group discussions and seminars, personal sessions with scholars and practitioners, laboratory apparatus, and other resources which permit a step-by-step accomplishment of the intermediate goals previously designated. This becomes a self-teaching approach, without the pressures of external competition, and permits the maximum assistance from immediate and mediated teaching personnel and resources in terms of the individual's personal needs and abilities. Punishment through low grades, as practiced by virtually all academic institutions today, would be eliminated, and the student would be helped by positive rather than, as currently prevalent in education, negative motivation.

Education today by and large equates objective evaluation with mass testing. It dismisses the idea that an individual can be judged on the basis of personal worth or accomplishment and insists that all judgments of individuals be made in comparison to a mass. A full-page announcement in the *New York Times* several years ago illustrated this criticism of education. Next to a photograph of a somewhat disheveled-looking man, the commentary states, in part:

> He didn't say his first word until he was 3.
> At 7, his teacher said "nothing good" would ever become of him.
> When he was 16, he left his homeland to avoid the draft.
> He couldn't get a job at 19 because of his long hair and wrinkled clothes.
> Before he was 30, he revolutionized man's understanding of nature.

The photograph, of course, is of Albert Einstein.

Psychometrists attached to the Multi-media Resource Center would devise instruments and procedures so that the learner or receiving institution or organization may be able to ascertain at frequent intervals where the learner stands in relation to his or her own goals, and so that the tutors and guides may identify and assist with specific individual achievements and problems. Measurement would be of the diagnostic type: not a determination of the sum of knowledge, the approach currently used in virtually all educational and evaluative situations, but a determination of the learner's needs in an attempt to provide those experiences that enhance the learner's progress. Measurement would be oriented to the individual development of the individual person, as opposed to the standardized, normative tests usually used by educators and which are designed mainly to separate students into achievement-failure tracks.

This Multi-media Resource Center requires an organizational approach different from that used by the traditional media resources center. This Center would apply George Hall's concept of a cost-efficiency factor related to a wide range of print, audio, video and computer mediation apparatus designed to disseminate rapid low-cost instructional stimuli, some with active response factors. The Center's design and implementation team must take action on the specific instructional methodology proposed for each learner and for receiving institutions or organizations in terms of the most effective media combinations. Hall's organizational efficiency requires interaction among the following: the personnel, which includes scholarly, administrative paraprofessionals and others needed in a particular learning project; the facilities, including learning space for carrels, laboratory, office and production spaces; the media materials, laboratory supplies, equipment and other goods; the cybernetic factor, which includes the various administrative components by which the strategy for accomplishing one or many goals is devised; the time spans and articulated sequences by which the personnel elements and physical resources are to be deployed; and all information factors, specifically the content to be handled, usually expressed as mediating symbol-stimuli that are related to effective and desired response from the learner. All of these resources must be available to the learner in the order and mode required for his or her individual progress. The constant change in requirements demands designers who must conduct analyses on the acquisition, production and dissemination of materials—to determine the most rational choices and directions.

Instructional media specialist Ted Harris sees the Center as a series of modules, with each complex serving the function of interrelating various media and dissemination methods. In this respect, for example, the Center could have an "intermedia" complex, which would interrelate non-electronic media of communication, such as the performing, plastic and graphic arts, to the means of mass dissemination. In this manner a combination of stage, film, and television, through computer interface, would permit the learner to interact directly with a stage presentation which would serve as the primary content carrier for the particular learning experience desired at a given time.

An information access complex would be another element within the center, serving in effect as the "library" portion, providing storage for hard copy, microform, and audiovisual materials. All elements would be interconnected through a central data processing unit to provide both on-line and off-line remote accessing of hard copy, still-frame microform, audio and video tape, and audio and video disk materials. The complete collection would be indexed for rapid access to a specific point of utilization. Cross-indexing to the Library of Congress, the Educational Retrieval Information Center (ERIC), and other such sources would expand the facilities of the Center and of these other organizations. A central terminal would perform an automatic recording function to capture and store appropriate materials from various sources, with a similar terminal system used for instant dissemination of the same.

This terminal system, as Hall describes it, would be located in a central control complex containing systems for printing, processing, and reproduction as well as information accessing, program retrieval cueing, simulation and games capability, graphic and mathematical modeling, and computer-based instruction. This central control complex would provide the systems for reception, origination, and transmission of material through the various media, from cable interconnection to satellite. The storage and retrieval system would provide complete access, electronically, for all users.

Although what has been described here is one major multi-media center, there could be sub-centers of similar capacity throughout the world. To merely duplicate facilities would be to reinforce the currently wasteful duplication of resources in education (for example, print libraries in colleges and universities). Centers, however, that created, acquired, stored, and made accessible unique specified materials applicable principally or solely to people in that Center's service area would be justified, as would their function of electronically making materials from other parts of the world available on the local level. One special advantage of such sub-centers would be the involvement of the community—citizen groups, governmental units, social service organizations, individual educational institutions, professional and industry groups—in the development, acquisition and application of materials and in providing real-world input to the learning process of the participants. In this way the community itself would benefit from the operations of the Open University and School and the Multi-media Resource Center,[1] as would students and teachers through the sharing of real-scale problems in daily working contacts with the real world. It would be one more effective approach for tearing down the ivy-covered walls that continue to separate so much of formal education and so many educational institutions from social task and responsibility.

## NOTE

1. The Open University and School and the Multi-media Resource Center were originally developed by the author in 1971 for the International University of Communications, of which the author was the founder and first president.

# CHAPTER 5

# Television and Political Control: A Case for TV Literacy

In *Election Coverage: Blueprint for Broadcasters*, Carla Brooks Johnston analyzes the role of the media, specifically television, in determining who wins and who loses our elections. For several decades now, with few exceptions, there has been a direct correlation between the order in which candidates finish in a multi-candidate election and how much money each has spent on TV advertising. Beginning in 1952, when General Eisenhower's campaign managers decided that television ads should feature human interest background about their candidate rather than a discussion of issues, political advertising on television has been almost exclusively hype and slogans.

Television news personnel have reinforced this approach, concentrating principally on sound bites, personalities, and spin-doctor handouts, rather than on critical, unbiased analyses. Indeed, one often sees political reporters on television interviewing other television political reporters, inducing gullible viewers to believe that somehow this kind of incestuous reportage constitutes intelligent political analysis. Further, under the Reagan administration some of the equal time provisions for political candidates, as specified in the Communications Act of 1934, were vitiated. This has made it possible for station owners to give all the time on news and public affairs programs they wish to candidates they support and to totally ignore candidates they do not favor. The only equal time provision that can now be effectively applied is that relating to the purchase of paid political advertising time. A station is obligated to sell—not give—any candidate as much time as is sold to any other candidate for the same office. What that simply means is that the candidate with the most money can buy virtually unlimited air time, whereas a candidate with little money is entitled to as much time, but is financially unable to buy as much, thus giving the former—the one with richer backers—a clear advantage.

In a nutshell, the power of television to determine who is elected has resulted in enabling the richest candidate, in most instances, to literally buy the election.

Public perception and support of issues, as well as of candidates, are also determined by television. This was made manifest in the 1960s and 1970s, as described at the beginning of chapter 1. The media's bias in ignoring anti-war protests in the mid-1960s encouraged President Lyndon Johnson and the Pentagon in their Southeast Asia venture. But as protests grew and the mainstream media found itself forced to acknowledge what more and more of the American public was beginning to learn from other sources, the impact on issues and policies was enormous. President Johnson was compelled to withdraw from running for another term. The Pentagon, shown to have lied consistently on what was happening in Vietnam, lost public support.

Media coverage of the Republican and Democratic conventions of 1968 reflected the growing counter-culture movement, in the eyes of some critics giving it the impetus that marked it as the "sixties generation." Protesters gathered in Miami, where the Republicans met, and in Chicago, where the Democrats were. The protesters, mostly middle-class college students, were oriented to Ghandian and the U.S.'s more recent Martin Luther King, Jr., approaches to nonviolence. They principally wanted to convey their issues to the public, to clarify their opposition to the stands of the leading candidates of both parties. (One Democrat, Senator Eugene McCarthy, had earned the support of many of the protesters with his stands against the war and his support of counter-culture philosophies. Another Democrat, Senator Robert Kennedy, had had the support of the more establishment-oriented protesters, but his assassination a short time before the convention fueled even greater discontent.) At both convention sites the authorities were pressured by embarrassed party officials to keep the protesters' voices from being heard. The police responded by barring peaceful marches and rallies and violently turned on the protesters. Media coverage immediately moved from the issues to the violence. The police even used violence against the media's camera crews in an attempt to prevent them from showing the public what the police were doing. Viewers saw brutal beatings by the police and, principally, saw protesters who looked and dressed oddly. The media concentrated on the counter-culture appearance of the protesters, ignoring those whose dress and demeanor were that of mainstream America. The media emphasized stereotypes, which to this day are still the public's concept of the 1960s and 1970s counter-culturists. Most hurtful to the protesters, however, and most satisfying to the established political parties, was that the protesters' issues were buried under the media's emphasis on events and not ideas. (Similarly, in 1999 and

2000 the established media not only conveyed the same false stereotypes of those who protested at the World Trade Organization conference in Seattle, the International Monetary Fund and World Bank meetings in Washington, and at the Republican and Democratic conventions, thus obfuscating the issues presented by the protestors, but even more grievously ignored the police brutality and the gross violations by the authorities of the protestors' civil rights and liberties.)

In 1968, however the crux of the protests had nevertheless, been made known to the majority of the public, and the counter-culture movement had tremendous political impact over the next few years. Eventually, five years later, it forced a re-elected President Richard Nixon to withdraw from the war in Vietnam. What became crystal clear, however, was that through their decisions on what or what not to cover in electoral races and controversial issues, the media controlled the political processes of America. The media's—especially television's—ability to influence the public's minds and emotions continue, at the turn of the new century, to give the media unparalleled power over our institutions and our lives.

The following is an amalgamation of an address, "Alternatives for Education: To Improve Learning," to the 22nd annual convention of the Association for Educational Communications and Technology (National Education Association), April 18, 1972, Minneapolis; and an address, "New Responsibilities for Instructional Materials," to the national audiovisual convention of the Educational Media Producers Council, January 20, 1973, Houston. These materials were updated for two later articles, "Are You a Television Illiterate?" *Emerson Beacon*, Winter, 1984, and "Ethics, Education, and the Necessity for Media Literacy," *Media Ethics*, Fall, 1988.

When American television was young, in the 1950s, Edward R. Murrow interviewed a teen-age gang member indicted for the murder of another youth. Although the accused boy could neither read nor write, he watched television a lot. He explained his act of aggression by comparing himself with his favorite invincible hero, "Mighty Mouse." He could not differentiate between the fact and the fancy of what he viewed on television. He saw, but could not interpret. He was not only a print illiterate, but more significant, perhaps, in the current media context of America, he was also a television illiterate.

Even today a woman goes to her physician with symptoms of breast cancer and, despite recent alternative methods of treatment, she accepts with little question the diagnosis and prescribed mastectomy. Her principal knowledge of medical doctors comes from television, where doctors are gentle, altruistic, infallible, and look like Robert Young. [*An actor who played the role of a compassionate physician in a long-running television series.*] The television reinforcement of the image the medical profession projects for itself influences her even against her own self-interest. She is a television illiterate.

During a political campaign a man learns about the candidates principally from television, where the need to get attention and make a point in a short space of time results in condensed thinking and the capsulation of significant issues into 30-second spots. He comes to conclusions and casts his votes on the basis of symbols. He exercises his most precious democratic right through superficial, manipulated judgments rather than through evaluation. He is a television illiterate.

A homemaker goes out and buys a television-advertised detergent for her husband's shirt collars instead of telling the clod to wash his neck more often. She is a television illiterate.

At the very least we are confronted with an issue of morality—the morality of our being controlled without our knowledge. We need to know what is being done to us, how it is being done, and how we can cope with it.

Most of us are television illiterates—that is, we cannot analyze and evaluate and come to objective conclusions about what we see and hear on television—although many of us, because we are highly literate in print, think we are television-literate as well. The success of Madison Avenue in selling us products and services that we may not really want or need and may not be either the best buy or good for us is proof that we are not.

An American Association of Advertising Agencies study showed that more than 90% of television viewers misunderstand some part of what they see, no matter what kind of broadcast they are watching, and that there is only a "slight relationship" between the level of understanding and education and age. Sophistication and traditional learning are meager defenses against media brainwashing, as the relatively highly educated society of pre-World War II Germany found. It cannot be overemphasized: Those who control a country's media control its political processes. Unless we become literate enough to understand and control the effects of television, it will control us.

Both the fault and the answer lie in our educational system. We require formal preparation of all of our citizens in print literacy. Almost without exception, graduates of secondary schools in this country have had 12 years of courses in composition, literature and other print-competency areas to enable them to communicate in print and have some critical facility with print communications. Almost every college graduate has had at least two years of required courses in print-competency. However, almost every human being—and that includes those of us who are older than television and even older than radio—will spend most of his or her communicating hours with visual and aural rather than with print materials. Yet, there are very few elementary and secondary schools or colleges and universities that require even one course in visual and aural literacy. If we do not formally educate our people—young and old—to at least as much competency with visual and aural media as we do with print media, we will be—we are—setting the stage for eventual control of them—of us—by those who control the media.

We have become weary of hearing statistics about television watching. They have become so familiar that we no longer take sufficient account (if we ever did) of how they affect us now as well as their effect as part of a Future Shock or Third Wave. Maybe we had better take another look.

How many hours a day do you spend reading? One? Two? Three? Four? Five? Six? Because you are reading this book, it is likely that your time spent reading is more than the two hours per day of the average American—which includes signs, packages, labels, advertisements—with less than half-an-hour devoted to books, magazines and newspapers. Compare that with this statistic: the television set in the average American home is on six hours each and every day of the year. And 98% of the households in the United States have at least one TV set.

The average student, by the time he or she has graduated from high school, has spent some 10,800 hours in the classroom and over 12,000 hours in front of the television set. We are a society that is communicated to and is learning to communicate by visual and aural means primarily, rather than through print, which, before the electronic revolution of this century, was the only medium for communication by the mass and, concomitantly, the only mass medium. Before television and radio, we relied for hundreds of years on print as the medium through which we could communicate long distances and with large groups of people simultaneously. We could do that only because, early in the fifteenth century, Gutenberg developed movable type, which subsequently resulted in what many people then thought was the ultimate desecration of all that was good and holy and cultural and religious: the Bible was put into the mass media. It was published.

The same accusations of desecration were being made against television 500 years later.

Because something is powerful and new doesn't necessarily mean that it's bad, unless we arbitrarily consider any change as bad. Of the three great revolutions of the twentieth century—energy, transportation and communications—communications appears to be the most pervasive. Television and radio are the most powerful forces in the world today for affecting the minds, emotions and, through them, the behavior of humankind. The effect of television on society depends on how we use it.

Mussolini said that without radio he would never have gotten the control over the Italian people that he did. Goebbels praised film as his most important and successful tool in solidifying national support for the Nazi program. And senior citizens and historians can testify to the power and influence of Franklin D. Roosevelt's fireside chats.

When a political revolution occurs anyplace in the world, what is first taken over? Not the Treasury. Not the Post Office. Not the schools or universities. Not the factories or department stores. Not even the printing presses. But the television and radio stations!

Political control through television is not necessarily overt, obvious or sometimes even discernible. The communications revolution has affected us in ways we are not even aware of and, if we were, we would find it difficult to acknowledge or comprehend. Television has affected us far beyond its ostensible purpose of informing and entertaining. Just as the automobile changed our lives in considerably more ways than in our mode of transportation. In the first half of this century in this country, automobiles had greater impact on the development and changes in sexual attitudes, behavior, and relationships among young people than any other single factor. Electronic visual and aural communications have similarly affected interpersonal relationships. We have frequently read that in a number of countries throughout the world power failures shutting down television stations have resulted in surging birth rates exactly nine months later. Summer television rerun schedules have had the same effect.

New forms of art have been created. Picasso said that the twentieth-century developments in communications and transportation freed us from having to look at objects, including people, on the traditional fixed plane. It became both physically and attitudinally possible to see things across space and time quickly and virtually simultaneously from many angles and viewpoints. *Voilà*: cubism. John Dewey's greatest contribution to education, for some people, was his dictum that education should bring the real world to the classroom and the classroom to the real world. Yet, it wasn't until a half-century after he wrote this that television made it literally possible for it to happen in every classroom for every student.

Communications Professor Dallas W. Smythe [now deceased] of Simon Frazier University, Canada, has long been in the vanguard of those who have recognized both the potentials and the responsibilities of the mass media in the real world. In the 1960s, as the cold war got hotter, he wrote: "We know that the public is largely apathetic and alienated from concern with the vital issue of survival. What has been the contribution of the mass media to this apathy? . . . As Lazarsfeld and Merton argued . . . the escapist nature of most of the content of the mass media has for the citizen a 'narcotizing dysfunctional' effect."

Current events make Dr. Smythe's comments as applicable today as they were then. By demanding passive response, television exercises virtually as heavy a control over people's minds—that is, successfully neutralizing their concern with and participation in the social and political events of the world—as by actively persuading them to take a particular stand on something. It worked for a long time in the 1960s, allowing our Vietnam venture to go on until word of mouth and alternative established media resulted in a growing opposition to the war that the mainstream media could no longer ignore. By finally making it an essential part of their total coverage, the media hastened the end of the war. By the end of the 1970s the pattern was repeated, with the media largely ignoring the growing nationwide protests against the continuing production and deployment of nuclear weapons, protests by a substantial number of the 85% of Americans who wanted an immediate bilateral, verifiable freeze.

In support of Professor Smythe's concerns, I asked in an article written in the mid-1960s: Is there any doubt that the most important criticism of the mass media should relate to their roles as information and educational agencies in matters relating to the life or death of humankind?

I met with some of our consular officials in Calcutta while on official business for the State Department. Those of you who have been there know the impossibility of describing the extent of poverty and degradation: millions of people are born, exist, and die on the streets, never knowing a roof over their heads, decent food in their stomachs, clothes other than rags on their backs, or medicines for diseased and ravaged children. I suggested to one of the U.S. consular officials that television sets placed on top of lamp posts or poles on street corners throughout the city would reach millions of people with information on sanitation, on sources of health aid, on the needs and methods for contraception, and perhaps even, as has been done in some countries, with elemental material on training for various job areas, including agriculture, that might ultimately help some of them become at least minimally employable.

"That is not possible," I was told. "It is politically dangerous. The kinds of things they might see could foment a revolution." And then, as if the implications were too overwhelming without counterpoint, "How're you going to keep 'em down on the farm after they've seen TV?"

So powerful is the television medium that whoever controls it virtually controls society. The control of the political processes of a country through the control of television—whether by a government in power or by media barons in the private sector—is already a reality in many countries. In only a handful of countries, the U.S. among them, are television and radio insulated to any substantial degree from the direct control of the government. In many countries the systems and stations are government owned and operated. In the United States, however, except for partial federal, state, and local government support for public television and radio, the broadcasting system is not only operated but supported entirely by the private sector. The responsibility in the United States for determining the content of television programming lies with the people, through their influence on the private sector—the advertisers who sponsor the programs, the stations that carry them, and the state and local governments, institutions or organizations that support and operate public television.

Before you exercise such influence, however, ask yourself whether your judgment is based on ignorance and prejudice—making that judgment perhaps even less valid than that of a controlling government—or on intelligent, literate evaluation of what you see and hear. Perhaps even more important is the effect on our thoughts and feelings of those things that we make no judgment about because we do not understand enough about the medium's psychological and aesthetic impact. Those things may be, in fact, the kinds of things we have little problem making evaluations and judgments about when we see them in print because we've had enough education in reading, writing, and literature to be literate in the print medium. Many of us who are print-literate wrongfully assume that we are television-literate as well.

Even in a democratic country such as the United States, efforts to control television politically have sometimes been less than subtle, by both public and private sources. Control of the purse strings can affect media content indirectly if not directly. Sponsors' beliefs and interests have frequently determined the political orientation of programs, so subtly in many cases that unless you are a television literate you probably didn't realize how you were being proselytized.

In the late 1960s a National Conference Board study, which asked leaders in various professional areas to rate the most significant issues they thought would dominate the 1980s, found that one important concern was the possible control of the political process through the control of television by government or private interests. Government documents released in the late 1970s confirmed what many people in the field knew of earlier in the decade: the attempts by the Nixon White House to use television to forward its political purposes and to intimidate the television industry into restricting materials the White House considered politically unfavorable. Although this pressure did not succeed in the long run, it was not without some temporary success in both commercial and public television.

History and current events have shown us unequivocally that those who control television and radio are likely to control the political processes of any given country or society, with few exceptions. This is a dual truism: those who gain control of the broadcast media are most likely to gain political control; those who already have political control invariably solidify it by taking, or by attempting to take, control of the broadcast media. In only the rarest of situations, given the political systems in today's world, is there a practical possibility that individual citizens might gain direct access to mainstream TV and radio—that is, for citizen groups, including minorities and the poor as well as the elite, to own and operate their own stations. Indicative of the democratic practices of the U.S. compared to most countries, even though the United States' broadcasting system is one of the freest and least politicized in the world, the potential dangers of concentrated control led to FCC rules limiting multiple station ownership in individual cities and throughout the country, including, in certain situations, television-newspaper combinations. This presumably has prevented a given entity from being in a position to control the information and ideas disseminated to a given large segment of the population. [*These protections, among others, were vitiated in the 1980s by the Reagan administration and were virtually eliminated by the Clinton administration-backed Telecommunications Act of 1996.*] The only citizen alternative, therefore, is to gain control of the products of the media—to be able to analyze objectively and evaluate critically the content of television and radio so that it does not influence our thinking, feelings, and actions without our intelligent and informed consent. This is what we mean by TV literacy.

For politicians, an even greater fear than their lack of control of the people through the media is the corollary: if the media do not control the people, the people may ultimately control the media. The implications of this are earth-shaking—or, if you will, earth-mending. For the first time in the history of the world we have the opportunity and means for small and large groups of people to reach out to each other in every way except actual touch. Through their direct control over television programming and international patterns of transmission, immediate and live, people in all parts of the world, even those ostensibly enemies or at odds over presumed political, social, ethnic, religious, economic, or other differences, can talk with each other, begin to understand each other, sense a commonality in each other's needs and problems, see that basically all people are more alike than different in their common goals of survival and self-realization, and feel the bonds of sharing and interdependence rather than the breaches of divisiveness so frequently imposed by leaders whose maintenance of power is predicated on dividing people through extreme nationalism. [*Apply the above to the potentials of the Internet in this new century.*]

Giving control of the relationships among people to the people themselves in this way could potentially create traumatic changes in some of the traditional patterns of existence for many of us: no more disliking other people because of their skin color or country of origin or pronunciation of their names or because their arts or culture or ways of making a living are different; no more subjugating of people whose economic bases are not as strong as others; and maybe, even maybe—and don't let this throw you because it is so drastic a change in what we expect in our lives—maybe even no more wars.

Modern science, specifically communications technology [*read "Internet"*], can be used to achieve these purposes, if we wish it to. It is pragmatically feasible; communications have already been used to serve the opposite, antihumanistic goals. Throughout history totalitarian countries, in whatever political form they existed, usually attempted to maintain a high rate of print *il*literacy. They knew that without the ability to communicate effectively and to critically evaluate communications received, people were at a continuing disadvantage in understanding their political alternatives or organizing to do something about them. During the past few hundred years, with the invention of movable type and the printing press, print literacy began to spread, resulting in a gradual series of political revolutions, not the least of which was the one on the North American continent in 1776.

As long as print was the principal medium of sophisticated communications, the rise in literacy provided—I do not say guaranteed—the bases for people-oriented governments. The development of non-print media as significant means of communication permitted, in some countries, a return to totalitarian control over minds and emotions, including countries where the people's high degree of print literacy lulled them into the false perception that they could not be controlled through any form of communication. Germany in the 1930s is a prime example. Authority has always recognized print as a medium requiring the active participation of the reader, making it easier for the individual to exercise control; therefore, authority has tried to suppress it. On the other hand, recognizing TV as a medium of passive participation, less easy for the individual to control, authority has tried to dominate it. In the coming decades we may see an even greater power struggle between authority and the individual, if the present interactive potentials of computer communication become technically and economically feasible for large numbers of people, on the national and international levels both.

Print illiterates are especially vulnerable to control by television and radio because they cannot take advantage of the multiple-source alternative information and ideas that are possible in even the most repressive societies through underground newspapers, clandestine pamphlets and smuggled books. Television and radio are especially powerful in developing countries, where they are the principal instruments of control of thought and feeling. The more developed countries, however, are not immune. Even with—or, perhaps, because of—our extensive and intensive exposure to television, we Americans are not literate enough to immunize ourselves objectively from its persuasive powers. Print literates are vulnerable to control by television and radio because they have a false sense of security about their ability to evaluate critically and cope with the effects the electronic media has on them.

If our educational institutions truly believe that they are educating people for participation as thinking, contributing, competent human beings in a free, democratic society—and that is what educational institutions tell us they are doing—then it is incumbent upon them to introduce curricula that will graduate people who are visual and aural as well as print literates.

Certainly, there is some question as to whether we are now turning out even print literates. Perhaps part of the problem is that we have created a schizophrenia in learning: attempting to concentrate primarily on print and being unsuccessful because the real world in which the student lives and operates is principally a visual and aural one.

Just as a young person graduating from high school has had twelve years of required courses in print literacy—composition, literature, and other subjects that generally come under the heading of English—so should that person have at least an equivalent education in visual and aural literacy, such as courses in television and radio criticism, the analysis and preparation of visual and aural communications materials, and writing and producing visually and aurally as they have learned to do in print. The same consideration applies to college and university learning as well. All students in all fields of endeavor, including those going into economics, engineering, medicine, history, sociology, business, law, and other professions, and not just majors in journalism, film, TV or radio, should have at least as much exposure to visual literacy courses as they do to print literacy composition and literature courses required for graduation in most institutions of higher education—if they are to function in and contribute to their society effectively.

The same people who in all sincerity would make their educational institutions the best schools or colleges of the nineteenth century are likely to object strenuously to the introduction of mass media courses as an essential part of the curriculum. But just as the monks with the mortarboards and gowns who railed against the intrusion of books into their memorized monopoly of all of the world's knowledge had to adjust to people's desire for uncensored learning, so will those who are now fearful of the people's right to learn how to cope with perhaps a less obvious, but more insidious, kind of censorship and control.

In the 1970s the Federal Interagency Committee on Education held two conferences in Washington, D.C. on education and technology. One of the recommendations that came out of both conferences and was endorsed by all federal agencies with educational responsibilities was that "every citizen should have access to the highest quality communications, information and knowledge resources and should be provided with the opportunity for developing competencies in print literacy, electronic literacy, computer literacy and telecommunications literacy." In this respect, at least, our frequently foot-dragging federal bureaucracy is far ahead of our educational establishment.

Those who are concerned about our national illiteracy and want to do something about it do not have an easy road. It means changing education. It means convincing school boards and superintendents and principals and teachers and trustees and professors and students and parents. It means more than talking about it. It is easy to get agreement when only words are at stake. It is exceedingly more difficult when action is required and political control of a people is the prize.

If we believe in the desirability of a society governed by the educated will of the people, we will have to take action—perhaps, in using George Bernard Shaw's description of Savanarola, as saints perceived as public nuisances—that will make us all literate enough to critically evaluate and control the effects of television, or we can be certain that television will eventually control us.

# CHAPTER 6

# Communications and Minorities

While America's great revolution, the War for Independence of 1776–1783, solidified the power of the elite over the masses, who in turn imposed their concepts of culture and lifestyle on subsequent waves of new citizens, two revolutions of the twentieth century attempted to take back some prerogatives. These revolutions came at about the same time, in some instances stimulating and complementing each other. One is the focal point of this book, the counter-culture revolution of the 1960s and 1970s. Many of those who joined that cultural revolution against authority and conformity had participated in the revolution that immediately preceded it, to some extent inspired it, and continued after it: America's civil rights revolution.

Like the counter-culture revolution, the civil rights revolution had as its principal cadre, at first, college and university students. The 1960 Greensboro, North Carolina, lunch-counter sit-in, considered the first significant group action in the South, was engineered by college students. Protest marches, other sit-ins, petition drives, and boycotts relied principally on college students, although as the civil rights revolution progressed through the early 1960s, older concerned citizens and many clergy—of all denominations—joined in, many in leadership roles. The early reliance on college students stemmed from good reasons. First, college students, no matter how lacking in sensitivity their formal education might have been, were still generally more aware than most people of the historical, social, and political factors governing society, and concomitantly more aware of the ethical failures of that society. Second, college-age youth were stronger and healthier than most of the rest of the population and could better withstand the physical punishment that civil rights activists were subjected to in the South. In addition, anyone in the South, especially an African-American, who participated in civil rights protests was, almost invariably, immediately fired from his or her job; college students generally did not have families dependent for survival on the income from their jobs.

African-Americans had to fight for the right to vote. In the South many were murdered, many more physically and economically intimidated by southern whites to keep them from the polls. A number of protest groups developed, including the Southern Christians Leadership Conference (SCLC) led by the Reverend Dr. Martin Luther King, Jr. More aggressive groups such as the Student Nonviolent Coordinating Committee (SNCC, popularly called "Snick")—described by one leader, Andrew Young, as "aggressively non-violent"—played an increasingly important role. In 1963 Dr. King's March on Washington drew positive national attention to the civil rights struggle, prodded the Kennedy administration to send federal troops to protect the rights of African-American citizens in the South, and presaged the Voting Rights Act enacted under President Lyndon Johnson in 1965.

Meanwhile, the fight for equal rights spread from the South throughout other parts of the country, especially to urban areas where economic and in many cases social and political policies had ghettoized African-Americans (and other racial minorities) into situations that denied them opportunities and rights equal to those of the governing white male majority. (The term "white male" is used here advisedly, inasmuch as women of all races were also denied equal rights and opportunities, later leading to another political-economic aspect of the counter-culture revolution, the women's movement that began to grow in the 1970s.)

The racial equality battles in the North were not over voting rights, but principally over schools, jobs, and housing. While the "separate but equal" school approach that resulted in vastly inferior schools for African-Americans was not an official policy in most of the North, the geographical ghettoizing within cities resulted in the same thing. Rabid racism existed in the North. In some areas, such as Detroit and South Boston, the problem was virtually as bad as in the South, but was generally smoothed over by the media. The South was more openly racist and, therefore, the focal point for action and for public attention.

As the Civil Rights movement grew, so did official resistance to the idea that equal rights for African-Americans might actually be achieved. Police brutality in many northern cities led to the establishment of the Black Panther Party in 1966. The Panthers posed a significant threat to the status quo, given that group's willingness to fight violence with violence, although its principal concerns were to improve education, housing and jobs within the African-American urban communities, such as providing breakfasts for children in ghetto schools whose parents were too poor to give them anything to eat before the school day. With chapters in 25 states, the Black Panther movement grew so strong and was considered so threatening to the establishment that in 1968 FBI director J. Edgar Hoover called the Black Panther Party "the greatest threat to the internal security of the country." Not long afterwards the FBI raided the Black Panther's principal headquarters in Chicago while its leaders were asleep and assassinated most of them in their beds.

Although Martin Luther King, Jr. received the Nobel Peace Prize in 1965, the policies and practices of the majority whites who ruled the national, state, and local structures changed but little. The Civil Rights movement, having won legal support, now had to put the rule of law into practice. The only way was for African-Americans to enter the political arena and gain some measure of representation and perhaps even some control over their own communities. The most likely places to do that were the cities, urban areas where large concentrations of African-Americans and other racial minorities lived. In 1967 Carl Stokes was elected mayor of Cleveland, the first African-American to become mayor of a major U.S. city. The heady progress of the civil rights revolution, coupled with the continuing anti-establishment actions in the counter-culture revolution, promised significant change and movement toward a literal rather than figurative democratic society in America. As time has shown, the first flush of progress was given only lip-service in too many instances, and although important gains ultimately were made by African-Americans, equal rights and opportunities and affirmative action to provide such rights and opportunities gradually waned and virtually disappeared as the country turned conservative and supported the regressive policies of two Reagan administrations.

But during the 1960s and early 1970s the revolutions continued. SNCC and Dr. Martin Luther King, Jr. took strong stands, along with white college students of the North, against the Vietnam War. Individual icons, such as boxing champion Muhammed Ali, spoke out against America's venture in Southeast Asia; Ali refused to submit to induction into the armed forces on moral, ethical, and religious grounds. He was vilified, blackballed in the boxing industry, and prosecuted by the government, but was later vindicated by the Supreme Court and by his ultimate triumphs as a boxer.

The situation was one of ferment and hope, however, in the mid-1960s, when it seemed that the civil rights revolution had an excellent chance of changing the educational and social blight imposed on the country's inner cities. There was a strong possibility that education, with the proper support and use of technology, could reach the inner-city racial minorities and poor in a way that might begin to be equal to that afforded children in more affluent and white communities. Coupling this with the potential of the media to have a profound effect on education, both formal and informal, and for children and adults both, it seemed logical to push for changes in urban education that would take advantage of the new media-assisted learning opportunities.

While the emphasis was on African-Americans and recent Black immi-grants from other countries—those who constituted the principal progeni-tors of the civil rights revolution and principal subjects of urban education reform—the concerns and needs of other racial minorities required equal attention, and some of these constituencies began to organize to obtain it. In urban areas with large Asian populations, primarily Chinese at that time, the 300,000 Chinese-Americans in the United States were moving ahead mainly on their own. As the U.S. News and World Report noted in 1966, although many of the Chinese in cities were poor, they applied "traditional morals of hard work, thrift, and morality." There was little organized effort from outside of their own communities to help solve their educational or other problems.

Native Americans, although no longer the object of genocide by white European-Americans seeking to take their land, were nevertheless in a continuing situation of ghettoized—on reservations—poverty. Unem-ployment, inadequate housing, lack of medical care, and high infant mortal-ity were ways of life. Education leading to professional status was virtually nonexistent. The U.S. Bureau of Indian Affairs (BIA) enforced both physical and psychological segregation. Most BIA schools did not provide the courses necessary for subsequent admittance into secondary schools and, most emphatically, did not provide preparation for entrance into higher education. Part of the educational problem was the isolation of Native Americans imposed by the U.S. government and within the Native Ameri-can communities among the Native Americans themselves, a dichotomy between preserving tradition and breaking away from their own civiliza-tion into the white majority's world of higher education and its social and employment marketplace.

Hispanics—now more often referred to as Latinos—were in the 1960s, as reported by U.S. News and World Report, "a silent majority start[ing] to speak out." Latinos constituted large populations in a number of U.S. cities, principally in the Southwest and South and in some northeast cities, such as New York, were beginning to make up a sizable percentage of the popula-tion. In many cases the lack of bilingual education doomed many Span-ish-speaking children, new arrivals to this English-speaking country, to inadequate schooling. Unlike African-Americans, who by the 1960s and 1970s had organized for political action, Latinos were comparatively quiet and even apathetic—due in great part to the language barrier and inade-quate education about U.S. customs and processes. Nevertheless, some na-tional organizations, such as the GI Forum and the Mexican-American Anti-Defamation League, were letting the nation at large know that Latinos and Latinas, also, needed assistance and equal opportunity if they were to obtain the educational and economic situations that would enable them to make their potential contributions to American society.

The following is an amalgamation of an address, "Communications and Crisis," to the American Management Association's Third Annual Conference on Education and Training, August 9, 1967, New York City; an address, "Communications and the Urban Crisis: Doing Our Own Thing," to the American Management Association's Fourth Annual Conference on Education and Training, August 13, 1968, New York City; an address, "Minorities and the Communications Field: A New Educational Ethic," to the Broadcast Education Association annual convention, March 16, 1974, Houston; from the report and dissenting statement at the 1968 national conference on telecommunications sponsored by the Joint Council on Educational Telecommunications, University of Georgia; and from notes from other meetings and panel presentations.

With the exception of those who have learned and maintained the subculture of an immigrant parent-grandparent ethnic group or of a particular geographic-economic-political-social group, most Americans are oriented to a predominantly single-plane white middle-class majority culture. As complex as it may sometimes be, by and large it is not as complicated as the minority sub-cultures with their additional, necessary self-protective mores and practices. Communication to and with a group or individual whose subculture is more complicated, more cohesive and, in its self-protective way, stronger than the majority culture is difficult and sometimes ironic.

The middle-class white sometimes identifies progress as verbal effort. Because the middle-class can afford more time with passive verbal progress than can people who urgently need to change the material realities of their economic and political situation, it gives more importance to words than to actions. White America, for example, does not know the Black subculture. (On the other hand, Black America knows the white majority culture, having had to learn it well in order to survive.) The lack of understanding, the lack of identification of White America with Black America hinges on the inability to communicate and on the assumption that verbalization, particularly the white concept of Black language, is synonymous with communications.

For example, a "Doonesbury" strip by Garry Trudeau showed a group of whites being taken by a Black tour guide through the inner city. The guide points to a group of young Black men headed their way whom he describes as "evil dudes." His white tour group is frightened. When the Black men arrive they greet the tour guide as a friend, and he tells them that the white group is his tour party. The members of the white group, trying to show a camaraderie with the Blacks, say such things as "Hey, guys, what is happening?" "Check it out," "Right on, man," "All power, fellas." The

Blacks, of course, laugh, and the tour guide, embarrassed with his charge, suggests that they move on.

We are dealing with a lack of communication and a lack of knowledge of how to communicate. Yet, for years, White America has been telling Black America (and other minority groups) how to use communications and what to communicate. Even when white radical Americans, in the years when working for integrated, democratic economic-political opportunity and social relationships was far from acceptable, tried at their own socio-political-economic risk to provide access to communications for minorities, it was principally in terms of their white majority concepts, understandings, and needs. Even in the late 1960s—following the burning of cities and the notice served by Black America on White America that subjugation and frustration do, indeed, lead to revolution—when the media magnanimously began doing some programming for Blacks, the materials were determined almost totally by whites who somehow assumed they knew what was needed by Blacks.

In the summer of 1967 I spoke at the annual education and communications conference of the American Management Association in New York to several thousand people representing management (middle and upper income, educated, and with some social commitment) of industry, education and government. That was a summer of revolt; Black people in the inner cities desperately reaching out in the only way they had, to communicate to the world the despairing frustration of what it is to live in oppression without hope. My speech dealt with "Communications and Crisis." It suggested that what was happening in Newark, Detroit, Milwaukee and East Harlem was more significant in revealing our failures and potentials in the field of communications than were all the government-industry-university experiments and research.

Because those in the controlling majority had denied the people of the inner city direct access to the means of communication, there was no choice but for these people to scream out with the kind of action and intensity that gets the attention of the rest of society: riots, violence, arson. What desperation a person must be forced into to be willing to destroy everything they have, including their own lives, if necessary! What hopelessness and despair force people to acts of self-destruction! What a tragic cry for help is an inward act of violence! What a forsaken wilderness of education and communication is revealed between the majority and large groups of minorities in our society!

Although the situation at the time revolved around Black uprisings in Black ghettos, the concerns then and now are not limited to one minority group. They relate to the emerging militancy of Latinos and to the needs of Asian-American ghettos, Native American reservations, and poor-white slums as well.

My speech called for a realistic, practical effort on the part of industry, education, and government to provide communications media for the inner city, to be run by the inner city for the purpose not of communicating to those living in the inner city (who, living in the ghetto, has to learn from the media what life in the ghetto is like?), but for the purpose of solidifying intraghetto communications for more effective group action and for communicating to the predominantly white suburbs not only what was actually happening, but what was likely to happen if the people of suburbia continued to ignore the inner cities.

In 1967 the concept of urging the establishment to use communications for social reform was relatively new, particularly the use of media to directly solve the problems of the inner cities. Hadn't the Civil Rights legislation of 1964 and 1965 taken care of everything? We could be shocked into action by riots, by burning, by looting. But somehow we were not willing to be as openly and publicly concerned and motivated by the continuing conditions that caused them.

One year later, in 1968, I spoke on the same subject at the same conference of the American Management Association. My speech was entitled "Doing Our Own Thing." It stressed the need to put Black-oriented communications into the hands of the Blacks, and that the majority white society should use white-oriented communications to change its own racist patterns of behavior. Martin Luther King, Jr. and Robert F. Kennedy had just been assassinated.

I asked the business and industry executives, many of whom reported active projects to recruit members of minority groups for their companies, if they were providing opportunities for educated minorities to work in executive positions commensurate with their education, or whether they were putting them into the category of trained, as opposed to educated, personnel? Was training being provided not only for minority employees to qualify them for equal opportunity jobs, but, perhaps more importantly, also for company executives who needed to acquire the attitudes and practices necessary for providing equal opportunities?

I suggested that perhaps one of the most effective uses of communications to assist minorities was by educating white America. Thanksgiving baskets carried by ladies in crinoline skirts, no matter how altruistic and sincere the motives, are not answers. Paternalism—or maternalism—is not the solution. Minorities, I suggested, want their own prerogative and independence of action, want the pride and self-respect of making their own decisions, want to determine their own futures.

Middle-class liberal white America is not Machiavellian. It is, primarily, the victim of inadequate understanding and feeling, of inadequate communication. An occurrence at the Dalton School in New York City illustrated this gap. The parent-teacher organization of that private school of good reputation in an affluent area sponsored a program to bring the predominantly white parents of children at Dalton and the parents of children at a special school in Harlem—children with learning problems—together to learn how to help their children learn to read better. "A more satisfactory way than writing checks," one of the sponsoring Dalton School parents said. The $26–$40 costs for the sessions paid by each Dalton parent were not charged the parents from Harlem. What a disappointment for the white parents when only 13 of the 40 expected parents from Harlem showed up—13 out of a total of 100 adults in the program.

The white parents were puzzled. But listen to a young African-American interviewed by the *New York Times*: "We don't say keep out of our lives, but we say make Black people so strong they can do their own thing—whatever their thing is—by themselves." And another young African-American: "Black people want Black control of their lives and activities more than anything else. If they make a mistake, let them be Black mistakes—we're tired of white mistakes in our lives."

Isn't this simply the kind of independence and privilege most of the majority society has always taken for granted for itself?

Where does that leave those who strongly believe that as white individuals they not only can help alleviate the urban crisis, but have a responsibility to do so? Again, a quote in the *New York Times*, expressing even in 1968 a growing sentiment among minority group people: "The missionary area for white people is not in the ghettos, but in white suburbia."

The audience reaction to this 1968 speech was surprisingly strong and supportive. How one year and a couple of assassinations can bring consciences out in the open! Yet, as the years continued to pass, minority progress in the control of communications media remained—and still remains today—painfully slow.

One significant method for obtaining access to the media for minority groups has been to challenge the license renewals of radio and television stations. A landmark case that set the stage for future challenges began in 1965 when the FCC renewed the license of the Lamar Life Broadcasting Company licensee of WLBT in Jackson, Mississippi, despite evidence that the station was discriminatory in programming and personnel policies. In 1966, following suits filed by the Office of Communications of the United Church of Christ on behalf of the minority challengers in Jackson, the courts reversed the FCC and ordered that a new hearing be held with applications for the station license considered from other parties besides the station owner, Lamar Life. In 1970, after receiving several applications and holding a hearing, the FCC granted the application of Communications Improvement, Inc., an organization composed of minority group interests, and took the license away from Lamar Life.

It was continued court insistence that the regulatory agency serve the public interest that opened the way for more citizen participation in communications development and resulted in subsequent FCC actions that made stations more responsible to minorities. Another such instance occurred in July, 1971, when the United States Court of Appeals reversed a January, 1970, FCC Policy Statement not to consider license challenges to stations that were considered to have "substantially" met the programming needs of their communities. The suit had been brought by Black Efforts for Soul in Television and the Citizens Communications Center. In ordering the FCC to conduct full comparative hearings in cases where there was a challenge, including reconsideration of challenges it had dismissed since January, 1970, the court stated:

As new interest groups and hitherto silent minorities emerge in our society, they should be given some stake in and chance to broadcast on our radio and TV frequencies. According to uncontested testimony no more than a dozen of 7,500 broadcast licenses are owned by racial minorities. The effect of the 1970 Policy Statement, ruled illegal today, would certainly have been to perpetuate this dismaying situation.

As a result of continuing pressures, the FCC adopted in early 1971 a requirement that every commercial station (by mid-1972 pressure had begun to build to include noncommercial stations as well) do an ascertainment of community needs as a guide in determining the kind of programming that would best serve the community in which the station was located. In addition, in 1971, the FCC required each station with five or more employees to adopt an equal employment opportunity program and to file a yearly statement showing its efforts in this regard. However, there was little self-initiated effort on the part of the FCC to enforce its rulings. It remained for minority groups themselves to initiate and follow through on action to obtain access to the broadcasting media, building on organizational patterns and tactics developed during the 1960s civil rights efforts. The early 1970s became a time of ferment, and news stories, such as this one in *Broadcast Magazine*, began to appear:

The renewal applications of 14 Rochester stations were the object of a single petition filed by 36 residents of the city, for themselves as members of a number of community groups representing the city's poor. The petition charges that "nearly all" of the stations' surveys of community needs were inadequate, in that they discriminated against participation of the poor and minority groups and that the stations' public-affairs and news programming bears no "identifiable relationship" to the needs that were ascertained in surveys. ("More local news was available to the 87,000 citizens of Aristotle's Athens than is available to the city which is a black Rochester today—a communications disaster area," the petition said.) The petition also said that none of the stations had implemented an affirmative action hiring and promotion program.

Another news story, in the *New York Times:*

A coalition of black community organizations announced yesterday that it had reached agreement with two of the three network-owned New York stations for a voice in management, planning and production of black-oriented programs.... Under the agreements, the stations have agreed to increase their over-all black employment in the next three years, make every effort to increase the number of blacks in management-level decision-making positions, and to increase the number of on-air personalities in both news and entertainment.

Through their own efforts, to go beyond the tokenism of most of the commercial networks and stations, Blacks set about to develop their own communications resources, and in mid-1972 the first Black-owned, Black-oriented national radio network went on the air. The National Black Network (N.B.N.) featured public affairs programming, sportscasts, and live coverage of events of special interest to Blacks. It also carried on-the-hour newscasts with a Black perspective. N.B.N. started with an affiliated group of some 40 so-called "soul" stations that have predominantly Black audiences.

The success of Black efforts prompted Latino groups to begin to bring pressure on radio and television stations, especially in the Southwest, to serve the needs of the Spanish-speaking communities. In many instances, under threat of local pressure and of legal action against renewal of broadcast licenses, many stations began to change programming and to hire Latinos in more than menial positions. In mid-1972, for example, coordinated action against the sale of Time-Life stations to McGraw-Hill resulted in a breakthrough for all minorities in broadcasting. Following FCC approval of the sale of the stations, a five-city coalition of eight Mexican-American organizations and one Black group filed suits in the U.S. Court of Appeals to overturn the FCC decision. In exchange for withdrawal of the suits, McGraw-Hill signed an agreement providing for national and local minority advisory councils on programming, extensive production of programs dealing with Mexican-American history and culture and other minority topics, greater employment of Hispanics and Blacks in professional and managerial as well as other positions, the establishment of minority training programs, and local public access through free public service announcements.

The agreement was significant in that it had the most far-reaching effect up to that time on broadcasting's commitment to serving the nation's minorities. It clearly established the right and ability of minorities to use the judicial process to enforce the responsibilities of the regulatory agency when they feel the executive branch has failed in that regard.

The increased service to minority listeners and viewers was not always because of force or altruism. Some networks and stations recognized the financial as well as public service benefits. Advertisements seeking advertisers for Spanish-speaking and Black audiences began to appear. These were breakthroughs in providing minority service, albeit the appeal to potential advertisers was based on the traditional bottom line. One advertisement, headlined "A Spanish Radio News Network? Si!" stated: "Now, for the first time, advertisers can reach the U.S. Spanish market on a national basis with network radio. On May 1, MUTUAL SPANISH NETWORK began reaching out to 11 million Spanish-speaking Americans with once-hourly newscasts and additional drive time sportscasts, delivered simultaneously to Spanish stations coast to coast. . . . With the MUTUAL SPANISH NET-WORK it's easy to buy the U.S. Spanish audience . . . one order, one billing covers outstanding Spanish radio stations in all the important U.S. markets."

Another advertisement stated:

Black America wants information, too. News of significance to blacks. The day's happenings . . . told with emphasis on how they relate to the black experience. On May 1, Mutual Black Network began to reach black Americans on a national basis with *network radio*—over local black-oriented radio stations. . . . One order, one billing covers outstanding black radio stations in all the important U.S. markets. You can *sell* Black America through Mutual Black Network's all-encompassing schedule. . . . Because it is written, produced and broadcast by blacks, Mutual Black Network is unique in its access to and interpretation of news from the perspective of black Americans. Almost 17 million blacks live in America's cities. And the big majority listens to black radio. Mutual Black Network will deliver your message, coast to coast, to the largest black audience ever.

There was progress during the 1970s. Minority employment grew, stereotyped portrayals on television and radio diminished, and more attention was paid to the needs of all citizens in a community in preparing programs. However, compared to the needs and the potentials, the results fell far short.

During America's counter-culture revolution there were attempts to use the media in ways that would give actual rather than lip-service support to minority progress, attempts that still have not been fully realized. In the 1960s, for example, after many months of U.S. planning and work, the U.S. Office of Economic Opportunity (OEO) established a government-industry-education community project in a mid-west city. The state bar association, a respected and somewhat conservatively oriented organization, wished to alleviate the urban crisis by disseminating materials dealing with the legal rights and responsibilities of ghetto residents. The association's first approach was to develop the ideas and to have them produced by an outside organization. The results were less than satisfactory. Finally, it was decided that each group concerned would do their own thing. OEO coordinated and funded the project; the bar association, in cooperation with a ghetto organization (a Black nationalist group, incidentally) determined the basic problem areas; the bar association, on its own, developed the legal approaches to be used; the Black citizens group, on its own, produced the communications materials for mass distribution. Suddenly, it was realized by the majority society that it no longer had complete control over the minority society. By control over at least a part of the communication process, African-Americans were not only participating in, but making decisions concerning their own governing process. The project was stopped.

At about the same time, Canada experimented with a highly dramatic plan that had direct application to majority-minority relationships in the United States. The National Film Board of Canada, in cooperation with Memorial University of Newfoundland and the community of Fogo Island, filmed in depth the people and problems of Fogo Island, then played back these films to the people to help reveal, modify, and develop individual and group attitudes. The entire community was involved at all stages in decisions to be made and in the entire process of self-analysis and problem-solving. The people selected the topics, participated in making and editing the films, and determined the modes of distribution. Some of the goals included developing insights into community problems and a desire by the community to act on them, fostering more effective community-education-government cooperation, promoting greater understanding and desire for action in communities with similar problems by showing the films there. Perhaps most important, all groups in the Fogo Island community were brought together as a result of using the films as a base for ameliorating real or imagined differences among the groups, thus creating a strong, unified community for mutual self-help and action.

On the basis of the Fogo Island experiment, OEO set out to do the same kind of thing in two communities in this country, one on the West Coast and one in New England. The success of this approach here could have been a milestone in using communications to bring minority groups together to solve problems by internal and external action. It could have significantly strengthened the progress and place in the total society and in local government of disadvantaged groups, which had little or no access to or control over means of communication. Following the two efforts in this country, with a realization by the white controlling majority of what the success of the projects might mean to the existing power balance, the projects were abruptly dropped.

In 1968 the Federal Interagency Media Committee, consisting of representatives of thirty-two federal departments and agencies with communication responsibilities, recommended to the White House the establishment of a Communications Liaison Office on Minority Group Matters. This office would, among other things, cooperate with industry and other public and private organizations in facilitating the development, distribution, and use of materials oriented toward minority group needs, specifically including the needs of the urban ghettos. The agencies would be encouraged and assisted in diversifying materials, not only for informing minority groups of services available to them, but for assisting intra-minority group communications and for educating the majority society on the special problems and needs of minority groups. The Office would also develop a broadcasting skills bank of minority group personnel so that agencies, through employment of more minority group members, could better understand and serve the needs of those groups in the country. In addition, through greater use of minority group performers in film, television, and other audiovisual materials produced by federal agencies, members of minority groups seeing these productions would be able to identify more with the overall growth and goals of their country and be more greatly motivated to become an integral part of it.

Endorsed by representatives of various federal agencies, this proposal was sent to the Johnson administration. No action was taken on it. When the Nixon administration came into office a few months later, the proposal was again sent to the White House. Again, no action was taken.

Was the establishment trying to tell us something?

Sympathy, dedication, concern, willingness and even militancy on the part of a member of the majority is not enough if communication has not also established understanding, identification, and the kind of sensitivity that one develops usually only by living an experience, not learning about it.

A typical example of such insensitivity to the needs and feelings of the minority, even by the well-meaning, occurred at a 1968 national conference sponsored by the Joint Council on Educational Telecommunications, under a Ford Foundation grant. The purpose of the conference was laudable: to explore the application of telecommunications to national policies for education. It was held in a relaxed atmosphere at the conference center of the University of Georgia. Task forces were assigned to wrestle with various areas of human concern and to come up with solutions through the application of communications. I served on the urban task force.

The composition of the urban task force resembled that of similar conferences, seminars, and meetings. Of the thirty people in the group—most quite prominent in their fields—who were deciding on policy for the application of communications to inner-city needs, one was Black: Elizabeth Duncan Koontz, then President of the National Education Association and later to become Assistant Secretary of Labor and Director of the United States Women's Bureau. There were no other identifiable minorities on the task force.

My comment at the beginning of the opening session was one that I invariably make under such circumstances: "We are here to decide how to use communications to meet the needs of people who are poor, Black, and live in the inner city. I don't see anyone here who is poor, Black, and lives in the inner city."

With the kind of typical stereotyping that each person involved would deny as being racist, eyes immediately turned toward Dr. Koontz.

"I'm Black, but I'm not poor and I've never lived in the inner city," she said. Dr. Koontz went on to say that without direct knowledge of economically disadvantaged inner-city problems and needs, the group could hardly be expected to develop any meaningful recommendations. She suggested that, at the minimum, the group should be provided with mediated materials from inner-city residents, if not the participation of the residents themselves. I announced that I was participating with the reservation that, under the circumstances, the validity of whatever recommendations the urban task form came up with would have to be seriously questioned.

For two days the group dealt with generalizations. Koontz had been right. Most suggestions were from the white, middle-class viewpoint. Television for vocational training. Television for literacy. Television to serve consumer information needs. Finally, I suggested that we ought to at least try to judge what the poor ghetto Blacks themselves might be concerned with. Like jobs. Housing. The PO-lice. (The need to explain the pronunciation of that word was an ironic comment on the ability of White America to understand even the simplest language of Black America.)

Finally, the task force arrived at some principles of communications activism that seemed to relate to the realities of the inner city: to provide direct information and education through materials that the inner-city residents themselves develop according to their needs and understanding; to provide means by which the ghetto residents can communicate with each other, through an efficient and quick intraghetto system; to provide communication from the ghetto to suburbia on the problems, needs and dangers of discrimination and segregation to all of society as they really exist. A specific breakdown of the kinds of materials, media, and uses was included. The report, as it was developed for final adoption, was strong insofar as it implied the need for inner-city development and control of its own facilities and programming, and by such an implication indicated that the majority society had thus far failed to meet the communications needs of the country's urban minorities.

But final adoption never came. A substitute resolution was offered which deleted the specifics and offered a general suggestion for the need for "a coordinated program of research, implementation and evaluation to determine which media performing which functions can best meet any given urban need." It recommended that "a comprehensive approach to the use of communications technology be undertaken in one or more selected 'model city' programs."

Dr. Koontz joined me in a concurring vote and in the issuance of an additional statement, as follows, that we believed dealt with the core of the problem: "This commission operated under the handicap of attempting to deal with urban problems without having a representative from the inner-city on the commission, and of directing its attention to areas primarily affecting Black people without having knowledge of their attitudes and feelings, or of those of all the other minority groups involved. We wish to make it clear, therefore, that these recommendations must be oriented toward an acceptance of the needs and desires of the people concerned, in their environment, in terms of what they want done, and not imposed in terms of what we think should be done."

The sponsoring organization, the Joint Council on Educational Telecommunications, ceased inviting me to its conferences.

Not a single other person in the group was willing to sign their name to the statement when it was read. One did, later. William Harley, the President of the National Association of Educational Broadcasters (N.A.E.B.) and a member of this urban task force, walked past me a bit later as I was typing up the dissenting statement for formal submission. He walked past two or three times, stopping each time to look over my shoulder at the statement, then finally said, "Bob, would you add my name to the dissenting statement?" At the time the N.A.E.B. had been delaying efforts by some of its members to have the organization set up an Office of Minority Affairs. Following a vote of its membership at its 1968 convention to set up a committee on minority affairs, the N.A.E.B. administration did not hold a meeting of that committee for nine months, and did so only after public pressures from one of the committee members, Dave Berkman, and a story in a national magazine implying bad faith on the part of the N.A.E.B. in fulfilling its members' wishes on minority needs. The office subsequently was set up. Shortly afterward, at an N.A.E.B. convention, several association officers led the membership in voting down a resolution calling for the setting up of a civil liberties office to combat censorship and other pressures on educational broadcasting and in defeating, as well, a resolution that called for censuring one of its members, the Alabama Educational Television Commission, for discriminatory programming and employment practices, for which the FCC subsequently revoked its licenses.

It should also be noted that two years after that, in 1972, the convention program of the N.A.E.B. contained not a single session on minority group needs. The director of the N.A.E.B.'s Office of Minority Affairs, Lionel Monagas, an African-American, was considering boycotting the convention. It was at this convention that F.C.C. Commissioner Benjamin L. Hooks, the first African-American to sit on the Federal Communications Commission, told the convention delegates that there was too much racism in the country and in public/educational broadcasting and that noncommercial broadcasting's record of minority hiring and minority participation was abysmal. He attacked the lack of "Blacks and Chicanos and women" at noncommercial stations and stated that he could not be the friend of public broadcasting he would like to be "until you get your own house in order."

The controllers of communications have acted only when they have been forced to. Although the 1960s and 1970s can be said to be decades of progress, the progress has been slow, painful and insufficient. When the pressures get so strong that something is about to burst, it appears that only then do we take action. Unrelenting pressure resulted in increased minority ownership of stations, with the FCC adopting in 1978 a policy to permit capital gains tax deferrals for sales of stations to minorities and to permit "distress" sales to minorities of stations that may be about to lose their licenses in a hearing. As significant as such actions may be, however, they still were of the band-aid variety. [*Even this action was repealed by Congress as it continued deregulating broadcasting in the 1990s.*] They are similar to the "cool-it" approach taken by broadcasters during the urban disorders of the late 1960s, when they put "reasonable" Blacks on the air to cool the ire of "unreasonable" Blacks.

Majority America has got to stop judging minority America in terms of its own white middle-class values. How often have we heard white broadcast executives complain that minorities don't appreciate what they are trying to do for them? Ironically, while white America still does not understand America's people of color, minorities—through bitter years of learning how to survive—understand majority America only too well!

Approaches that were necessary to spark the efforts of minorities in the 1960s and the 1970s unfortunately continued to remain valid. For example, from a story in the *Washington Post* in 1972:

Tony Brown, dean of the Howard University School of Communications, yesterday urged a group of black journalists meeting at Howard to become activist writers involved in promoting the interests of black people. He also criticized the traditional journalistic idea of the uninvolved writer as inadequate for black advancement and said white-controlled media had promoted negative images of blacks. A solution, he said, would be for blacks to gain access to the media and tell their own story. "Our primary concern should not be the sensibilities of boards, commissions, committees, and so forth of whites, but the education of black children and adults," he said. "Black people have spent most of their lives fighting the struggle of self-hate that every white institution in America teaches blacks. By promoting black pride through the use of black journalism, we can provide an antidote to this psychological self-destruction."

And from the *New York Times* that same year: "A gloomy picture of a white-controlled communications industry that ignores or distorts the true needs, aspirations and lifestyles of black Americans was painted for the Congressional Black Caucus today." A few days later, in *Broadcasting* magazine: "The Congressional Black Caucus laid it on the line last week: In its opinion, the mass media are pervaded by racism in employment and news coverage and moreover are engaged in a conspiracy—conscious or unconscious—to prevent the public from learning that blacks and the poor are exploited by media advertising."

The statistics in the late 1970s [*and, significantly, 20 years later*] show more Blacks employed in the broadcasting industry and more prominent Black personalities on the air, but as stated in the title of the Civil Rights Commission report of 1978 on the status of minorities and women in broadcasting, it is "Window Dressing on the Set." Broadcasting is still clearly and unequivocally under the control and the decision-making of America's white majority, with minorities still discriminated against, the sincere and sophisticated understanding and motives of many white broadcasting executives notwithstanding. For many now at the top, especially those who consider themselves "liberals," ego may have to be sacrificed for purpose. It is a very threatened ego that needs to build itself up at the expense of others, a very weak one that needs an underdog to survive. People will have to learn to be willing to "share" rather than to "lead" or "help."

The disappointment in the failure of the hope and promises of the 1960s and in the tokenism of the open doors of the 1970s was compounded by the recession-inflation of the 1980s, which was beginning to turn many minorities back to the militancy that at least created conditions for change during America's counter-culture revolution. In the 1990s the strong economy obfuscated the continuing frustration. But it is still there. To avoid a national trauma that will not be salved or solved by a band-aid approach in the new millennium, minorities will have to have the opportunity for an equal measure of control over those forces in society, including communications, that affect them. The white majority might well use its measure of control to sensitize and educate white America until such time as equality of opportunity, prerogative, and control has been attained by *all* Americans. The answer may be, perhaps—to borrow a phrase from the 1960s—in all of us simply doing our own thing!

# CHAPTER 7

# Education, Media, and the Inner-city Child

In the mid-1960s the civil rights revolution brought a revolution to education in America's urban areas. The white middle class accelerated its exodus to the suburbs. City populations were increasingly composed of people of color. The urban public schools, already in many instances objects of continued neglect, were incapable of serving the needs of their students. Many, if not most, were understaffed and underfinanced. Shortages of textbooks, desks, and even classrooms and teachers made adequate learning almost impossible. In some schools the overcrowding was so bad that many students had to sit in makeshift classes in damp basements, in hallways, in bathrooms, and in auditoriums and gymnasiums where other activity interfered with any normal educational process. Many buildings were crumbling—broken windows, unsanitary toilet facilities, leaking roofs, broken stairs, and peeling walls. In some schools double shifts were required, some students going to classes from 7 A.M. to Noon, and others from Noon to 5 P.M., the starting and ending times in the dark days of winter hardly safe for little children. Many children in the crowded classrooms had to sit on floors. And even when children in schools in African-American and Latino ghettoized neighborhoods were able to attend classes, many of them came from families so poor that the children were sent to school without any breakfast, their physical conditions seriously interfering with their ability to learn.

One example took place in Queens, New York, where one of the projects of a Black Panther chapter was to provide breakfasts for such children as they arrived at school. Before the Black Panther project, these breakfastless children registered low scores on IQ tests; three months after they began to have something to eat before school their IQ averages shot up by 30 points. (So much for the validity of IQ tests and, by extension, other standardized tests!)

As Peter Schrag wrote in his book, *Village School Downtown*, urban education in America was becoming "Negro" education. Increased racial strife and insensitivity and, in many cases, racism on the part of teachers and school administrators, further demeaned the learning process for children of color. This occurred not only in the South, but in many cities in the North, as well. South Boston, in Massachusetts, was a prime example of bigoted parents and a compliant community, rioting against the busing of African-American children into South Boston schools and, in fact, even viciously attacking children who were bused in. It is significant to note that in the 1990s, after several decades of affirmative action that provided equal opportunity to African-American children for a decent education in decent schools, the city of Boston reverted to the racist separate-but-equal doctrine—patently, ghetto schools, with few exceptions, have always been unequal—and discontinued affirmative action placement for ghettoized children. In the 1960s, even when African-American children were permitted to attend the white schools, which had more funds, staffs, and resources, many principals and teachers found numerous ways to obviate the equal opportunity. For example, at the Murch School in Washington, D.C., where the author's children were pupils, the principal made certain that the bused-in African-American children were put on buses back to the ghetto at 3 P.M., as soon as classes ended, thus preventing these children from participating in the school's extra-curricular activities or socializing with their white classmates. In other schools, some teachers sat white pupils in front and pupils of color in the rear of the classrooms. In some schools where the majority of the students were African-American, some teachers were not only insensitive, but used racial slurs while teaching. Teaching and learning materials—especially by African-American authors—relating to the Black experience in America were in some cases ignored or banned. Textbooks were almost invariably "white"—photos and illustrations did not depict families or children of color. The pupils, living in urban areas, virtually saw only pictures of white children in suburban houses with wide lawns and late-model automobiles in driveways.

The 1968 Kerner Commission Report on violence in America, which included an analysis of the reasons for urban problems, plus the assassination of Dr. Martin Luther King, Jr. later that year, both exacerbated the problem and brought it to a head. The Kerner Commission Report got to the nub of the matter when it said: "What white Americans have never fully understood—but what the Negro can never forget—is that white society is deeply implicated in the ghetto. White institutions created it, white institutions maintain it, white institutions condone it."

Conditions in the ghettos, including urban education, had to be revolutionized if education was to meet the needs of its new constituency. It was clear that it was up to groups and organizations representing the urban population to do it themselves. They tried. Picketing. Boycotts. Rallies. Political demands. Eventually, community political action—community involvement in putting up school board candidates and getting out the vote—opened the doors for change.

The following is an amalgamation of two presentations; an address, "Media and Education: A Look At It Like It Is," to the District of Columbia Association for Supervision and Curriculum Development," June 7, 1968, Washington, D.C., and an address, "Communications and the Urban Crisis: Doing Our Own Thing," to the American Management Association's Fourth National Conference on Education and Training, August 13, 1968, New York City.

Disadvantaged children are put into classrooms surrounded by print material that they cannot read, given tasks that they cannot do and that have little meaning in relation to their real world, and talked at by white faces in suits and ties that drive out of the ghetto every afternoon to a different society. These are conditions of Kafkaesque terror for any child; they are unreal, they have no positive meaning, and it is incredible that anybody can be expected to learn anything under them.

It is no accident that a study some years ago by the U. S. Commission on Civil Rights reported that not a single compensatory educational program in the United States had been successful. It is no accident that a study by the Center for Urban Education showed New York's "More Effective Schools" program to have had no significant impact on the academic achievement of pupils. It is no accident that New York University's Clinic for Learning in a junior high school in Brooklyn's Bedford-Stuyvesant area "got the hell kicked out of us" and abandoned its efforts. It is no accident that the millions upon millions of dollars being poured into special education for disadvantaged children seem to produce little or no positive results.

As I have often stated, all children today, including and maybe especially the ghetto child, live in an aural and visual world. Yet, virtually every education program in the country is rooted in the print world of fifty years ago. How can we expect any child to learn when we continue to use nineteenth-century methods and techniques to try to solve the problems of education that are rooted in the twentieth-century revolutions of energy, transportation and—especially—communications?

It is significant that the term "ghetto" came into increased use following the disorders of the 1960s. We used to call those areas slums. Now we use a term that refers to a group deliberately isolated—the traditional concept of ghetto as developed in organized discrimination against the Jews in Europe throughout the centuries. Isn't the term "ghetto" more descriptive and explanatory of what has happened and what is happening than the word "slum?" Have you heard of poor whites living in ghettos? They live in slums.

The federal government, ostensibly in a position to diagnose the inner-city problems and provide solutions along a broad front, has failed to adequately differentiate between cause and symptom and has failed to relate the psychological and experiential input of people to their verbal and physical output. For example, in 1968 the Advisory Commission on Intergovernmental Relations devoted much of its Ninth Annual Report to racial unrest and civil disorder and to urban problems. It searched for causes that would fit the traditional solutions and proceeded to ignore the most important single element that is at one and the same time the lack, the cause, and the solution: communications.

On the other hand, the Report of the National Advisory Commission on Civil Disorders that same year went further than any other national official statement up to that time on the subject of communications. It recognized the need to provide programs of special interest to the ghetto and to represent more objectively the needs and actions of the ghetto to the population as a whole. It suggested increased racial desegregation in the field of broadcasting. Although, compared to previous documents, it was a good start, it nevertheless did not yet reach into the heart of the problem. For example, although the Commission dealt with the problem of educating the ghetto child, it approached it in terms of traditional techniques and did not deal with the place of communications in ghetto education. It did not recognize the need for communications among citizens of the ghetto, the role of media in serving that need, or the specific kinds of communication that would be most effective into and out of the ghetto.

Professor John C. Robertson, director of the already noted unsuccessful New York University Bedford-Stuyvesant "Clinic for Learning" project, hit at the crux of the matter when he wondered, following the failure of the experiment, how the children could be expected to be reached if the curriculum and the teaching had no relevance to their lives.

The same is true for the adult in the inner city. Communications have not been adequately used to distinguish between the real and the imagined world.

The adult is forced into a ghetto. She or he is surrounded by brick and concrete and wood barriers that are blank and threatening, with no free access to the outside world. She or he is given promises that are not kept, projects that are temporary make-work with no true relationship to one's own or one's family's future, organizations that result only in talk, and people who come from a society of jobs and homes and travel mobility that are totally unrelated to and barely understanding of the Barrio or the Black ghetto. Here, too, is a Kafkaesque world.

What really happened in the summer of 1968, when we seemed to be on the verge of physical revolt by a substantial portion of our citizenry? In none of the cities where disorders occurred were they planned. There were no organized riots. Instead there were the vivid pictures of what we continue to fail to learn from history: how hopelessness and despair force people to acts of self-destruction! What a tragic cry for help is an inward act of violence!

Violence in the inner cities has been principally anti-Black, coming from Blacks against Blacks, and from the police and other armed forces against Blacks. The initiation of violence was personal and inward, the deep gasping of people for fresh air, revealing a forsaken wilderness of communication between the total society and a large segment of its population.

This lack of communication was accentuated in 1977 in New York City when, following extensive looting and some destruction in the ghetto areas of the city during a 25–hour blackout caused by the failure of Con Edison services, public officials, journalists, social scientists and others were unable to determine or agree on the motivation for the disorder. Some attributed it to "human nature"; some said it was "the character" of the people doing the looting; some blamed it on a lessening of "moral standards"; others felt it was caused by a relaxation of "law and order"; some saw it as a result of high unemployment; and still others believed that the hot, humid summer created frustrations that needed an outlet. No one, at least as reported by the press and the broadcast news, seemed to understand why there was such turmoil in 1977, and why, by contrast, in 1965, during a previous New York City blackout, there was no violence and no looting.

In 1965, with the apparent success of the civil rights revolution and the passage of the Civil Rights Act, the people living in the ghettos had hope. There was the promise of opportunity, of an end to discrimination, of an equal chance to become part of the larger community and get a piece of the economic, social and political pie. In 1968, with the murder of Martin Luther King, Jr. as part of the attempt to revoke that promise, the violence was as much a statement of determination as it was of anger. They could kill the symbol, but not the dream. By 1977 the dream had dried up. The ghettos had seen much lip-service and little real progress. The hope of a decade before was gone. If there was no apparent future for a better life outside of the ghetto, then what else remained but to unleash the torment and frustration and anger into a destruction of both the symbol and the reality of the hopelessness, the ghetto itself.

The people of the ghetto unconsciously as well as consciously tried to communicate their frustration and anger to the people outside of the ghetto, hoping that the majority society would finally begin to understand. In a number of instances the looters had the television news teams turn the bright lights on the shops they were looting so they could better see what to take and so that the rest of the world could better see what it had so long tried to ignore. Some city officials said later that the rumor on the street was that the next time there was an opportunity for mass violence in the ghetto, the ghetto itself would be put to the torch. If white, affluent suburbia refused to pay attention to other forms of communication, what about a huge, red, fiery light reaching out and up into the sky?

What we also continue to fail to learn from history is that although hopelessness and despair are self-destructive and nonrevolutionary, frustration and anger are not necessarily so. The violence eventually turns outward and, as with the unfulfilled demands by Americans for equal rights and a redress of grievances two centuries ago, leads to active revolution.

Between the lines of hysteria and behind the pictures of fear two consistent issues continue to appear: education and communications.

The Report of the Commission on Civil Disorders verified what had slowly begun to get through to some of the public: the 1968 riots were not the result of incitement but of deprivation. One significant part of that deprivation is effective education. Following the disorders, Senator Robert F. Kennedy said, "We pass bills and appropriate money and assuage our consciences, and local school systems keep right on doing things the way they've done them for decades." New York Senator Jacob K. Javits stated that education has to be part of the solution to offset the "frustration, despair and anger" that "create the conditions which bring on riots."

The other significant part of that deprivation is communications. Mayor John Lindsay noted that, in his own New York City, appropriate agencies had not been able to "make contact" with the teenagers who made up most of the disorderly mobs. In Philadelphia a high official of the school system told me of the threat of a riot, an attack upon a school in a so-called white neighborhood. The white people were the incipient rioters, objecting to the fact that a number of nonwhite children came into their area to attend that school. The white children of the community were part of the threatening mob. The difficulty, said the school official, was communication—to reach these white people with information and understanding to "cool them" and to help them learn responsibility.

In the continuing urban crises of our time we come back again and again to these two interacting areas: education and communications. We come back to the need for people to learn about the special problems and needs of other people. In an article in *INTERCOM* magazine, Dr. Seymour Fersh stated: "The best way—though certainly not an infallible one—to learn about other peoples and cultures is by direct experience. The least effective way is by words, because words themselves are a man-made product of one's own culture." The most direct experience possible for most people is not the ideal one of touch and smell and taste that requires a physical presence possible only for the relative few. Fifty years ago experience was limited to second-hand sight—through the inert words or photographs or drawings in a book. We now have first-hand sight and hearing—through real-time live television and radio.

Our continuing efforts to communicate and educate with nine-teenth-century techniques is a major reason why disadvantaged communities, including the schools in the ghettos, continue to be cut off from the mainstream of society. Many of us still do not recognize that the cathode ray tube and the transistor have replaced the printing press as the primary means of communications. Think back to photographs and news films of inner-city disorders. You didn't see any teenagers or adults reading news-papers or books while violence was all around them? But you did see many with transistor radios pressed up against their ears. [*Unfortunately, in too many cases the same thing can be said of cyberspace and the Internet vis-à-vis traditional television, cable, and film at the turn of the twenty-first century.*]

Television and radio are not just adjunct tools or aids in teaching and learning, but are integral parts of the entire education process. The child in the ghetto says s/he doesn't find anything interesting in school. What the child means is that s/he's bored because s/he can't read the book used as the core of instruction. We cannot teach that child to read the book as easily as we might teach children who have not suffered the psychologically destructive deprivations of the ghetto. We must first motivate the ghettoed child toward the personal worth and confidence that will give him or her a base for being willing to learn. We must use those means to which that child is already tuned in: radio and television. To continue to push print as the primary approach is to continue to create an ever-concentric surrounding circle of stone walls.

Outside of school the ghetto child thinks, uses his or her mind. Inside the classroom s/he is shut off from the world. Television and radio must bring that world in. We must relate the child to the world. We must use the mass media not only to provide motivation through visual action—rather than through non-meaningful (to that child) print symbols— but to provide a socializing situation for the child, to make the real world a part of the classroom, to provide the problems of the real world as the learning problems. The solutions learned—or at least the understanding obtained—is what constitutes education. If we can do this first for these children, then we can make it possible for them to learn to read.

The visual and aural input into the classroom must turn the classroom away from itself, must remove the four walls. It must bring in experiences and people that are meaningful to the children. Most of the attempts to do so have been misleading, although not necessarily deliberately so. Those who develop and produce educational media materials may conscientiously believe that they are making unique and appropriate contributions to minority, inner-city learning. Sometimes their products are even publicized as panaceas. "Sesame Street," for example, has developed effective, stimulating, motivating techniques for getting the attention of children, for conveying to them factual information relating to skills, and for reinforcing the memorization of these information bits. Not as effectively, perhaps, as some programmed or computer-assisted-instruction materials, but a significant advancement over what relatively low-cost-per-viewer mass television has previously done.

In seeking support to provide educational experiences for disadvantaged children, the Children's Television Workshop, the producers of "Sesame Street," originally stressed the considerable difference in cost between educating the "5 million children 4 years of age [who] are candidates for pre-schooling . . . in conventional schools" and in the manner proposed. In light of some of the subsequent criticism of "Sesame Street," it is worth noting that this innovative media project, with unparalleled opportunity to turn children on to learning, justified its efforts by implying that its principal contribution would be to provide the opportunities of conventional schools, only at lower cost.

The stated purposes of the Children's Television Workshop in producing "Sesame Street" were "to stimulate the intellectual and cultural growth of young children from disadvantaged backgrounds . . . to capitalize on the medium's potential by teaching numbers, classic stories, the alphabet, language and the art of reasoning." There was no clarification, however, of whether or how the program would serve the primary needs of the disadvantaged child: self-motivation, self-understanding, and ego-building identification with one's background and immediate self.

"Sesame Street" has a setting that middle-class white suburbia might mistake for a block of the disadvantaged inner city. There is serious question, however, not only about the validity of the setting, but the relationship of the program's other materials to the ghettoed child's cultural background and their applicability to that child's immediate learning needs. As disturbing as they might be to the psyches of the white middle-class producers and viewers of "Sesame Street," some of the more important things the ghetto child needs to learn are how to escape being beaten by the police, how to avoid being gang-raped by a neighborhood teenage gang, how to scrounge a dime or a quarter from the slumming white tourist to buy a candy bar or a loaf of bread, how to talk back to the white neighborhood merchant who has cheated you without getting your family's credit cut off, how to avoid being hooked into a momentary ride out of the ghetto through powder or pills that some of the kids have tried and offer to let you in on. On the other hand, this kind of learning is just as important for white suburbia, which needs to become more sensitive to the need to do away with the conditions that create these situations.

The white middle-class kid thinks "Sesame Street" is great. He or she can learn easily from it principally because s/he's already had a head start. The ghetto kid may also think it's great. It's funny, it has attractive animation effects, and the Muppets are marvelous. The characters are no more unreal than many of the characters one sees on television and more real than most. The child who sits and watches does learn much information and some concepts very effectively. To what degree, however, is that child helped to understand and cope with the special problems of his or her disadvantaged life, and to learn what is necessary not only to survive, but to be prepared to change that condition?

The criticism is not that "Sesame Street" has been lauded for what it is. It deserves accolades for its new techniques in presenting factual information on television, and in effectively adapting the most creative of television practices, including the commercial announcement, as a means of effective and entertaining presentation. It also has been criticized for what it is- n't—materials that presumably are strongly helping disadvantaged, mi- nority children learn and grow. In this, "Sesame Street" falls far short of its potentials.

Educator John Holt, who has been in the vanguard of those attempting to make the American educational system more responsive to individual learning needs, wrote the following about "Sesame Street":

The show is much better than most of what has been offered to children on TV. . . . Nonetheless . . . [it] has aimed too low, has misunderstood the problem it is trying to cure . . . has misunderstood the nature and underestimated the opportunities of its chief subject, the three R's, and its medium, television. . . . [I]t is like a conventional school run by super-gifted teachers . . . assumes like most schools that nobody ever learns anything by himself. . . . Everything, however trivial, must be deliberately *taught* . . . cut off from any connections with the rest of life. . . . [L]earning on "Sesame Street," as in school, means learning Right Answers, and as in school, Right An- swers come from grown-ups. We rarely see children figuring things out. As in school, we hear children responding, without much animation or imagination.

In the development of some of its learning programs for children, Can- ada, in the opinion of many, has surpassed the techniques of "Sesame Street." One example is a series produced by James Dormeyer for the Cana- dian Broadcasting Corporation (CBC), incorporating film, electronic edit- ing techniques, self-study and evaluation by the participating children of their own reactions to their learning experiences and, through phone hook-ups, direct individual guidance for the children at home in the learn- ing situations presented over television.

In planning its future programming for children, the CBC set up a com- mission to study and evaluate "Sesame Street." It found "Sesame Street" greatly lacking and of virtually no value for Canada's future planning. The British Broadcasting Company (BBC) came to the same conclusion, and de- cided not to use "Sesame Street" on BBC, citing the program's "authoritar- ian aims." The BBC questioned the value of "acquiring knowledge in a passive, uninvolved fashion," criticized the program's "essentially middle-class attitudes" and noted its "lack of reality and its attempt to prepare children for school but not for life."

Maybe if you haven't thrown in millions of dollars a year of your own tax money for the Emperor's New Clothes, you can more objectively see them for what they really aren't.

A recognition of "Sesame Street's" shortcomings as well as its contributions might have prompted funders and producers to adapt from and improve upon it, and move the art of children's educational TV programming forward. However, the U.S. Office of Education's and the Ford Foundation's next major step was to fund the Children's Television Workshop's "The Electric Company," a duplication of "Sesame Street" for the elementary school level. In the 1970s funding for new children's programs appears to be based by and large on comparisons with "Sesame Street." Except for some of the programs funded under the Emergency School Aid Act by the U.S. Office of Education, designed to help children in school learn to integrate their attitudes and actions with those of children from different backgrounds, few children's programs have emerged that go materially beyond the traditional information-learning concept. As in commercial TV, the approach seems to be that if you have a popular show, duplicate it.

Most children's educational programs on television are pretty good in terms of preparing children to survive in the schools of America—not an easy or inconsiderable task—by helping them learn what is expected of them in virtually all formal education situations: passivity, conformity, and non-critical information learning. The alternative is to change the schools to meet the needs of the learner. Yet, maybe the U.S. Office of Education [*in 1980 the Department of Education*], the Ford Foundation, and other past and present sources of support for children's TV know exactly what they are doing. They are not called the *establishment* for nothing!

Because so many people consider "Sesame Street" the sine qua non of educational television, it would be fair to take these comments as, perhaps, not so much a criticism of that program as of the inadequate progress television has made in terms of the learner's requirements and of its own potential.

Maybe someday somebody will come up with a program for children that will deal with a real street—like 125th Street in Harlem or 7th Street N.W. in Washington, D.C. or Olivera Street in Los Angeles—instead of a magic street that is just so much fiction for the minority group or ghetto child—where rat, rape and revolution come closer to the real three R's than a whole cave full of make-believe jewels that only the white and/or middle-class child will have access to, anyway, in the real world.

The child in the ghetto, just to survive, must make meaningful, effective judgments and decisions every moment of the day—and night. This takes an additional kind of intelligence that most of us have not had to develop or exercise. When talking about survival in the ghetto, it is not like the experience of most middle-class children playing in the back yard. It is an experience usually lacking the guidance of an adult. It requires an intelligence of a high practical order that is not reflected in the verbal-oriented cultural achievement evaluations we call IQ tests. It is the kind of ability many industry people say they are looking for, but for which they have not yet really been willing to provide opportunities.

The intelligence and potential are clearly there. They must be motivated and matured through communications and education. They must be communicated with and given an opportunity to communicate.

Dr. Theodore R. Sizer, when he was Dean of Harvard's Graduate School of Education, repeated, in a report deploring the conditions of the slum schools, the frequently heard statement that "Nobel winners do not abound in the slums." The tragedy is that potential Nobel winners do abound in the slums as much as anywhere. How many children are growing up today unexposed to the fullness of the world about them, unaware of what is possible, what is probable? How pitifully few of all those—including the children in ghettos—who might eventually make important contributions to the peace, dignity, freedom and well-being of humankind will ever be given the opportunity to do so!

# CHAPTER 8

# Urban Communications: A Plan for Action

The commentary at the beginning of chapter 7 referred to the 1998 Kerner Commission Report. This special commission was appointed by President Lyndon B. Johnson in July, 1967, as more than 150 disturbances, including riots, were sweeping throughout America that summer. A key quote from the study, noted in chapter 7, is worth repeating: "What white Americans have never fully understood—but what the Negro can never forget—is that white society is deeply implicated in the ghetto. White institutions created it, white institutions maintain it, and white society condones it."

Another key quote from the report generated the title of a best-selling book and sums up the conclusion of the report: "Our nation is moving toward two societies, one black, one white—separate and unequal."

The inner cities—"ghettos" was the term applied in the 1960s and 1970s—were developed by an influx of African-Americans from the South, especially the rural South, in the first half of the twentieth century. In 1910, 91% of African-Americans lived in the South; by 1966 there were an estimated 21 million African-Americans in the United States, with almost 15 million in metropolitan areas and almost 50%, slightly less than 10 million, living outside of the South.

While the immigration from the South to the urban areas of the North promised better economic and educational opportunities and greater personal and political freedom, the prejudice against people of color did not disappear. The Kerner report found that white Americans were far more prejudiced against African-Americans than against European immigrants, consciously as well as unconsciously limiting the options and opportunities for African-Americans. The media were more receptive to other so-called minority groups, especially white ethnic minorities, than to African-Americans. Although housing in northern cities, according to the Kerner report, was significantly better than in the rural South for African-Americans, the inner cities, or ghettos, had grossly inadequate housing, and overcrowding was common. In 1967 the unemployment rate for African-Americans was twice that for whites. African-Americans were more than three times as likely as whites to be in low-paying, unskilled, or service jobs. The report indicated that the concentration of African-Americans at the lowest end of the occupational scale was the single most important cause of poverty, with 11.9% of the country's whites and 40.6% of non-whites living below the poverty level in 1966.

The lack of equal opportunities for jobs, plunging so many families into poverty, was devastating to African-American communities. Men chronically unemployed or underemployed often are unwilling or unable to remain with their families. Children growing up without fathers and, in many instances, with only part-time mothers—as women were forced into low-paying but necessary jobs to keep their families alive—experienced debilitating deprivation. This culture of poverty, the Kerner report verified, generated a system of ruthless exploitation within the ghettos. Prostitution, drug addiction, and crime created an environmental "jungle" of tension and personal insecurity, an atmosphere primed for civil disorder. The lack of adequate health and sanitary conditions and facilities in the inner cities resulted in higher mortality rates for African-Americans. A major grievance of the African-American population was the alleged insensitivity, discrimination, aggression, and even brutality on the part of the police—a grievance that continues into the new century.

In 1967 Black Power advocates Stokely Carmichael and Charles Hamilton wrote of the concerns of African-American communities. These concerns included economic exploitation by merchants and landlords, corruption by whites at the expense of Blacks, official neglect of the infrastructure needs of Black areas, and the effective exclusion of Blacks from the political process and, therefore, political control. In addition, they noted the absence of pertinent curricula in ghetto schools, citing, for example, history books that overlook the achievements of African-Americans and other people of color and concentrate on white-viewed events. They pointed out that the school boards are controlled by whites. The Kerner report noted that in 1967 one in every five African-Americans living in urban areas was ghettoized into squalor and deprivation. Both the Kerner and Carmichael-Hamilton reports stressed that the deplorable and volatile situation in the inner cities is caused by the lack of decent housing, decent education, and decent jobs.

Unfortunately, a third of the century later, in the year 2000, the problem still exists.

It was against this background that in 1968 the author was asked by Senator Robert F. Kennedy to prepare a plan for the use of television and radio as part of the Senator's rehabilitation program for the Bedford-Stuyvesant section of Brooklyn, New York, a long-neglected and deteriorating, predominantly African-American area. Most of the material in this chapter was originally included in that plan. Other material in the chapter comes from papers and speeches prepared in the 1960s and 1970s, most specifically an address, "Communications and Crisis," to the American Management Association's Third Annual Conference on Education and Training, August 9, 1967, New York City. Chief Justice Harold A. Stevens of the New York Supreme Court Appellate Division, an African-American, called this address "magnificent . . . reveals an insight and understanding of the problem."

What is true for the child in the classroom is also true for the adult in the tenement. The traditional methods of communicating with adults have failed again and again in Bedford-Stuyvesant, in Harlem, in Watts, in Detroit, in Newark, in Milwaukee, in every community where aborted attempts to open up opportunities for equal access to the fruits of society have forcibly pushed the people into deeper despair and resentment.

The first step is not, as has been done traditionally, to organize a group to discuss housing problems or to set up an employment opportunity office or to bring in a task force of expert teachers to help children learn how to read.

The first step is to make a dent in the curtain of hopelessness that has been pulled down over every child and adult, every family, every racial, ethnic or other group that has been ghettoized into economic and cultural poverty.

The first step is to try to restore to each of these persons a sense of pride, of worth, of self-esteem, to try to bring some bit of reality to the dream—not deferred for these people, but shattered—that there is some hope for their children, if not for themselves, to break out of the conditions from which the best escape, for many, is now a nonviolent death.

Radio and television are the primary means of communication these people have with the outside world. There seems to be, however, a continuing reluctance to discuss television and radio in terms of the total impact they might make on and for the ghetto and on and for the white non-ghetto society. The emphasis has generally been only on the media's limited functions as informational, reportorial tools. Television's and radio's potentials, if fully realized, would be revolutionary. They would not only change the lives of the people directly affected, but would force a reorientation of the media, sociology, political science and other experts who continue to devote massive amounts of time, energy and money to urban projects that are largely ineffective and principally result in bureaucratic reports and increased inner-city frustration. Even if the apple cart is rotted through, it sometimes seems to be the easier course not to upset it!

The most comprehensive public analyses and recommendations to date concerning the relationship of the mass media to the inner city came out in the Report of the National Advisory Commission on Civil Disorders (the Kerner Commission report). With the prestige and expertise of the Commission behind the report, the recommendations on television and radio should have had a special effect on public understanding and acceptance. They were, however, buried by the White House.

Three of the Commission's major conclusions were (1) "radio, television, on the whole, made a real effort to give a balanced, factual account of the 1967 disorders," (2) "despite this effort . . . the overall effect was an exaggeration of both mood and event," and (3) "most important . . . the media have thus far failed to report adequately on the causes and consequences of civil disorders and the underlying problems of race relations."

The Commission's recommendations for steps toward solving the problems indicated in these conclusions were primarily for improving media coverage of riots, including better communication among the individuals involved, discussions of the problems of all concerned, establishment of media information police officers, a central information center, helping "out-of-town" reporters understand the community's needs, and the development of guidelines on procedures and behavior in reporting riot news. The Commission also recommended greater opportunities for "Negroes" [*term used by the Commission and many other official organizations at the time*] in the fields of journalism, including radio and television, and the production of more programs validly reflecting, in casting and in content, the place of African-Americans in society.

As a step toward accomplishing the above, the Commission recommended the establishment of an Institute of Urban Communications, which would educate journalists in the field of urban affairs, would prepare and place African-Americans in the field, would serve to coordinate effective police-press relationships, would serve as a public nongovernmental watchdog on media coverage of riots and racial issues, and which would organize a quality urban affairs news service.

Reporting adequately on the "causes and consequences" and the "underlying problems" is a critical need, and positive use of television and radio in these respects can contribute importantly to the eventual fulfillment of inner-city needs, particularly through educating a white public that still refuses to recognize its own responsibility for the urban problems. However, although the Commission had an opportunity to make a real breakthrough in communications with and for the inner city, its recommendations related only to part of the total problem and potential:

toward improving the reportorial aspects of the media, toward *telling*, rather than *doing* something about the inner city.

The report did not recommend how the inner city itself should communicate with the outside world. It did not show how the media should be used to affect the thoughts and feelings of white America in respect to the problems of the inner city. In the section on education, the Report did not show the need for increased and imaginative use of radio and television to provide urgently needed higher quality education for children and adults. It made no recommendations on using radio and television's subjective, psychological non-content effects on both the inner-city and outer-city resident. It stressed instead the role of the media as neutral, objective information carriers.

To its credit, the Commission did note briefly in its report the existence of the media's other potentials, such as "its role in shaping attitudes, and the effects of the choices it makes on people's behavior." It suggested that such areas were worth "intensive scholarly exploration" by the Institute of Urban Communications.

Tradition-rooted, limited evaluations of media potentials are not limited to government bureaucracies. At a conference at Syracuse University on Media and Race Relations, the audience was asked to answer the following question by selecting one answer: "Do the mass media have a (positive) (neutral) (negative) influence on race relations?" After concluding that the questioners were, indeed, not pulling the audience's collective legs, one finds it difficult to believe that there are people—especially experts in human relations—who still are not aware of the media's demonstrated effects on human thought and feeling. A three-year-old child exposed to the television set knows, even if unable to verbalize it, that the media are anything but neutral; they have both positive and negative influences. Indeed, what are all the efforts for of those concerned with the social impact of media if not to find ways of more creative and effective use of the positive influences?

We cannot continue to play academic games with the media because we cannot continue to play academic games with our urban problems. We have, by a lack of boldness and courage and through scholarly cob-webbing, permitted persistent deterioration to reach a condition of crisis. Now, we have no choice but to finally break from the past and go beyond the continuing use (and failures) of the traditional approaches to communication, as well as to training, education, housing, and jobs.

Communication for what?

Training for what?

Education for what?

Education and training for their own sakes are luxuries that the people of the inner city cannot afford.

Housing task forces meeting frequently to discuss the problems in the community are diversions for which the people of the inner city cannot take time.

Job centers referring people to prospective employers whose jobs exist principally in publicity announcements, or referring unqualified people for jobs they cannot do and must be rejected for, are exercises in callousness.

Storefront vocational training programs and degree-granting college programs preparing people for jobs that are unavailable to them are cruel deceptions.

We expend too much time, too much effort, and too much of people's hopes on the *appearance* of accomplishing something. We must take a practical look at the needs and at the long- and short-term goals and not be afraid to reach out realistically for what is probable and possible. There are some basic approaches applicable to almost every inner city, and some specific purposes applicable to each separate situation. For example:

What are the goals in the area of housing? To harass landlords? To obtain legal action for repairs and better housing? To lobby for housing legislation for the poor? To establish a funded cooperative to build adequate housing for nonprofit rentals?

What are the goals in the area of jobs? To establish cooperative industries to employ the employable? To make a mass militant effort to break down the illegal but still flourishing patterns of discrimination in hiring? To seek governmental—federal, state, local—action in creating public job opportunities? To lobby for an annual guaranteed wage-job law?

What are the goals in the area of education? To train people for the few jobs that are available to minorities? To educate youth for professional careers that are still largely closed to minorities? To raise the literacy and cultural level of younger children through a crash program designed to establish a base for future learning? To retrain workers for specific fields? To prepare youngsters to be able to seek—though not necessarily find—jobs upon graduation from high school? To motivate and prepare them to seek as much higher education as possible, whether or not job opportunities rise concomitantly?

Seeking any particular goal must be related to the practicality of its accomplishment. Too often we have succeeded only in creating activity without fulfillment because we have not made certain that we have also established an outlet for a successful conclusion.

For example, the often-suggested sidewalk college/storefront classroom/walk-in schoolroom idea is basically a good one. But it has not been successful in a vacuum. Before we bring back a single dropout to the 11th or 12th grade under the guise of this being a means whereby he or she can then get a decent job, we must be sure the opportunity exists for that job. Too many promises have been made that have been broken. The inner-city resident has learned through bitter experience that another year or two of high school or in a special training program usually makes little difference, and the entire inner city turns even more vociferously against the illusion of education. If, with specific programs, we first make certain that jobs will be ready and available and that people are actually placed in them after they complete their education or training, word of mouth will inform the rest of the inner city and other urban areas that there are alternatives to the usual exercises in futile good will. There will be new attitudes and new motivations and cooperative efforts to change a quality of life that depresses all of America. The people of the inner cities are fed up with empty promises represented as hope. It is past the time for euphemisms and into the time for action, for practical results.

No purpose can be unrelated to any other purpose. Jobs, housing, education, medical attention, nutrition, legal aid, and other critical concerns must be interrelated. Goals set for one area must be in terms of their relationship to other areas. As with the interdependence between education and jobs, only through combined efforts can meaningful results be achieved.

There are many who would decry what they perceive as a forced relationship between education and jobs, and say that education is, or at least should be, undertaken for its own sake. Until the economic base of our society is changed, however, education for its own sake is a luxury afforded only those who have achieved the means for sufficient economic security to permit them the time and energy for non-vocational educational self-realization.

We have heard too long about what the "outside" world is doing for the people in the inner cities. The people of the inner city must themselves be involved, first through the creation, through radio and television, of a sense of personal worth and, second, through management and operational activity in all phases and on all levels of operation of whatever program is being brought into the ghetto. For those outside of the ghetto, their investment is only that of time, effort, ideas, responsibility, conscience, emotion, and money. For the people in the ghetto, their investment is their entire future, and the success or failure of a given program can be as critical to them as the success or failure of life. They cannot go back to Sutton Place or Chevy Chase or Grosse Pointe after a "good try."

Urban programs, to be successful, can no longer be Thanksgiving Basket paternalism. The programs must be under the control and direct day-to-day operation of those people in and from the inner city who understand and have the background and ability to see them to fruition. Where people from the inner city are not available to do the job as it has to be done, then people who have escaped from the urban ghettos, but who still know it and feel it, must do the job. The white "establishment"—admirable as its talents and motivations may be—is nevertheless a physical and psychological stranger to the specific immediate need, and its contributions should be advisory, as needed. Let's look at how this might work in setting up a communications project in Brooklyn's Bedford-Stuyvesant, for example.

First, planning task forces composed predominantly of African-American professionals and citizens of the area should be set up in two major areas: (1) Media and (2) Social Organization. These should operate simultaneously, with the Social Organization Task Force determining the needs and the specific goals, the problems within and without the community that stand in the way of accomplishing the goals, and the factors within and without the community that can be of value in reaching the goals. The Social Organization Task Force would provide this information to the Media Task Force, which would then determine to what motivational, informational and educational uses the media should be put, the kinds of media and extent to which they might be used, and the specific programming that would best meet the area's needs.

The Media Task Force should include funding, technical, and public relations subcommittees that would work toward obtaining the media tools, including radio; several forms of television, including cable, closed-circuit, instructional and operational fixed microwave, and broadcast; and the visual, performing, and graphic arts.

Most important, in this particular situation, is radio. Any campaign to attract people to watch TV programs at optimum time—assuming such time were made available—would face the competition of the prime time hits, "Laverne and Shirley," "The Jeffersons," "Charlie's Angels," "Dallas," and similar fare. And who, after working 12 or 16 hours a day, or facing the destructive tedium of futile job-hunting, or fighting the moment-to-moment-horrors of hunger and disease and vermin, can be expected to give up the opportunity for a momentary escape from the real world? Even in poverty areas, however, transistor radios glued to the ears of the youth and close by the adult are in proliferation. Radio is the most immediate, direct, and effective way of reaching people in the inner city.

If properly promoted and programmed for a combination of entertainment and information and education, radio can motivate entire groups for action in a way that no other mass medium (besides TV) can do. [See chapter 5, "Television and Political Control."] In many urban communities "soul radio" has become an important part of the community's vicarious cultural existence. Surveys indicate that more people listen to radio in the course of an average week than watch TV: about 96% of the population tunes in radio some time during the week as compared with about 95% who watch television. But the purposes of inner-city radio stations are not, as presently constituted, directly oriented toward solving the problems of the ghetto. A broadcasting journal headlined an article as follows: "All-News, All-Music, All-Ghetto Radio is a Success"; and then, for fuller explanation: "Special interest broadcasting—a nearly sure-fire method for getting a fat slice of the pie."

What is needed is a radio station owned and operated by a community-controlled organization. This could be done either by purchasing an existing station (extremely costly in any high-density urban area), or cross-filing at renewal time for the license of an existing station that has not been serving the community's needs, and the subsequent assignment of that license by the FCC to the community group. There is no likelihood of finding an unused frequency in any city large enough to have a sizable inner-city population. [*By the 1980s the challenging of licenses declined and by the time of the Telecommunications Act of 1996 had virtually disappeared, as FCC deregulation extended license terms, lessened broadcaster responsibilities, and made license renewals virtually automatic.*]

The funding, technical, and public relations subcommittees should arrange to purchase and staff the radio station (which could be self-supporting, if necessary, through commercials) and also arrange for the use of television where possible, such as: (1) installation of cable into dwelling units, with the cooperation of the cable system in providing a free access channel; (2) closed-circuit systems; (3) instructional and operational microwave systems to selected receiving sites; (4) time on commercial and educational or public broadcast stations. Where it is not possible to obtain major TV station cooperation, small independent stations may provide some program time. Although "prime time" may at first seem most desirable, most people, including urban residents, prefer narcotizing entertainment during the evening viewing hours. Therefore, very early morning hours and late night hours might be the most effective television times for reaching the largest number of people. On radio, of course, programs and other communications can be scheduled at virtually all times (with the exception of trying to compete with prime-time TV viewing hours), including during the working day.

The public relations committee should use all available media for a crash program to attract listeners/viewers to the initial programming, on whatever medium it may be.

A "motivation and programming" subcommittee of the Media Task Force should work closely with the Social Organization group in (1) identifying community needs (i.e., children need to develop a feeling of personal dignity to cope with the humiliation they experience in so many classrooms; adults have to be convinced there is practical value in joining a block group to work on a housing problem); (2) determining how to meet the designated community needs through the media, including a clarification of which media will most effectively achieve which purposes, which ones the residents of the community are most likely to respond to, and in what manner; and (3) selecting the kinds and contents of materials to be aired.

Traditional approaches to programming will not work. There must be flexibility beyond the existing formats and the arbitrary program lengths and placements. In radio, conversations, questions and answers, counseling, exhortation, concrete and abstract sound stimulation, and other kinds of content and non-content motivation, including audience participation, in and out of the studio, should be explored. Unique uses of visual demonstration and stimulation should be sought for television. The key word is "communication," not "programming."

In some instances radio, not limited by the confines of sight, can loosen the imagination of the viewer to a much greater degree than can television. Some examples are Norman Corwin's radio scripts and the Orson Welles-John Housman "Invasion From Mars," which permitted—forced—the listener to create images that would be impossible to duplicate on television. On the other hand, where content requires sight as well as sound, and where sight-sound combinations have highly effective psychological effects, television is more desirable than radio.

This is not to suggest that programming, as currently conceived, is not of value. It can not only be used to convey ideas and information, charge emotions, and prime attitudes, but, most importantly, it can be used to motivate the audience to action. Not a small part of such motivation is to get people to listen to and watch the inner-city community radio and television stations in the first place. This means the development of programs of significance and interest to the inner city, rather than to advertiser-sought suburbia. In Bedford-Stuyvesant, the kinds of programs that could attract and motivate at the same time, depending on the specific content and technique used, would feature performers and personalities most admired in the African-American community. This would transcend entertainment alone, although entertainment would be used to attract as large an audience as possible, and might include, for example, Andrew Young on a panel analyzing the political power and prospects of Black votes, Muhammad Ali interviewed on his identification with the goals of the people in Black inner cities, and Ossie Davis and Ruby Dee in dramatic interpretations of the listeners' problems and fears, desires and expectations.

Given the purpose of their participation, there is no question that prominent African-Americans, Hispanics, Native-Americans, Asian-Americans and other minorities would generously donate their time to reach out to the people in the respective ghettos, barrios, reservations and other economically and culturally isolated islands—prominent people whose emotional empathy will permit motivation and persuasion not otherwise possible.

Finally, the Media Task Force, coordinating with the Social Organization Task Force, determines when to program what. For example, a housing committee may decide that a certain date is best for establishing block groups. The media must be used to inform the people about the issues, convince them of the value of such an organization, and motivate them to come to an organizing meeting. In addition, the media should prepare the rest of the community, in and out of the inner city, to support or at least accept the block housing group plans and efforts, and to raise financial backing for it, if possible.

The Social Organization Task Force should be divided into committees related to the important needs of the community: Safety, Housing, Transportation, Education, Jobs, Energy, Health, Welfare, Legal—in effect, reflecting the services of the federal, state, and city governments that somehow have not been as effective as the inner-city residents need them to be. Each of these committees immediately should ascertain needs in terms of practical solutions and plan for specific projects that are likely to accomplish specific purposes. Because many of the projects would be sub-local in nature (for example, the Housing Committee might have a problem applicable to a row of same-owner houses, or deal with sewer repairs in a two or three block area), small teams of task forces should be prepared to work with block leaders on individual streets. Where a project might be larger in scope (a storefront college or community job-opportunity campaign, for example), representatives of individual blocks would join together into larger groups. In every case, a resident of each block affected should be part of the representing team. The greater participation of residents, the better chance, obviously, any given project has of success.

The approach outlined above represents only a beginning for motivation, socialization, preparation for action, and for further intensive formal and informal education. Variations and extensions will evolve naturally out of the need and direction of the people involved as they develop their personal abilities for more effective individual and group self-realization. These abilities may range from political skills in organizing housing protests to artistic creativity in using the media.

Innovation does not mean haphazardness. Nor does it necessarily mean success. Radio and television alone cannot do the job. They happen, in this instance, to hold the promise of being the most effective means. But they must be used flexibly to meet specific situations. Joel L. Fleishman, Director of Duke University's School of International Affairs and former Associate Provost for Urban Studies and Programs at Yale University, states that "as a matter of educational strategy, schools ought to deal with those substantive matters by means of those media of communication which are both relevant to the experience of the child and to his personal interest." He adds, rightly, that he would not limit any program to radio or television, but would utilize whatever media are most effective.

A basic problem we face is that virtually all other media, especially print, have failed. What we must do is to concentrate on those media—especially radio and television—not yet really tried in terms of their full potentials. Individuals can be reached, organized and worked with through a continuous relationship with mass communications in ways not previously attempted.

We have no guarantee that this approach will work. But we do know that the traditional approaches for reaching and organizing and activating and educating have not worked. We cannot do worse—and we may do better. But we must be prepared to go all the way, not to hedge our attempts by using the mass media secondarily or only partially. We must be willing to break through the communications sound barrier.

What has been discussed thus far relates primarily to communications into the inner city and within the inner city and to the use of television and radio beyond their informational reportorial functions. That is not to say that the informational reportorial functions should be ignored. On the contrary, they have distinct, significant roles to play. What is suggested here is that communications should not be limited to informing and reporting, as seems to be the case in recommendations, discussions, and actions thus far by government, foundations, and public and private organizations. In addition, the burden seems to have been placed largely on broadcast stations for the production of applicable programs and materials, and though the stations and networks should not be relieved of such responsibility, neither should they be expected to carry the total communications load. Other means of dissemination are needed to realize the full potentials of radio and television.

Keeping in mind, then, that this is only part of the total picture, let us examine some of the informational-reportorial requirements and possibilities. In 1968, Federal Communications Commission Chairman Rosel H. Hyde told the annual convention of the National Association of Broadcasters that "broadcasting clearly is in a unique position to assist in achievement of . . . the fullest possible reporting on the causes and consequences of civil disorders and the underlying problems of race relations. If we are not to have a retreat from national progress, the nation must come to understand much more deeply and meaningfully its problems and the courses open to it."

The disorders of the summer of 1967 forced broadcasters to pay more attention to the long-neglected inner cities, and even as the violence of April 1968 was making headlines across the country, stations and networks were announcing new informational-reportorial programs to both the inner cities and the suburbs. In subsequent years a number of programs and series—although not as many as some people think there should have been—have been devoted to African-American history and concerns. (Other minorities, absent the political and public pressures of African-Americans, have been given virtually no attention by broadcasters.) One outstanding series was CBS's "Of Black America," which dealt with Black history and contributions to the progress of America, and has helped young Black people identify with the dignity and success as well as the struggles of their forebears. Another was Westinghouse Broadcasting's "Black African Heritage." But only one—and that not until 1977—utilized the emotional as well as informational impact of television and created new feelings and actions as well as thoughts on both intensive and extensive levels. That series, of course, was "Roots."

It is pertinent to note that in 1962 National Educational Television (NET), the predecessor to PBS, produced and distributed an excellent 15–program series entitled "Dynamics of Desegregation," showing the history, development, contributions, problems, and social-political-economic relationships of Black America with white America. Yet, only about half of the public television stations on the air were willing to carry it. One example: I was a member of the University of North Carolina television advisory committee at the time. A minority on the committee fought to have the University's TV station carry the series. But the station manager and the chairman of the committee (ironically, a member of the Department of Education) fought for two years to ban it and, with the ultimate help of the administration of the Chapel Hill branch of the University, succeeded.

For several years following the rumblings of revolution in the inner cities, radio and TV stations were beset with good intentions, some of these intentions actually seeing fruition. Most of the projects carried out were on public TV stations; WTIF in Hershey, Pennsylvania, for example, prepared documentaries used in conjunction with "mini-town meetings" at which representatives of the inner city, business, education, church, and other community groups discussed problems and then met once a week to watch a live telecast of an open-ended report of their sessions and to seek agreement of changes needed to meet the problems analyzed. This kind of approach takes television and radio beyond their neutral positions as merely tools and integrates them into the problem-solving functions of their communities.

Many public radio stations, notably the Pacifica stations, have long had special programs and communications to, for, and from the inner city, and a number of stations have had two-way communication (i.e., the telephone question-discussion shows) on the problems of the inner city, involving African-Americans and other minorities on both sides of the microphone. An example of the impact of this approach was a program series entitled "Carolina Roundtable," originated by radio station WUNC-FM of the University of North Carolina at Chapel Hill in the early 1960s—quite different than the University's aforementioned television station at the time in recognizing and serving minority needs. WUNC radio was probably the only station in the state to have a continuing series which dealt predominantly with civil rights problems. The program featured African-Americans and whites of all attitudes and opinions as equal partners on panels—a rare occurrence then in southern broadcasting. The African-American churches in the listening area brought together residents of the community the nights the broadcasts dealt with civil rights. They phoned in questions and followed up the broadcasts with discussions. During those critical civil rights struggle years this program became a principal source of information and motivation for understanding and action on the part of many Blacks and whites in the area.

Some special events have provided the opportunity for excellent media contributions. On the night of the funeral of Dr. Martin Luther King, Jr., educational radio station WRVR, New York City, put together a hook-up of some 40 noncommercial and commercial stations across the eastern half of the country, through which individual listeners, phoning in, were able to talk with civil rights leaders.

Perhaps the best known and most successful of the public affairs media programs for a minority group has been "Black Journal," initially produced by National Educational Television and, later, independently by a Black-owned production firm. Letters from Blacks on all economic and educational levels throughout the country praised its contributions to raising Black pride and ego and for candidly dealing with Black problems and accomplishments. Although, as with most minority-oriented programs, public support and funds soon petered out, the efforts of producer Tony Brown have maintained it as one of the few programs that continue on the air dealing in depth with issues significant to various minority communities.

A look at the 1960s and 1970s shows that when there have been summers with a decreasing number of violent protests in the cities, there has been a concomitant decrease in the amount of time devoted by broadcasting to minority concerns. Are the media managers telling the people of the inner cities that there is only one way—fomenting violence—to get the media to pay adequate attention to one of the most critical of this country's problems?

Informational-reportorial programs must go beyond the innocuous stance of "factual presentation." Too many documentaries are a good two or three centuries (either chronologically or philosophically) away from our current critical problems and do not relate concretely to them.

The residents of the inner cities need to have access to the media and control of their own stations. They need the opportunity to communicate on their own terms within their communities and to the outside world, including other minority groups in other parts of their cities.

We need have no doubt that the daily and nightly electronic visions about all those families with pleasant homes in the suburbs and nice cars and well-dressed and well-fed kids make a person very uncheerful about the two rooms his or her family shares with the rats. Television has shown the urban man, woman and child the promised land; shouldn't television go on from there and help them to reach that land?

And there's the rub! The Report of the National Advisory Commission on Civil Disorders indicated that the educated Black man and woman are at least as angry and at least as ready to go along with violence as is the less well-educated person, precisely because they have made the educational hurdle and are still barred from the economic benefits.

It is not enough, therefore, for television only to educate the disadvantaged. If domestic peace and justice are to be achieved, will television not also have to educate the rest of us to accept the practice of what we preach?

We must educate the inner cities, yes, but we also must educate the suburbs—the people on the outside of the urban ghettos who still practice a TV kind of paternalism. How long do we think society can keep saying, "Look—but don't touch!?"

We are talking about television and radio, and we are all of us tuned in. The Bible says that the child is father to the man. Freud said that what a child will be is determined by the time he or she is three years old. And the latest statistics say that two-year-olds spend about 20 hours per week watching television.

We—all of us—need the education that television and other electronic media can provide. Just as we want the people inside the inner city to learn, those of us outside of it have also got to be ready to learn. For those of us who have been emotionally raised in a world of platitudinous beliefs and verbal rationalizations, it isn't going to be easy. But in realistic terms, even for those of us who can't see it from other than a personal, narrow self-interest point of view, I suspect that it beats having to choose between hiding out forever in the crab grass or being beset by irrational prejudices and fears when visiting the art museum in the center of the city.

# CHAPTER 9

# Women and Communications

The 1960s and 1970s saw a dichotomy in the role of women. The greater personal freedoms within society and the influences of alternative lifestyles resulted in an alteration of the traditional roles for women, including that of the obedient, selfless, family-serving, dependent housewife. The newly discovered sense of self plus a yearning for the fulfillment of their personal abilities—a fulfillment automatically granted to their husbands whom they were expected to uncomplainingly serve and support—prompted many heretofore subservient women to seek personal freedom in the labor force, thus injecting women as a key factor in America's business, professional, and economic society. But it was not easy, given continuing male governance of both the legal and moral rules of society and business. The threats by women to uncontested male dominance resulted in strong male reaction, including the denigration of women's efforts for equal rights.

For example, the word "feminist," an apt term to describe those who put forward in word and deed the notion that women were entitled to the same opportunities and compensation for their labor as were men, was immediately colored in meaning by the male-controlled media to suggest something negative, antisocial, and, indeed, even unfeminine. So successful were those who opposed women's rights that even thirty years later, at the turn of the twenty-first century, many women who have achieved some measure of success only because of the earlier efforts of the "feminists" protest that they are not feminists. Younger women, with no knowledge of the fact that the opportunities open to them were unavailable to women scant decades before—opportunities achieved only through the sacrifices of the feminists—proudly announce that they are not feminists.

The growth and, to many, the peak of the women's movement, coincided—and had a symbiotic relationship—with America's counter-culture revolution of the 1960s and 1970s. The women's movement had several components and went through several phases. In the early 1960s a principal aim of the movement was to raise female consciousness, first to provide rationale and support for individual women to attain some measure of respect and dignity in situations where they had little or none, and, second, to politicize women to understand and take political action to remedy those laws and society-imposed restrictions on their personal freedoms and potentials. In 1966 Betty Friedan and several other women established The National Organization for Women (NOW), which became the principal arm for representing and seeking women's rights. NOW's purpose was—and still is—"to take action to bring women into full participation in the mainstream of American society now, exercising all the privileges and responsibilities thereof in truly equal partnership [with men]." (Unfortunately, a generation later some NOW chapters, such as the one in Boston, abandoned its principles in favor of individual political advancement for some of its leaders.) Other organizations seeking similar goals and providing broader bases and expansion for the women's movement included the National Women's Political Caucus (NWPC), and the Women's Equity Action League (WEAL). Some organizations of women were dedicated to targeted issues, such as Women's Action for Nuclear Disarmament (WAND).

In the early 1970s women took their fight to the streets, in marches in many cities throughout the country. One 1970 march in New York City was declared "the beginning of a new movement. . . . [T]oday is the end of millenniums of oppression." Through organizations, through marches and meetings, and through individual efforts, proponents of equal rights for women finally convinced Congress to take action. Title VII of the Civil Rights Act enabled women to sue firms for discrimination in hiring and in job compensation; Title IX mandated equal support for women's athletics as well as other activities in educational institutions, making possible a remarkable growth of women's professional sports in the last decades of the twentieth century. Ironically, many of the women athletes who benefited from the feminists' success in making their athletic careers possible either have no notion of who their benefactors were or what they did and some—hypocritically or stupidly—look askance at feminist organizations, refusing to acknowledge their debts and just grabbing their sports money and running.

A most significant effort of the women's movement, however, did not succeed: an Equal Rights Amendment to the U.S. Constitution. Although Congress passed an Equal Rights Act, the "old boys" controlled legislatures, coupled with some prominent, politically self-serving women, prevented ratification by the required three-fourths of the states.

One major women's movement success, albeit temporary, was in the area of media. Coinciding with racial minorities' participation in the licensing and license renewal process of the Federal Communications Commission, women's organizations also represented their concerns about discrimination by radio and television stations in programming and in employment. NOW established a special office to deal with media discrimination. In many instances women's groups' representations at FCC licensing hearings—or the threat of such representations—convinced numerous stations to begin changing their stereotyping of women in commercials and programming, and to provide women with employment opportunities above the clerical level. The FCC included women as well as racial minorities in its rules for affirmative action in hiring and in promotion, with emphasis on managerial positions.

Subsequently, in the 1980s, the Reagan administration obliterated almost all affirmative action regulations, and many stations retreated to their old discriminatory practices. But the door had been opened and the many women in the media today, on camera, in the studio, and behind executive desks, owe their positions to the feminists' efforts during America's counter-culture revolution.

The following is an amalgamation of materials from a number of addresses and papers presented in the 1960s and 1970s, in which women were included as a minority in terms of opportunities in and treatment by the media.

Minority status is not measured by numbers alone. Minority also refers to those who lack the same opportunity, power, and prerogative afforded the majority or the controlling force in any given society.

Although women may constitute the numerical majority in the United States, they do not have the economic and political prerogatives or opportunities that men have. They are a minority group. The evolution of humanity is so slow that even though there have been many centuries of so-called modern civilization, the physical basis of power—Neanderthal brute strength—still dominates human relationships. It dominates it on an individual level, the subjugation of women in the traditional one-to-one male-female relationship, just as it does on a large group level—the accumulation and use of physical weapons of strength capable of mass murder in a country-to-country relationship. In both cases economic and political subjugation are part of the purpose and the result.

The use of communications to visually and aurally verbalize the subjugated nature of their roles in society, to reach out to society at large, and to organize action to free themselves from their status has been explored by women in much the same way it was applied by racial minorities. The self-directed African-American revolution for human dignity and freedom provided impetus for a similarly self-directed revolution by women; the latter began to gather momentum in the 1970s. It should not be forgotten, however, that it is really a re-revolution, a resumption of women's rights and suffrage movements of 100 and more years ago that resulted in some of the more humane and progressive laws enacted in this country, and which provided experience and impetus for subsequent efforts by other minority groups, including African-Americans. As the impact of communications on human motivation and societal change is more and more understood, more and more minorities will be using the media to achieve their goals.

Media, particularly television, comprise a significant part of the women's revolution. Dial Torgerson, in an early 1970s *Los Angeles Times* article on "The Status of Women Around the World," wrote: "As it did a decade ago with the disadvantaged minorities of the United States, television is raising the expectations—and stirring the desires—of women on the bottom of the status ladder. Women in the provinces see how freer counterparts live in sophisticated capitals. Women whose lives are dominated by men and poverty see dubbed versions of American TV series in which women live in luxury and hold men in amused contempt."

Women through the 1970s are where African-Americans were with media some ten years earlier: not yet in a position to use communications as a positive force to organize and motivate because they still have to fight to change the negative images that dominate the existing media. It is significant that at the latter part of the 1970s African-Americans no longer have to fight wholesale negative images on television—but women do.

One of the first and perhaps most publicized efforts in the new era of women's liberation was the invasion of the offices of the *Ladies' Home Journal* just as the 1970s got under way. The purpose of the 100 or so women who staged a protest was "to change attitudes," including the replacement of the magazine's editor—a man—by a woman, and a discontinuance of advertisements that were "exploitative" of woman's minority role in our society. Although the principal immediate gain was only an eight-page supplement in the *Journal* on women's liberation, the action did call to public attention not only the need for change, but the fact that women were ready to take militant action to achieve that change.

Some seven years earlier, in *The Feminine Mystique*, Betty Friedan wrote about *McCall's*, considered then the country's most popular "women's" magazine: "The world that emerges from this big, pretty magazine is young and frivolous, almost child-like; fluffy and feminine; gaily content in a world of bedroom and kitchen, sex, babies and home. The magazine surely does not leave out sex; the only passion, and the only goal a woman is permitted is the pursuit of a man. It is crammed full of food, clothing, cosmetics, furniture and physical bodies of young women, but where is the world of thought and ideas, the life of the mind and spirit?"

At the same time efforts are being made to eliminate negative images, concomitant efforts must be made to introduce positive images—the ego, pride, and self-concept discussed earlier for minorities. This is easier to do in the print field than with the electronic media. There is no physical limit to the number of magazines that can be published and, given sufficient resources, anyone can publish a magazine. But the number of television and radio channels in any community is limited, providing at least a partial monopoly for those relatively few able to obtain a license. This is, of course, why government regulation to serve and protect the public interest is necessary for broadcasting, and why the generally laissez-faire prerogatives of magazines and newspapers cannot be applied to television and radio. A number of low-budgeted women's liberation publications, including *Aphra* and *Off Our Backs*, were developed in the early 1970s for relatively small audiences, something that could not be done in broadcasting. The first issue of *Ms.* in the spring of 1972, aimed at the women who were committed or ready to become involved in self-liberation or group action, was an immediate success. Several less militant journals and even non- or anti-militant journals (combining traditional features with an interspersing of "free woman" concepts) such as *New Woman* and *New York Woman* presaged a bandwagon of so-called women's magazines that attempted to relate to, if not support, the developing women's movement.

Establishing new ideas or changing old concepts in television and radio, however, has been exceedingly more difficult. From the soap opera to the dramatic series, the woman is portrayed as either incompetent or overbearing. Even in programs where women behave in adult, responsible, respected ways, there is always the tragic (or, more accurately in terms of media practice, "comic") flaw that makes the woman less than the ideal image presented of the male. (This is not to ignore the countless "father-knows-worst" kinds of programs that show the male, as well, as an incompetent bumbler.)

Perhaps the most flagrant area of anti-woman media practice is in commercials. Judith Adler Hennessee and Joan Nicholson wrote an article in the *New York Times* on TV commercials vis-à-vis women, entitled "NOW Says TV Commercials Insult Women." They illustrated, with specific examples, concepts of women as presented in commercials, ranging from the sex object "Fly Me" to the woman-as-chattel "My wife, I think I'll keep her." Through all the commercials, they pointed out, no matter how insulted or misused women are, they always smile: "Women smile a lot. It goes with the shuffle."

A study by the National Organization for Women (NOW) of 1,241 TV commercials showed women's place was in the home in almost all of them. In 42.6% of the commercials women were doing household work; in 37.5% their role was to provide help or service to men; and in 16.7% their main purpose was for male sex needs. In only 0.3% of the commercials were women shown as independent individuals.

Hennessee and Nicholson describe some of the commercials:

The bride and groom have run directly from their wedding without bothering to change their clothes to go on their honeymoon, to the appliance store. The salesman is telling the groom (not the bride) how terrific the G.E. Toaster Oven is. The bride is standing around in a daze, having just achieved the greatest ambition of her life—a husband. The two men decide that the groom should buy the product and then, as a polite afterthought, they turn to the bride and ask her what she thinks. Oblivious to everything she replies, "I do."

The Downey Fabric Softener commercial offers an explicit definition of a wife. "Honey, here's your laundry," the new bride says brightly. "Did I wash it right?" Her husband registers his approval and she is fulfilled. "He noticed," she says euphorically. "I'm a wife."

The product [Geritol] has given his wife the energy to take care of the baby, go to a school meeting, shop for groceries and cook dinner. Through it all she has still managed to stay attractive for him. "My wife, I think I'll keep her," he says.

Women never tell men what to do, but men are forever telling women what to do and how to do it. Even in their own private beauty realm, women aren't quite with it. "I'm all thumbs," the helpless woman in the Revlon Fabuliner ad says. "It won't skip? It won't run?" The male voice-over keeps telling her, with decreasing patience, that no matter how clumsy and inept she is, she just can't mess herself up because "it draws a perfect line every time." She finally learns the lesson and repeats, with slow, dawning comprehension: "It draws a perfect line every time." She really ought to haul off and sock him.

All the ads for educational opportunities and careers invite only men to participate—except for one, the U.S. Auto Club Driving School. "There is a special division for women students," the male voice-over says patronizingly. Women are some strange sub-species whose coordination is questionable at best.

[N]ot even the few professional women whose lives definitely do not revolve around a stove escape. In a Dove commercial, a professional actress is shown hand-washing the dirty dinner dishes of 150 people. The important thing is not that she is an actress but that she is a female, and females wash dishes. Her career, her real work, is valueless.

We all know what "Fly Me" really means, and why all the men in the office cluster around the Olivetti Girl. She is a plaything, a sex object. With the typewriter fixing up all the errors, she will have more time to entertain her bosses. "Two brains are better than one," says Olivetti, but she doesn't really need a brain at all. In the marketplace of television, women are just another commodity, peddling their wares like the model in the Shop Rite pantyhose commercial who becomes the product. She sits there in the grocery cart like a big doll, smiling, her legs in one of the classic cheesecake positions, waiting to be picked up and bought.

The Hennessee-Nicholson study was published in 1972. Has much changed? On your television set this evening you will probably see some male who is too lazy to wash his neck regularly, yet his wife will be blamed for his "ring-around-the-collar." The *Good Housekeeping* survey finding that one-third of women viewers have at one time or another turned off commercials because they found them offensive is not surprising and is as pertinent today as when it was conducted in 1971. (A later "Doonesbury" cartoon shows a woman character telling male friends that her husband invited some male friends to dinner and at the end of the meal one of them complimented her on her cooking, and her husband said "with a big stupid grin": "my wife, I think I'll keep her." "I broke his nose," she adds.)

Even seemingly innocuous "Sesame Street" is not immune. In 1970 NOW expressed to the Children's Television Workshop, producers of "Sesame Street," its concern with the "portrayal of women and girls" on the program. In its third season, 1971–1972, "Sesame Street" accordingly expanded the cast from one woman to three (increasing the males as well), including the addition of the role of a letter-carrier who is female. It also cut down the woman-in-the-kitchen sequences. In its 1972–1973 season "Sesame Street" developed a female Muppet character, discarded some Muppet segments "because of their unsatisfactory portrayal of women," and developed other sequences in which girls would be shown in assertive non-stereotyped roles.

The stress by women's liberation organizations on the need for self-awareness on the part of women is reiterated by some of the leading women in the communications field, reinforcing the necessity for media creation of positive images of women, not only to influence men, but to affect women as well.

Joan Ganz Cooney, president of the Children's Television Workshop, has stated: "Doors are opening for women, but I'm afraid many won't seize the responsibility because of fear. Women are conditioned to be supportive and submissive from childhood. They must fight the fear of failing." Francine Wilvers, as executive vice president of the Marschalk advertising agency, said: "Women are underachievers. They don't use all their gifts and strengths. Women's liberation has started opening their minds up, but it's something that has been conditioned in them since childhood."

In a study entitled "The Image of Females as Presented on Children's Saturday Morning Network Television," Mary Ellen Verheyden-Hilliard, coordinator of the NOW National Education Task Force, found that females constituted only 23% of the characters the children saw, although females make up 51% of the population of the country. She also found that female roles were limited in initiative, mostly verbal and rarely action, with virtually all initiatives on all programs taken by the male characters. In moments of crisis the female character usually turns over the initiative to the male even before she tries to do anything. Verheyden-Hilliard asks:

What is the explicit and implicit message which is being conveyed to boys and girls concerning the role of the female? The female is peripheral. She is in many cases non-existent. If she should have intelligence or capability, it is wise to hide it. She is subservient and serving to the male, whether he is a seven-year-old peer, a teen-age beau, a son. The only way she may dominate, and this in a negative way, is as a wife. She learns that boys do not like the clever girls and do not listen to them. A show of brains is never rewarded. Acting dumb is.

The behavior patterns which girls may be storing are ones which encourage them not to compete, not to indicate intelligence, to let the man do the big, important job, to be a follower, not a leader. And the boys, what are they absorbing? Boys learn that girls rarely have an idea worth listening to, that they will fail in a crisis.

Why is such pervasive denigration of females shown on network television? Why do the networks allow it? Is television simply a mirror of society? Can it be, should it be more? No network would, any longer, put on five hours of programming every Saturday morning in which Blacks acted dumb, fell over their feet, and were happy at anything as long as their white friends loved them. Why have Blacks been able to change their TV image and females have not?

Male chauvinism, like racial prejudice, does not come about because of some inborn characteristic, although both eventually become part of the subconscious and take on emotional as opposed to rational qualities. Both result from, and in turn feed upon, the need to maintain an economic condition. Television, like all communications media, can create and support intellectual and emotional stereotypes. The public image created of a handicapped person or a race or an ethnic group or of women affects the acceptance of that individual or group into the mainstream of economic endeavor—including the job market and those opportunities that ultimately affect one's qualifications for entry into the job market. Given the current situation, where male-dominated business and industry keep women's pay lower and deny women equal opportunity to compete with men for top-paying jobs, it would not be paranoid to suggest that there is an unconscious if not conscious "hidden agenda" behind the commercials and other representations of women in the media. This is not to imply that there is a conspiracy by writers, producers and ad agency representatives to keep women in a certain economic and, hence, socio-political-sexual place; nevertheless, the product they turn out cannot be ignored.

It wasn't until the early 1970s that overt, organized pressure by such groups as NOW and WEAL began to have results. One step forward was the FCC's addition of women to its equal employment opportunity program station filing requirements in 1972—a year after the program was adopted. Its addition was also a step forward for federal bureaucracy. It is pertinent to note some of the FCC comments in the official Report and Order, dated December 19, 1971:

Women . . . constitute over 50% of the population, and the history of employment discrimination against women is amply demonstrated by the comments in this proceeding. It is fully appropriate, in our judgment, for the attention of broadcasters to be drawn to the task of providing equal employment opportunities for women as well as for Negroes, Orientals, American Indians and Spanish-surnamed Americans. We do not believe it follows, as the NAB [National Association of Broadcasters] suggests, that the extension of the application of Section VI to women will require its extension to such groups as Armenians and Tasmanians.

[*In 1976 the FCC adopted a ten-point program for implementation of equal opportunities in broadcasting for women as well as for minorities. In 1977 the FCC exempted from its requirements, however, all stations with ten employees or less.*]

Not satisfied with words on paper alone, less than three months after the 1972 rules went into effect, representatives of NOW, WEAL and Federally Employed Women (FEW) met with the FCC Commissioners over the latter's waiving of the requirement for New York and New Jersey license renewals, which had been submitted on March 1, 1972. The insistence of these groups resulted in the FCC writing to the New York and New Jersey stations requiring compliance and making certain that the May 1 applications from Pennsylvania and Delaware would also comply. By the end of the meeting the Commissioners were urging women's groups to involve themselves with the community ascertainment programs of their local stations.

Although some FCC Commissioners were reported to be visibly and even angrily disturbed by the continuing pressures brought by women's groups, a conscious awareness did take place. In July, 1972, following analysis of the Pennsylvania and Delaware license renewal applications, the FCC asked 30 stations to explain their employment records in light of the FCC rules concerning equal employment opportunities for minority persons and women. This did not resolve the issue, however. In the fall of 1972, after a review of equal employment policies and practices of stations in Maryland, Virginia, West Virginia and the District of Columbia, the FCC renewed the licenses of 418 stations and deferred action on the applications of 49 stations—26 AM, 18 FM, three commercial TV and two educational TV—pending receipt of further information.

FCC Commissioner Nicholas Johnson, who had been a principal motivator for immediate and positive steps for equal employment, dissented from the FCC decision, citing inadequate action on behalf of women and racial minorities. His statement is considered by many to be still pertinent.

### Equal Employment—Washington Renewals
*Dissenting Opinion of Commissioner Nicholas Johnson*
In August of 1972 the Federal Communications Commission decided—after long procrastination—that it ought to make an effort to enforce its own regulations against discriminatory employment practices. (See Pennsylvania and Delaware Renewals, FCC 2nd (1972).) That effort was weak, but it was at least something.

In our August decision, we directed the Broadcast Bureau to send equal employment opportunity inquiry letters to 30 broadcast stations which had ten or more employees and which:

(1) had no women employees, or showed a decline in the number of women employees from 1971 to 1972, or

(2) were in areas with a minority population of 5% or more and employed no blacks or showed a decline in the number of black employees from 1971 to 1972.

The purpose of these letters was to solicit from the stations their reasons for their employment patterns—to help us determine whether the stations might be engaged in the sort of discriminatory practices against which our regulations are directed.

As I have noted on prior occasions (see my concurring and dissenting statements in Pennsylvania and Delaware Renewals, FCC 2nd (1972) and Pennsylvania and Delaware Equal Employment Opportunity Inquiries, FCC 2nd (1972)), I had considerable reservations about the standards employed by the Commission in selecting out stations meriting letters of inquiry because those standards ignored many patterns of possible discrimination—such as a station's refusal to employ minority group members and women in high paying positions. Nevertheless, I went along with the majority on the theory that some remedial action is generally preferable to none at all.

The Commission's subsequent reaction to the stations' responses to our inquiries—blithe acceptance of the stations' explanations, refusal to delve deeper, and simple renewal of those stations' licenses—cast considerable doubt upon this theory. The majority's refusal to put teeth into its letter of inquiry program sapped that program of its potential and converted it into a joke. Still, despite my reservations, I went along because I believed and still believe that the very fact of our letters could bring some needed changes in broadcasters' hiring practices. (See my statement in Pennsylvania and Delaware Equal Employment Opportunity Inquiries, supra.)

Today the Commission converts its laughable equal employment opportunities program into a total farce. Confronted with the specter of having to send out letters of inquiry to a large number of stations in the Washington-Maryland-Virginia-West Virginia area—stations which have shown some decline in the number of women and blacks employed, or which have not employed any women or blacks—the majority hurriedly sought the shelter of its staff. The Broadcast Bureau—without the aid of any standards whatsoever—was advised to trim this list of stations and to return with a more "manageable" group of stations to be sent letters of inquiry.

The staff has dutifully complied, and, with nary a word, the majority accepts every single staff decision. And this in spite of the fact that, in a number of cases, the staff has offered no good reason for its favored treatment.

For example, in its very first case, the bureau excludes from our letter of inquiry program Washington station WOOK (AM & FM) even though that station shows a decline in the number of women employed from 1971 to 1972. The staff justifies its decision on the sole ground that this "decline was among office and clerical workers. All female employees," adds the staff, "are in these positions."

Surely this is an odd reason for declining to inquire further of this station's hiring practices. Indeed, the justification—bizarre as it may be—would seem to suggest that WOOK might well be discriminating against women. Apparently, however, WOOK employs a considerable number of blacks. The majority may thus be holding that if a station does not unlawfully discriminate against one group of Americans, it may discriminate against another.

WRFT, in Roanoke, Virginia, is also excluded from our letter of inquiry program for similar reasons. While that station does show an increase in black employment, it shows a decline in the employment of women. As the staff rather curiously notes, "females were not employed in other than office and clerical positions." That's enough for the majority. WRFT doesn't receive a letter of inquiry, and its license is renewed.

These are merely two examples. I have, rather arbitrarily, selected the first and last stations dealt with by the staff to point out the very troublesome nature of the majority's own arbitrary approach.

I would send out our letters of inquiry to every station which has failed to meet the standards—meager as they may be—which we adopted in August. Those standards were the product of considerable statistical analysis; they are objective indicia of certain trends in employment patterns which ought to arouse our suspicion if we are, indeed, concerned about unlawful discrimination. Further, on the basis of these suspicions, we are not punishing any station; we are merely investigating further in order to discover more facts.

Even that investigation troubles the majority, and the majority's problem with so mild a measure—a technique whose sole purpose is to decipher the truth—is terribly disturbing to me. Equally disturbing is the totally *ad hoc* approach now relied upon by this Commission to "implement"—or, more properly, to emasculate—its letter of inquiry program.

That program, like the equal employment opportunity program it is designed to effectuate, is no longer merely a joke. Indeed, it is not even just a farce. It is a mess.

I dissent.

Women's organizations began to use an approach already found most successful by other minority groups in changing the practices of television and radio stations: challenging a station's license renewal.

One milestone in such challenges was the 128–page petition filed by the New York Chapter of NOW in 1972 against WABC-TV following an 18–month study. NOW specifically complained that the station had failed to comply with the FCC's community needs ascertainment requirement and its fairness doctrine by not ascertaining and not presenting meaningful programs on the needs and interests of women. It charged that the station showed women as "unintelligent, irresponsible, dominated by men, defined by their anatomy and incapable of independent thought or action." It also charged the station with failure to implement the FCC rules on equal employment opportunities for women.

Another significant action was in Syracuse, New York, where a number of citizen organizations opposed the transfer of station WNYS-TV to new owners and the license renewal of station WSYR-TV on the grounds that programming and hiring practices of the two stations were prejudicial to women and to other minorities. The challenge against the WNYS-TV transfer was withdrawn when the prospective new ownership agreed to actively recruit women and other minorities, to expand its public affairs programming with women and other minorities on the production staffs, and to avoid unnecessary use of racial and ethnic identifications on programs. The agreement further stated that "disparaging and out-of-context references to sex roles will be avoided. Cliches and misleading description, including but not limited to 'women libbers,' will be especially avoided."

Simultaneously, efforts were made to convince state legislatures, civic groups, universities and other noncommercial organizations involved with media to recognize the needs and rights of women and to adopt positive media practices to meet these needs. Dr. Sandra Bennett, testifying before the State of Ohio Centennial Commission Hearings on Women, said: "We must focus our energies on the use of media to take the university out of the campus classrooms and into the community where the women are. Into the homes, into the lounges of the factories and public schools, hospitals, libraries, and, thereby providing opportunities to train, to re-train, or to continue training."

Programming for women audiences has been changing. One of the best statements of goals was developed by four women in public/educational radio broadcasting: Mary Roman (Pacifica), Marion Watson (KUOM), and Barbara Patterson and Elaine Prostak (WFCR). In preparing for a session on "Women in Public Radio" for an annual convention of the National Association of Educational Broadcasters, they established the following guidelines:

1. Topics such as cooking, sewing, child-care, housekeeping and food shopping should be considered of general interest and not, as traditionally, materials stereotyped for women.
2. The audience listening at home includes, along with housewives, the infirm, the elderly, the retired and the unemployed.
3. There are topics of particular interest to women, such as legal rights for women.
4. Community awareness should be increased as to what women have done and are doing in politics, arts, sciences and technology.
5. Women's awareness should be increased as to what it means to be a female, through such topics as female physiology and sexuality, female perspectives in public affairs, and female sensibilities in the arts.

Barbara Walters, who established the acceptance of a woman interviewer commentator on the "Today" show and who made a breakthrough as a news anchorperson on ABC television, believes that information-education programs which appeal to both women and men should be developed on daytime TV. Her own NBC network panel program, "Not For Women Only," covered such issues as drugs, nutrition, birth, marriage, death, and frequently included specific areas of women's rights. "To say a show is just for women is to put down women," Walters has said. "We feel the subjects are of interest to all people. Everything we do is ascertained as a community need."

A Group W program on WBZ-TV, Boston, "For Women Today," had an all-female production team, and was praised by a number of women's groups for its unbiased presentation of women's needs and organizational activities and its coverage of a broad range of topics from drugs to cooking to sex to sensitivity groups. Executive producer of the program, Raysa R. Bonow, analyzed the difficulty of getting women into key positions on network programs. "Psychologically both men and women have been indoctrinated into seeing only men in authoritative roles," she said. "Networking programming is determined by men who really believe that women are not a salable item." Sherrye Henry, who conducted New York's WCBS-TV show, "Woman," stated: "We assume women can keep house, clean their ovens, and make tuna crumble casseroles. There are wider horizons. We want to show what is possible for women, today and tomorrow, to present options, opportunities and the roadblocks in the way." Lee Shepherd co-conducted "Eyewitness News at Noon" on KSD-TV, St. Louis, which was principally hard news and had a predominantly female audience. Shepherd said: "We are not interested in how a politician's wife manages her children but how she feels about political issues." Washington, D.C.'s WTOP-TV program "Everywoman" was produced by women. The purpose of the two personalities on the program, Rene Carpenter and Jacqueline Tollett, was "to record the current revolution, to present women who are changing their life styles." ("Olivetti Girls Aren't Forever," *Broadcasting* magazine, August 7, 1972.)

In the early 1970s programs such as these were emerging on many stations throughout the country. By the mid-1970s, the first flush of lip-service turned into the same kind of inaction that previously characterized much of the commitment toward minorities, and the new wave of programs for women were being pushed into limbo. "Everywoman," for example, was changed from a twice-a-day program to a once-a-week presentation, with key members of its staff dropped. Some new important programs were developed, but not in the numbers or with the support anticipated.

The 1977 report of the United States Commission on Civil Rights, "Window Dressing on the Set: Women and Minorities in Television," noted that "recent trends toward relevancy and realism in television programming resulted in further entry of minorities and women into the television world. Both groups have been most successfully incorporated into the realistic situation comedies of Norman Lear and MTM productions. The popularity of these programs has resulted in numerous spin-offs and imitations. The proliferation of these comedies has provided, for the first time, a relatively diverse portrayal of minorities and women. Despite the relative realism of these series, they have nevertheless been criticized for displaying elements of racism and sexism. Public interest groups have found, however, that they can work with the production companies to improve the portrayals of minorities and women."

In 1975 NOW asked the broadcast industry to adopt guidelines governing the portrayal of women in television advertising. Among the proposals recommended for inclusion in the Television Code of the National Association of Broadcasters were the following:

- Advertisements should portray women and men in a wide variety of roles;

- The unbalanced portrayal of women and men as preoccupied with physical appearance and acceptability to the opposite sex is discouraged and members of both sexes should be shown dealing positively and realistically with the human process of aging;

- Portrayals of either sex as obsessed with domestic duties or inordinately uninformed about consumer matters should be avoided;

- Capitalizing on the women's rights movement by using feminism as an attention-getting or sales device should be avoided;

- Advertising should avoid depicting either sex as a sex object;

- There should be a better balance between the sexes as spokespersons for on-camera production representation and for voice-overs;

- Persons who relate sexually to persons of their own sex should be portrayed realistically and with dignity;

- Family size in ads should reflect the trend toward smaller families;

- Ads should reflect on camera the broad spectrum of racial and ethnic groups in the American population.

From your perspective today, to what extent did the broadcast industry adopt these recommendations?

Men run broadcasting, and even those with intellectual good will and awareness find it difficult to empathize with the degradation women feel when used as advertising sex objects unless they have had an experience comparable to that of "Tank McNamara" in the fictional comic strip, whose endorsement contract required him to stand in front of a display booth in his bathing suit. He objects that he would feel "like a piece of meat on display." A female colleague promoting the same product in her bathing suit says, "Congratulations, you've just had your consciousness raised." Afterwards he tells a friend that as he stood in front of all the women, in his bathing trunks and wet T-shirt, the women looked at him like men look at a pretty girl at a sales convention, and after a moment of male ego, he angrily realizes that "it made me feel . . . like . . . I was for sale!"

Women have learned, from their struggles to unionize, eliminate sweatshops, stop exploitative child labor, gain the right to vote, hold public office, and pass a constitutional amendment guaranteeing females the same rights as other Americans, that militantly active approaches are their most successful weapons. They have also learned, as in the case of other minority groups, that success also depends on the elimination of stereotyped and negative images. The media must educate and motivate women and men both not only toward acceptance, but toward the implementation of situations and relationships that will free both groups from their current stratified, artificial positions.

Romy Medeiros de Fonseca, women's rights movement leader in Brazil, stated that television "is the first means of education from which Brazilian men have not been able to bar their women. They stopped them from going to school, stopped them from studying, kept them at home and cut off all contact with the world. But once that television set is turned on there is nothing to stop women from soaking up every piece of information it sends out. They soak it up like a sponge, and they don't need to be able to read a word."

Women need and seek the same freedoms and opportunities available to the white males of this country that other minority groups also seek. The circumstances and the techniques may differ because of different attitudes on the part of the ruling majority and because of different conditions of servitude. But the goals are the same and in all cases use of the media is the key.

# CHAPTER 10

# The Arts: Stage, Gallery, and Museum (Out of the Tower through the Tube to the Multitude)

While the counter-culture revolution of the 1960s and early 1970s began to open traditionally closed areas of society to others besides the elite who controlled as well as inhabited them, many people remained relatively untouched. One of the bulwarks against progress were the museums, even though many of the counter-culturists were artists and craftspersons without whom the museums would have little reason to exist. Except for instances of exploitation of a new art form fad for publicity and fund-raising purposes, counter-culture art, reflecting the times, was generally ignored by most traditional museums (many art galleries, including new ones established for this purpose, embraced the "new" art). Museums, in general, continued to cater to those who were potential donors and members and they—the museums—did too little to serve or stimulate the artistic interests of those not in a position to materially benefit the museums.

Writing in the November 1966 issue of *Art News*, Thomas B. Hess (the journal's editor) noted that the American museum was a mirror-image of its mid-twentieth-century capitalistic society: in many ways imaginative, energetic, and creative—but blind. Comparing museums to big business, Hess stated that their principal program plans were for the purpose of doubling attendance, tripling facilities, and quadrupling funds by making news through spectacular acquisitions and exhibitions; exploiting their works in the mass media to increase attendance; using rising attendance figures as a rationale for seeking more funds from their communities; applying the new funds to put on more spectacular exhibits; and building larger facilities to accommodate the exhibits and the larger numbers of people attending them. Hess believes that to accomplish this the museums resorted to fads, to "discovering" 20-year-olds, regardless of the worth of their art, and ignoring proven artists.

Standards were compromised and standards remained rigid, both at the same time. Some of the public benefited and much of the public continued to be neglected. From time to time the federal government—whose responsibility, after all, is to serve the needs, including the artistic ones, of the American people—accepted the responsibility of strengthening the country's culture by offering support of the arts. One significant way was through the National Endowment for the Arts, through which federal funds attempted to implement the dictum that history has validated time and time again: a nation with guns and butter doesn't always survive, but a nation without a strong arts culture never survives. Frequently, it is only government that has the will, mandate, and resources to bring the arts to its citizens and thereby strengthen the country's culture. A government frequently destroys its own commitment by determining that it is the final arbiter of what is good or bad in art (as the U.S. Congress has frequently done—and is doing as this is being written in the late 1990s), and guts appropriations for the arts because it objects to the content or form of one or more given artistic presentation made possible through government funds. However, the obligation and potential of government to strengthen its own society through the arts is there.

A different face of elitist belief existed, as well, in much of the artistic world of the 1960s and 1970s. Television was looked down upon as an art. As the most dominant and far-reaching mass medium in the world, it was denigrated by many in the arts and by many in the museum field. Many artists and intellectuals "proudly" declared that they didn't and wouldn't have a television set in their home. The use of this mass medium to bring their art to the people was, at that time, rarely seriously considered.

In the summer of 1971 in a memorandum, President Nixon asked the head of each federal agency to prepare a letter to Nancy Hanks, Director of the National Endowment for the Arts, describing what his or her agency was doing for the arts and what arts and artists were doing and could do for the agency. Decades later there is little evidence that the federal agencies, other than the Endowment itself, have done anything significant regarding the arts. This is not surprising. If the people or the powers of America really believed that the arts were important to the progress of American life, something highly positive, rather than the negative censorship that has marked recent government actions, would have been done about them long since.

The following is principally from two addresses, "From Tower through Tube to Multitude," to the National Council on the Arts' seventh annual convention, September 5, 1968, Sarah Lawrence College, Bronxville, New York, and "A Museum on the Dining Room Table," to the 64th annual convention of the American Association of Museums, May 27, 1969, San Francisco.

Appropriations for the National Endowment for the Arts have multiplied since it was founded under President Lyndon Johnson a few years ago, in 1965, with a budget of $2.5 million. But increasing the budget for the arts does not alone guarantee the national growth. The arts still remain, by and large, the prerogative, plaything, privilege, pleasure and pride of the elite. Despite performing and visual arts centers being established in proletarian centers in some cities by a dedicated and courageous few, and despite arts festivals presented free in parks and other public access places in some localities, the arts are limited principally to those who have the money to attend performances at increasingly high ticket prices or pay the increasingly high fees charged by most museums, or who have the sophistication and education to seek out exhibits at art galleries usually located for optimum access by the middle- and upper-class patrons who dominate their mailing lists.

For example, the arts center in our nation's capital built and developed with the assistance of tax dollars, the John F. Kennedy Center for the Performing Arts, is located at one of the most expensive housing and shopping complexes in the country, Watergate, and is unreachable except by car and long bus rides. It is far removed from the lower economic and high population areas of non-white Washington, D.C., and it charges prices that strain the pocketbooks of even the middle-class. It is not surprising that the Kennedy Center has relatively few Blacks, Hispanics, self-supporting students or lower income people in attendance.

The arts were once part of the daily lives of the people and, as exemplified by the English Guild plays, medieval church drama, and traveling theatre, mime and music groups, were once brought to the people. As the arts became dependent on the financial support of well-to-do patrons, they were more and more oriented to a middle- and upper-class taste, placement and location. Only with the advent of mass media, at first film, then radio and television, were they made available again to the people. There have been a few exceptions, such as the Federal Theatre of the 1930s and the storefront and street theatre of the 1960s, which showed that when the arts are brought to the mass of the people, the people respond, although the lack of money by this particular audience has precluded the development of the financial bases necessary for the growth and expansion of "peoples" theatre and other arts.

The mass media—especially television—are the principal means by which the arts can be brought to the majority of the people today. If the government were really convinced that the arts were important to American life, the Federal Communications Commission would be taking at least as close a look at the arts and cultural programming of stations at license renewal time as it does at news and public affairs programming. But there is not the slightest indication at this writing that any regulatory attempt will be made to have the broadcast media strengthen our country's arts and culture. [*The government did try to do something in the early 1970s; it held a conference. The National Endowment for the Arts sponsored an "Arts/Media" symposium in Washington, D.C., the stated purpose of which was to explore creative ideas and projects which would meld media technology and the arts. The meeting turned out to be principally a showcase for the artistic work of a few people. The participants were mostly communications technologists, federal bureaucrats, educational administrators, and individual artists, with few having any experience in planning or administering the relationship of the arts to the electronic mass media. The Director of the President's Office of Telecommunications Policy, Dr. Clay Whitehead, counseled against the federal government requiring the communications industry to make room for the arts, and instead advocated a reliance on viewer demand for the kinds of programs the public would receive.*]

Many artists tend to look down on the mass media and are especially denigrating of television. In a society that places artists—performing, creative, interpretive—in a continuing precarious professional and economic existence that guarantees that 90% of them will be denied a living in the field of their talents year after year, perhaps they are entitled to some degree of snobbishness about their art so they might at least have ego support. For psychological survival, it may be necessary for them to look down upon or pretend to ignore mass media such as television as serious forms or carriers of art. Even many artists who have done fine work on television and have used TV to further their careers frequently are condescending toward the media. We are all protective of those techniques that we have learned to cope with and use best. Superciliousness is one way of dealing with something new that, however beneficial, may force upon us unwanted change.

Many of us pretend that we can hold at arm's length that which affects us most. Frequently, we hear and look at ideas and experiences as being around us, but not close to us in a way that we can taste them, touch them, smell them or make them a purposeful part of our inner selves.

For example, most of us consider food as an outside utilitarian requirement, necessarily part of our body fiber but at the same time not really part of us at all. The gourmet, however, makes food part of his or her total existence, consciously using food for emotional and aesthetic as well as physical growth and satisfaction. Many scientists work in a microcosm, seeking answers in isolated objectivity. How many members of the Manhattan Project realized only after they had contributed to the creation of an atomic bomb the implications of what they had done in regard to their personal lives and those of the rest of the world? Could any of them really not have known, while they were working on the bomb?

Television is a very real part of our everyday lives and affects us greatly. Yet, how many of us have written frequently or even occasionally to stations, networks, advertisers or the FCC concerning the quality of programs we've seen on television—programs that we personally felt like praising or condemning?

In much the same manner, many artists and teachers of the arts keep television at a distance. The world is watching TV and is being educated—and manipulated—by TV. It is no longer sophisticatedly snobbish, but shortsightedly senseless to say, "I don't watch TV, I spend my time reading books and listening to hi-fi and going to art galleries." Those who do so are alienating themselves from the world they otherwise pretend they are living in. Do you still meet people who say "I wouldn't have a television in my house!?"

By attempting to lessen the importance of the media, many people in the arts are concomitantly lessening the importance of the arts by limiting the scope and impact of their own creativity.

The term "create" is both awesome and confusing to some of us. Many of us think "create" means to paint a picture or compose a symphony or write a play. We may feel inadequate to such tasks and shy away. But "create" is not limited to that. It means something unique that we have brought to an experience—a recorded or transitory one. Einstein was a great creative artist—as were Darwin and Freud and Galileo—even though they may never have painted a picture or composed a symphony or written a play.

In the history of learning it has been the artist—the creative artist—Shakespeare, Leonardo, Beethoven, Pavlova and the Curies and Darwins and Einsteins—who have been the true learners, scholars, educated and educators. Only the artist, in whatever field of endeavor, has been free to develop ideas and actions simply because they are what he or she wants to do and can do and feels their processes and goals are important and possible of achievement.

Only when education is finally oriented to the creative artists' philosophy can we begin to realize our full human potentials to educate and be educated.

This implies significant responsibility for artists and teachers of the arts. They are in positions to affect directly and humanistically the course of events of the world through the power of the arts. They have within their grasp the forces to change world history: to create compassion or by default permit chaos; to achieve equal rights and opportunities or by indifference allow continued discrimination and segregation; to stimulate love or by neglect leave unaffected the sickness of hate; to move the world toward peace or let it move toward perdition.

It has been ever thus in history. Aristophanes took the responsibility. So did Molière. So did George Bernard Shaw. They used the mass media of their times. The play is still the most effective art form for achieving direct emotional and intellectual involvement. But the traditional theater is no longer the "mass" means. The hillside of Greece, the town square in France, the stadium in America do not now reach the largest audiences at any one time. One performance of a Shakespeare play on network television in the United States reaches more people than that play has reached in all its performances in theatres all over the world since it was first produced.

Are we restricting the arts to ivory towers, to the psychological self-fulfillment of a handful of artists, to the easing of jangled nerves of tired businesspersons?

In education, for example, are we using drama for the teaching and learning of history? Painting and sculpture for physics and chemistry? Dance for psychology? Music for mathematics and philosophy? Each of these arts provides a base for learning and a technique for application in various non-arts disciplines. Not only can the arts be used to convey information, stimulate thought, motivate ideas, analyze beliefs and clarify experiments in the classroom, but they can heighten the informal education of adults in all walks of life.

Unfortunately, although there is some excellent education in the arts, the arts in education are, like Sean O'Casey's police in *Juno and the Paycock*, "null and void" in most educational institutions.

Television, as both an art form and a medium of communication, has the ability to bridge the gaps of space and time and to provide a multi-view of and multi-experience in all of the other arts in addition to itself. It can reach out to us wherever we are and stimulate our artistic interest and even our personal creativity. But the creative force is not an easy thing to live with. It is not what many of us want in our classroom—or in our living room. If we invite it in, it means we must be part of it. We can no longer remain passive.

Television can show us what is creatively possible in the world, things we may not have been aware of before. That involves a choice—that *we* must make. It is more comfortable to believe that there is no choice, to foster a situation—a combination of concentric frustration and concentric tranquilization—where we are rarely given a choice. We can settle for the transience of the Roman games that ultimately destroyed Rome, or we can use the arts to build and develop a continuing and lasting culture.

Are artists and arts educators communicating an appreciation of the arts and stimulating a creative participation in the arts only to the relatively few students who enroll in arts courses and to the relatively few people who fill the auditoriums and exhibition halls, or are they reaching out to the total populace, the multitude? Are artists and educators using the most effective means available—television—to move the arts beyond their aristocratic and academic barriers: out of the tower through the tube to the multitude?

Are artists willing to make the arts part of the mainstream of current twentieth-century life? We complain that the arts are dying. We complain about declining audiences. We complain about the lack of public support and we call for increased subsidization. Does football need subsidization? Is not art as important as football to society? It won't be accepted as such so long as we continue to restrict the creative arts to an esoteric level of comparative privacy, instead of making them part of the everyday experience of all of the people.

As noted earlier, most people consider cooking a necessity, more of a routine chore than an art. Yet, through television, cooking has become for many people a participatory creative experience. If Julia Child can move cooking out of the "Cordon Bleu" and to the people, then it is certainly as important for artists and educators to move the arts out of the ivory-towered classrooms and the high-priced theatres and to the people.

What is true for the classroom stage and gallery is true, as well, for the museum.

A friend once told me about her childhood in a remote small southern town. "We didn't have much in the way of culture," she said, "but my brother and I, we did have a museum. Not in the town, though. We made our museum on the dining-room table."

Her parents had taken her and her brother to the museums in the larger cities in the state. (It is parenthetically pertinent to say that the color of their skin and their parents' economic status made it possible for them to enter museums, something which all museums have not always made possible for all people.) The girl and her brother were sufficiently motivated by their visits to wish there were a museum easily available to them. They established one the best way they could—on their dining-room table.

Today many museum directors and curators are beginning to search for ways to change museums' traditional isolation from the mass of the people. Most of us grew up thinking of most museums as stodgy, if not forbidding. A child's first experience with museums is frequently as part of a class field trip, heavy with teacher expectation of conformed observation and memorization. Often, there is even a feeling of guilt about enjoying a museum.

A "Peanuts" cartoon shows two girls on a class field trip to a museum. One is admiring a painting and says, "Isn't that beautiful." The other says, "Try not to have a good time . . . this is supposed to be educational."

Museums, like schools, are slow in becoming relevant to the needs of society. Dwindling funds, with little base of support from the community at large, have prompted many museums to take a new look at what they present and how it is presented.

Museums, individually and in concert, ideally contain people's goals, endeavors and creations, not only of what was and what is, but of what can be. They not only can show the past, but can lead the way to the future.

They can play important roles in establishing meaningful exchanges of culture among peoples of all countries to create mutual understanding.

But how often, for example, do you hear of museums having exhibitions on peace? They seem to be always on war. How often do we see exhibitions delineating controversial points of view on issues critical to society?

In the United States one of the first prestigious recognitions of museums' relationships to the world was the recent [late 1960s] mixed-media show, "Can Man Survive?," at the Museum of Natural History in New York City. Joseph Wetzel, creator and designer of the exhibit, said: "The museum has never made a statement about a contemporary problem before. They've always looked backward. That's a very safe thing to do. This exhibit says we shouldn't have too many kids; and it blames industry as being responsible for pollution. That's a risky thing for a museum to do. It's dependent on endowments that come from private fortunes and industrial fortunes." Eric Salzman, who composed the music for the exhibit, said: "We don't want them (the visitors) to walk out and say 'That was nice' or 'I learned a lot' or even 'That was an experience.' We want them emotionally engaged. We want them to come out and say 'I want to do something about this.' "

There are differences of opinion as to what a museum should be. John Kinard, as director of Washington, D.C.'s Anacostia Neighborhood Museum, said that American museums "have traditionally housed the interests of the rich" and have served the function of being "private purchasing agents for the same rich jokers that buy art." [*In the early 1970s, at the height of America's counter-culture revolution, director Thomas Hoving and president Douglas Dillon of the Metropolitan Museum of Art in New York stated that the "epoch of education and communication," as opposed to the emphasis on collecting individual, high-priced works of art, had begun. Mr. Kinard responded, "How can Thomas Hoving of the Met spend $5 million on a Velazquez painting when he says he's trying to help Blacks?" On the other hand, the director of the distinguished Brooklyn Museum, Duncan F. Cameron, said that Mr. Kinard's Anacostia Neighborhood Museum is "not a museum at all."*]

In a series in the *Washington Post* on "The Urban Museum Crisis," Elisabeth Stevens stated that the American Association of Museums Committee on Urban Museums "warns that 'total flexibility' is the first requirement for museums trying to develop so-called 'outreach' programs in the inner cities. Meanwhile, in many museums across the country, there are outreach programs that range from flexible and imaginative to patronizing and just plain awful. . . . Around the country, museum outreach programs usually consist of Sunday-school or missionary-style efforts and these are fast becoming the great middle way for a big urban museum to become 'responsive' and 'involved.' "

Most outreach programs consist of traveling exhibits or "mini—museums" under the auspices of a large, central, established museum. An example of the traveling exhibit was the New York Metropolitan Museum of

Art's "Eye Opener" mobile trailer, which carried some of the Museum's most important works throughout all the city's boroughs. The Museum has also circulated an exhibit on magic through the entire library system of the borough of Queens. An example of the mini-museum was the Akron Art Institute's establishment, with funds from the Department of Housing and Urban Development, of a Neighborhood Arts Institute offering participation in creating as well as viewing the arts. In a number of urban centers, including New York City and Washington, D.C., neighborhood children's mini-museums offer hands-on creative activities. One of the traditional approaches to community involvement is that noted by Ms. Stevens in reporting Washington, D.C.'s National Gallery's efforts to obtain foundation funds to bus "all D.C. third graders for a special black-oriented tour of the Gallery."

The most significant development in making museums responsive and responsible to the people probably has been the locally controlled neighborhood center. Most of these are not museums in the traditional nonparticipatory sense, but are principally workshops in which people in the community learn how to create as well as appreciate the arts. The neighborhood museums' exhibits usually relate to the lives and needs of the people in the community, rather than to the cultural values of those who develop and run the museums. For example, Washington's Anacostia Neighborhood Museum developed a "rat show" that was subsequently sent on tour to other neighborhood museums in the country. One of the first participatory centers, Studio Watts in Los Angeles, was started in 1964 by James M. Woods, who said, "We want to isolate non-dominant cultural values and make them a vital influence. We want to locate contemporary folk art coming from non-dominant cultures and get it into the museums."

As Ms. Stevens asked: "Can a major museum be more than a patronizing and jingoistic 'missionary' to an outlying or ghetto area? Can residents of such areas state their needs cogently enough to get what they want? Does anyone care?"

If more museums get into the business of becoming part of their larger world, and if more neighborhood museums are developed to serve the needs of their immediate communities, will that be enough? Will the proletariat be reached or will the outreach be merely to a different or larger elite? Will every person in the community have the opportunity for a museum experience as meaningful as if they had a museum on their own dining-room table?

Museums not only need to be in places where people can get to them, but they need to have exhibitions that are pertinent to the audiences they want to reach. The Smithsonian Institution buildings in Washington, D.C., are in the center of the city, yet there are comparatively few visitors from the adjacent inner-city neighborhoods.

Haryou Act in Harlem planned a community television system to go into store-front churches, laundromats, grocery stores and other places only a few steps from people's apartments. Haryou Act officers realized that they needed an alternative to getting people to physically come to their 125th Street center. Unlike most museums, television can go anywhere and everywhere.

Philistines in our communities frequently tell us that museums are frills, that they are not as important to society as are baseball parks or swimming pools or billiard parlors. And in their own Neanderthal way they are right. Right in that museums have been limited and restrictive, unrelated in large part to the real needs of society, and divorced from the continuing, every-day experiences of the multitude.

Not long ago I read a newspaper article on the departure within a very short period of time of three gallery directors in that newspaper's community. The article mentioned one museum's qualifications for a new director: "museum experience, a national scholarly reputation, and a deep grounding in art history." It is time to re-evaluate the qualifications sought in museum directors. It is time to take a fresh look at what the museums have been doing in society—or more appropriately, what they have not been doing. It is time to make the museums important enough to society so that society will no longer put museums at or near the top of the expendable list when it comes time to trim annual city, state, federal or private citizen budgets.

Museums might begin to think of director qualifications something like this: "an understanding of and commitment to relevance in content; a dedi-cation toward making visitors feel 'I want to do something about this'; an ability to involve visitors in the creating as well as an understanding of the arts that make up a country's heritage and stimulate its growth; and an un-derstanding of and commitment to relevance in technique."

Museum directors should understand that motivating people to want to go to museums, to appreciate museums, to develop their own mini-muse-ums does not come principally through deprivation. My friend's develop-ment of a museum on her dining-room table happened because her parents provided her with the opportunity to go to museums in the first place. Op-portunity, relevance, stimulation, and enjoyment are what turn youngsters into museum-goers.

The most important qualification for a museum director is a desire to bring the museum to all people, including children, everywhere, through the most effective means available so that there will be a reason and a mean-ing for everyone to develop their own museums on their dining-room ta-bles, not because they have to, but because it is important enough to them to want to.

# CHAPTER 11

# A Public Television Alternative to Public Television

In *Screened Out: How the Media Moguls Control Our Lives and What We Can Do About It*, published in 2000, Carla Brooks Johnston analyzes how the increasingly larger media monopolies not only decide what entertainment we should receive but also determine what news and information we should get. She shows how the media monopolies also restrict group and individual opportunity to exercise freedom of speech and press and concomitantly restrict the freedom of the public to see and hear any views but those the media moguls wish it to hear and see. The danger to America's democratic way of life is manifest. The public's right to know and to make known—in this country and in others throughout the world—has been screened out by the powerful media gatekeepers.

Is there a solution? The U.S. Congress thought so in 1967 when it passed the Public Broadcasting Act, initiated and endorsed by then President Lyndon B. Johnson. The Act envisioned the development of alternative broadcasting systems, not-for-profit operations directed by boards representing the public rather than private interests and dedicated to the public, not to private, interests. Under the aegis of a Corporation for Public Broadcasting (CPB), the Public Broadcasting System, PBS, was established as the television component of this alternative system. PBS's mission was to provide the public with a wide range of cultural, informational and educational programming not found on commercial television, and with objective content not controlled or censored by the owners or the advertisers upon whom the private stations were dependent for their continued existence and profits.

Unlike public television in many countries, where the government is itself a monopoly gatekeeper dedicated to programming that strengthens and keeps in office the party in power, the U.S. public television system is not run by the government, but by independent boards of directors selected locally in communities throughout the country. Public television was to be the model for First Amendment protections and privileges, where the public interest was the priority. But public television has not lived up to its promise or implied commitment. While it does, indeed, continue to provide more in-depth news, documentaries, public affairs, cultural programs, and quality entertainment than does the commercial broadcasting industry, it has not offered the full range of alternative ideas, beliefs, information, and culture that it is capable of providing.

It is often accused of being elitist—catering to the higher educated and higher income viewer and ignoring the needs of most ordinary citizens. Increasingly, like its commercial counterpart, public television reflects the dominant views of society and seems reluctant to offer too many alternative viewpoints. Too often it has withdrawn or censored programs because its underwriters—the same firms that advertise on commercial television—object to the content of one or more programs. Janine Jackson, when research director of Fairness and Accuracy in Reporting (FAIR), a media watchdog group, stated that "we must reinvent public broadcasting."

While public broadcasting as an alternative medium is increasingly vulnerable to criticism as the new century dawns, the signs of its willingness to yield to pressure were evident early in its formal life. Many and sometimes most stations declined to carry programs such as a series that dealt with the history of racism in the United States; or a program that showed the inhuman social and civil practices of an oil state with whom a given underwriter did business; or a documentary that revealed the corrupt practices of some American banks, upon whom many public television stations depended for corporate support.

This was all the more surprising because the public broadcasting system's backsliding from its mandate began during the height of America's counter-culture revolution in the late 1960s and early 1970s, when the doors were open for alternative media presentations, as they were for alternative political and social practices.

The following is principally from an article written in 1980 and submitted to, but not published by, a public broadcasting association journal; it includes parts of an address, "The Purpose of Public Broadcasting," to the National Citizens Committee on Broadcasting conference, June 24, 1977, Airlie House, Virginia.

Most of us would agree that public television has given us some outstanding cultural, educational and public affairs programs. Within the nationwide addiction that finds the average television set on 6.2 hours every day, creating what sociologists Merton and Lazarsfeld called a "narcotizing dysfunction," public television is often a stimulating breath of fresh air. Compared to most of the offerings of commercial television, it frequently is superb.

Why, then, are more and more critics making public television a target? Some of the nation's most astute and respected critics, such as John J. O'Connor of the *New York Times* and Tom Shales of the *Washington Post* have from time to time written about public television with less than adulation.

Shales, for example, has characterized public television's condition as one of "chronic, crippling befuddlement and timidity and lethargy from top to bottom." In an article reinforced by comments from Bill Moyers—who as a special assistant to President Lyndon Johnson was a prime mover in the passage of the Public Broadcasting Act of 1967, which set up the Corporation for Public Broadcasting and subsequently the Public Broadcasting Service (PBS), and who now is a shining star of public television programming—Shales gave examples of programs that do not reach people in many communities because "local stations who remain so loudly fearful of a Big Brother in Washington telling us what to put on the air have not always shown the greatest courage in presenting challenging or troublesome material, no matter how potentially valuable it might be." He added that "there are depressing indications that PBS officials are thinking in the same terms of audience lust that obsess commercial broadcasters and make commercial broadcasting so innocuous and escapist."

Shales reflects the belief of many other critics, viewers and public broadcasting practitioners that public television should not try to be the smarter sibling excelling at the same things as commercial television, but should be a clear alternative to it.

Under the present single public television system of 283 local stations and one national acquisition and distributing network (PBS, currently being divided into three services) controlled by these stations, public television is doing exactly what we might expect it to do. Each local station decides which programs it is going to carry. In making its choices, the station reflects the desire of the leaders of its community to avoid anything that might endanger what is conscientiously perceived by that leadership as the community's best interests. Therefore, "challenging or troublesome" programs—to use Shales' terms—frequently do not reach people in a given community because local stations refuse to carry them, or place them at inopportune times, or water them down through editing. In addition, there are those programs that could be produced, on both the national and local levels, but aren't.

Under the present system, local stations are controlled by local boards of directors. PBS neither owns or controls any stations. These boards, by the very nature of their members being in social, political, or economic positions that enable them to become members of a board that controls a television station, can be expected to represent and foster those ideals and actions that maintain a community in as full and consistent a state of stability as possible. Isn't this something most of us want in our lives, unless we happen to be part of, or are sensitive to, the needs of groups that have been largely excluded from the benefits of that stability?

Many station managers and board members, as part of the established majority in their communities, therefore often find it difficult to understand, much less identify with, the impatience of minorities and women and other groups that have not had access to or service from the media equal to the majority. For example, several years ago a long-time leader in public broadcasting and president of the principal public broadcasting association told me that many people in the field, including himself, didn't think I was on the side of public broadcasting because I had, with then FCC Commissioner (subsequently NAACP head) Benjamin L. Hooks, attempted to initiate a study of the minority composition of public television station boards.

Although many station managers and board members are intellectually sympathetic toward the needs of minorities, women, and other special groups, the efforts of organizations such as the Citizens Communications Center, the United Church of Christ, the National Organization for Women, the National Black Media Coalition, and Hispanic, Native American and other groups to satisfy those needs with "all deliberate speed" tend to be perceived as unreasonable pressure.

Sometimes a station manager may anticipate more concern about a program on the part of the governing board than actually occurs. Recently a station board's investigating committee called for new leadership at the station following the manager's decision to cancel a locally developed series because one of the programs included childbirth scenes the manager considered too explicit to be aired.

To a degree the FCC's Fairness Doctrine, which provides for the presentation of opposing views if only one side of a subject deemed controversial in a given community is presented, offers opportunity for diversity. But it does not guarantee presentation of any controversial view in the first place. Many legislators and opinion-makers, including those identified with civil liberties commitments, propose to eliminate the Fairness Doctrine on the grounds that it infringes on the First Amendment rights of freedom of speech and press, in this instance applied to the electronic media, and that its requirements for alternative views discourages the airing of any view. On the other hand, in 1969, in the "Red Lion" decision, dealing with the Red Lion Broadcasting Company's station in Media, Pennsylvania, the U.S. Supreme Court unanimously ruled that the Fairness Doctrine regulations "enhance rather than abridge the freedom of speech and press protected by the First Amendment." The Court held that broadcast station licensees "must give adequate coverage to public issues and coverage must be fair in that it accurately reflects the opposing views." [*In 1987 President Ronald Reagan vetoed a Fairness Doctrine bill passed by the House and Senate, effectively eliminating the Fairness Doctrine; at this writing, in 2000, it has not been reinstated.*]

In 1973 the FCC required public television and some public radio stations to conduct a continuing ascertainment of community needs and problems, a requirement for commercial stations since 1971. Presumably, such ascertainment has assisted and motivated public television stations to present more programs dealing more fully with problem areas within the community. Some proponents of the current trend toward deregulation of broadcasting, however, advocate the discontinuance of formal ascertainment. [*Ascertainment was effectively eliminated not long after Reagan assumed the presidency in 1981.*]

The nature of the current public television system sometimes limits even its own intentions. PBS President Larry Grossman frequently has given strong support to controversial programs, including a defense of the program "California Reich" despite sharp criticism from some station managers over the distribution of this denouement of the Nazi movement in America on the grounds that it was "controversial." Nevertheless, despite support of the program by PBS itself, only 145 out of 266 PBS affiliates carried it, just as only 22 public television stations preempted their scheduled programs to carry PBS-arranged live coverage of the May 6, 1979 anti-nuclear March on Washington. A December 9, 1979, highly controversial call-in program dealing with the energy program and oil distribution, produced by the Public Interest Video Network, an independent production organization, and carried live over PBS, was shown live by only 16 public television stations throughout the country (ten more planned to carry delayed broadcasts). One might read special significance into the fact that the program was carried live by some 400 commercial cable systems!

PBS can be considered a symptom—some say the victim—of the problem, not the cause. Fearfulness and censorship, or at the very least, aversion to material that might be considered by some to be controversial, were in flower long before there was a PBS. In the early 1960s, for example, "Dynamics of Desegregation" was a series lauded for its scholarship, objectivity, accuracy and television technique; its principal contributor, coincidentally, was an outstanding sociologist from the South whose forebears happened to be Confederate leaders during the Civil War. However, only about half of the PTV stations in the country carried the series, with a substantial number of rejections in the North. Other programs over the years have met with similar fates.

In addition to the matter of community beliefs precluding the carriage of some programs on some stations, criticism has also been drawn to PTV's alleged preoccupation with the size of its audiences. There is a difference between seeking large audiences for programs that are good and seeking programs that will draw large audiences. This difference reflects a long-standing dichotomy in public broadcasting. Most leaders in the field, including most station managers, believe that PTV should develop, acquire, and present those programs that attract as many viewers as possible. After all, they say, what's the sense of putting on programs if nobody or relatively few people are going to watch! Some stations, therefore, have even counter-programmed to compete directly with commercial stations in their communities. A few have been successful. [*The March, 1979, Nielsen ratings showed a monthly PTV audience of 49.1 million families (up 46% from 33.7 million in 1975), representing 65.9% (up 34% from 49.27. in 1975) of the total TV households in the United States.*] Some individual programs and series have made unexpectedly high rating showings. "The Incredible Machine," aired in October, 1975, was watched by 16% of U.S. TV homes. More recently, "The Scarlet Letter" received a 14 rating, or a 25 share of the audience over four evenings. National Geographic's "Living Sands of Namib" received a 15.3 share in New York and an 18.7 share in Chicago, and a Cousteau "Odyssey" received a 19.1 share. The average public television prime-time share is between 3 and 4. Compare these figures with current commercial network average shares of 30 and top-rated program shares of 45!

A minority of public broadcasting leaders argue that because even the highest-rated PTV programs are only marginally competitive with commercial broadcasting, PTV simply cannot compete, even if it wanted to, with the high-budget, personality-laden programs of commercial networks, and should concentrate on the alternative programming it presumably was originally established to do.

Some critics believe that when a principal criterion for choosing programs is to attract as many viewers as possible, there is a tendency, even an unconscious one, to gravitate toward the bland and noncontroversial. A frequently cited example is one of the programs chosen by PBS affiliates for networking, "Dancing Disco." It has been suggested that public broadcasting, instead of trying to reach the greatest number of individual viewers, should try to attract the greatest number of different audiences, providing materials to those groups whose numbers are too small to be served by the rating-directed commercial stations and whose interests and needs can be met only by noncommercial TV.

Public broadcasting is operating as effectively and efficiently as it can under the system of organization and control within which it exists. The Public Broadcasting Act of 1967 increased the federal commitment to public broadcasting and established a national organization, the Corporation for Public Broadcasting, to facilitate the growth of the field, but it did not change the essential nature of a system that was formed when the first non-commercial television station went on the air in 1953. To replace or drastically change the present system, as some critics advocate, would not only be politically impractical, but would endanger the core of its existence: the principle of local determination and control. We must not underestimate the importance of localism. Aside from its political significance, local initiative offers great potential for diversity of cultural and informational contributions to the country as a whole. In some countries a substitute for local diversity has been national conformity. A strong central authority in place of the present locally controlled stations is not the answer.

One single public television system cannot be all things to all people.

We need an alternative to do what it cannot do.

We need to establish an additional system, not destroy the existing one.

The answer is a public television alternative to public television.

The answer is two PTV systems.

If this seems like a spurious addition to the media bureaucracy, note that when Congress passed the Public Broadcasting Act of 1967 it stated "that expansion and development of noncommercial radio and television broadcasting and of diversity of its programming depend on freedom, imagination and initiative on both the local and national levels." Congress authorized the new Corporation for Public Broadcasting to *"assist in the establishment of one or more systems of noncommercial educational television or radio broadcast stations in the United States"* [emphasis added].

Alternative Public Television—APT—would be a second PTV system, a new system, an alternative system. It would not replace the present one, but provide what the present one is unable to.

Why is it necessary to set up a whole new system? Why not just make changes in the Corporation for Public Broadcasting (CPB is responsible for the establishment and principal funding of networks such as PBS and NPR [National Public Radio] and for the general growth of public broadcasting), or in PBS? In order to meet the changing needs in the field, to react to a proposed Congressional rewrite of the Communications Act of 1934 that would abolish CPB, and to acknowledge the recommendation of the Carnegie Commission on the Future of Public Broadcasting that CPB be replaced by a Public Telecommunications Trust, CPB recently approved an internal restructuring proposed by its President, Robben Fleming. It established two divisions: a Program Fund, with its own director and budget to handle selection, funding, and servicing of programming, and a Management Services Division to deal with planning, research, and other non-program responsibilities. Further, in response to dissatisfaction on the part of many of its member stations and to outside criticism, PBS recently approved a reorganization plan designed to strengthen its services.

In neither case, however, can or does the internal reorganization alter the basic nature of the system; the same controlling factors are still there.

For example, a major PBS change is its creation of three separate program services, adding, principally, regional and instructional services to its predominantly cultural and public affairs ones. The change is designed to provide additional program choices for its member stations. With only a few exceptions, however, each PBS member has only one channel in a given community and can present only one program at a given time. Even if PBS's new services do result in additional challenging programs, the same local stations under the same criteria will still select the programs they believe are in the best interests of their communities. (It should be noted that many local stations are in reality "satellite" stations; that is, they do not produce or carry programming selected by a local board and manager, but are part of a state system and carry the programs decided upon by the board and manager of the state system or its pilot station. Program selections generally follow the same procedure and are affected by the same considerations that guide the local station.)

We need to go beyond changes within old boundaries. We need to redefine our goals and operations in terms of the public rather than in terms of our organizations. We need to add what is new, while preserving what has been valuable and effective. It is important to reemphasize that Alternative Public Television would not replace the present system, but would add to it.

Alternative Public Television (APT) would be not only an uncensored outlet for controversial programs that now fall by the wayside before they reach all of the public. It would also permit the airing of materials considered too offbeat, lengthy, esoteric, unpopular, specialized, difficult to schedule or otherwise unacceptable for national or local distribution under the present system. The current PTV system has, with occasional exceptions, by and large followed the program formats and lengths established by commercial television. APT would encourage alternative experimental forms and allow programs to be totally flexible in time in order to most effectively achieve their purposes, not necessarily meeting the traditional half-hour or one-hour length requirements. It is about time we stopped putting artificial restrictions on television's fulfilling its aesthetic and artistic potentials. How outraged we would be if composers were required to write symphonies that were either precisely 30 minutes or 60 minutes or 90 minutes long!

APT would cover live, breaking events, controversial or not, that affect the public, no matter what time they occur, breaking into scheduled programs if necessary, without concern how the ratings might be affected. APT would use satellites to link classrooms, meeting halls and other group gathering places throughout the world, providing live forums for the exchange of views and feelings in order to achieve greater understanding among all peoples. APT would implement the potentials of participatory television. One example of such noncontroversial but currently lacking programming is national town-meeting citizen participation in activities of federal government departments and agencies. Through two-way video in some cases and two-way audio in all cases, groups of citizens gathered in town halls, community centers, school auditoriums, and similar meeting places throughout the country could sit in on open meetings, hearings and other "sunshine" activities of federal offices in Washington and be given the opportunity not only to observe but to ask questions of and offer comments to the Executive Branch officials whose actions and rulings so profoundly affect us all. This would bring the people closer to the government in ways not previously possible except on the local town-meeting level. [*By the end of the 1990s some of the above had been accomplished through the development and spread of the interactive Internet, seemingly unlimited in its potentials; and C-Span, on cable, has provided extensive coverage of government activities.*]

APT's distribution of programs would not be dependent, as under the present system, upon local stations which are responsible to the controlling attitudes of their individual communities. APT would be a multi-media national system, providing a television signal to as much of the population as possible through whatever means of transmission were most effective and economically efficient in serving a particular geographic area. These means would include broadcast stations, but would additionally consist of cable systems, video discs, high-power regional stations, translators (which extend signals rather than originate them), microwave and, if ultimately approved by the Federal Communications Commission, satellite-direct-to-home video transmission. [*This subsequently was approved.*] Local facilities would operate, at least at first, principally as distribution outlets for national and regional origination points, thus requiring only a fraction of both the capital and operating costs of the present public television system.

APT's financing would come, in part, from some of the same sources that support the present system: federal funds, foundations, viewer donations, industry. It would not likely have the benefit of budgeted state and university funds that stations licensed to those entities now have. It might, however, have a source of funds not now fully available to PTV: support of organizations and groups throughout the country whose needs it would meet and who are now not being adequately served.

The governing board of APT would be composed of citizens representing those publics and purposes not usually represented on the governing bodies of other public broadcasting organizations, nationally or locally. For example, the current board of PBS consists of 18 station lay representatives, 10 station professional representatives, six public members and the president of PBS, virtually duplicating the composition of the local boards. The APT board would seek people with alternative backgrounds and points of view from all geographical, political, economic, social, vocational, racial, and ethnic areas and levels.

Although operating as a national organization, APT would provide greater opportunity for local programming than does the current service. At present the availability of nonthreatening, attractive programs from national and international sources and the desire to attract large audiences discourage many PTV stations from taking advantage of many of the different ideas, cultures, and backgrounds which make up their particular localities and which, through TV dissemination, could enrich us nationally, whether in conformity with the beliefs or standards of any other given community or not. APT would deliberately seek not only alternative national programming, but would promote the production of indigenous local programming, thus strengthening local contributions to the nation as a whole.

The establishment of APT would not change the present PTV system. The latter's stations would have no relationship to APT except that they could send programs to or transmit programs from APT if they wished. They would continue to select and broadcast those programs from PBS and other sources that in the judgment of the given community, as reflected by the station's board and manager, best fit the community's needs. They would continue to reject programs they considered unsuitable. Stations would not be relieved of their responsibilities under the Communications Act or the FCC's Rules and Regulations because of the existence of APT, but would continue to ascertain community needs and be responsive to the Fairness Doctrine and other requirements that apply to them.

APT programs would not replace current PTV programming. The additional programs would be made available, through this second system, to those people in any community who wanted to see them. No one would be forced to tune in to a particular channel, just as no one is forced to read a particular newspaper or magazine. The strength of our democracy is based on the unrestricted flow of information and ideas to those people who want them.

Five major factors are involved in the implementation of an Alternative Public Television system:

1. FCC authorization of those means of transmission necessary to operate a national APT network, including: (a) continued reservation of frequencies for noncommercial television stations and the facilitating of drop-ins (channels put in communities where none are allocated) where existing facilities, including non-broadcast services such as cable, do not provide for adequate distribution. Presuming the system initially develops on a station-plus-cable-plus-other-non-broadcast media basis, there are currently sufficient channels—over and above those being used by the present PTV system—and other outlets to reach the vast majority of the 75 million television homes in the country. [*In the year 2000 there were over 100 million TV homes in the United States.*] Four hundred and nineteen of the 667 noncommercial TV reservations are still unused. Of the 50 cities with more

than one PTV reservation, only nine have more than one station in operation. Cable now reaches some 45 million homes, with satellite transmission able to serve at least some of the cable systems in each of the 50 states; (b) Flexibility in providing for use of non-broadcast services for public television purposes, if needed; (c) Eventual approval of direct satellite-to-home reception. Although the issue had been raised earlier in one FCC inquiry and proposed for another, the recent announcement by Comsat (the Communications Satellite Corporation, created by Congress in 1963 to develop America's space-age communications) that it is considering development of a subscription TV service to reach homes directly through satellite dramatically enhances the possibilities of such a system. Direct satellite-to-home transmission is technically feasible now; however, economic, political and regulatory factors would have to be changed before it is readily operational. One of these factors was the recent deregulation by the FCC of all receive-only earth stations, permitting anyone who wishes to do so to install a small terminal that can receive television signals from a satellite, without the requirement of FCC authorization. A number of countries are planning or developing satellite-to-home systems, with Japan and Canada, for example, both currently testing the possibilities through broadcast satellite experiments. Availability of direct satellite-to-home facilities would provide the most efficient distribution base for APT and could be the technical cornerstone of its success.

2. Commitment by Congress to both the diversity and national cohesiveness that can result from a dual PTV system, with adequate authorizing legislation and monetary appropriations.

3. An APT system that does not attempt to replace or duplicate existing services. Only through an additional network, uncensored by local determinants and with programming *in addition to and not in lieu of* traditional PTV fare, can we guarantee a free flow and full dissemination of information and ideas to every citizen who wishes to have them.

4. Opening up the new Alternative Public Television system to programming from all sources, including, to a much greater degree than at present, independent producers. Experimental programs would be encouraged, expanding TV's contributions not only in the exchange of ideas, information, culture and the arts, but in its psychological and aesthetic potentials as well.

5. Finding new leadership with experience. Too much of the old experienced leadership is either unwilling or unable to break away from the status quo. Too much of the new inexperienced leadership (recruited over the past several years, particularly by some national organizations, as an antidote to old leadership) spends much of its time and energy developing what seem to be exciting, innovative approaches which, when completed, most aptly can be called a reinvention of the wheel.

The key to Alternative Public Television's success is flexibility. It will not and should not achieve everything it initially plans to because the world is constantly changing and so, therefore, must APT's goals. APT must be prepared to adapt constantly in order to meet effectively the needs of the people, not only serving as an alternative to public television, but, if necessary, as an alternative to itself.

# CHAPTER 12

# An International University of Communications

As the new century begins, communications have moved to the forefront of societal development. Global satellite systems, run by ever-increasingly huge conglomerates, link every corner of the world. Traditional electronic media, principally television and radio, are not only being supplemented but gradually supplanted by the Internet. What was dreamed of and advocated as progress that was possible, but not altogether probable—because of the establishment's efforts to resist what was perceived as radical change during the counter-culture revolution and its legacy in the 1960s and 1970s—became reality just two decades later.

This book has concentrated on two themes: the potentials of media to affect the progress of humankind in a positive, humanistic manner; and the necessity for a new educational system, recognizing and based on the communications revolution and oriented to the needs of the learner and of society.

Two implementational aspects of these themes are (a) universal distance education for anyone, anywhere, and (b) responsible, ethical education in the understanding and use of the media. By the late 1990s the first was progressing apace, principally due to earlier application through television that paved the way for broader, instant implementation through the Internet. The second saw increasing recognition through the growth of media programs in higher education, but not yet an understanding that the global nature of the media required a globally based curriculum and a much greater commitment to teaching and learning about the international community and to serving the needs and interests of that community.

In 1970 the author founded and served as first president of a higher education institution in Washington, DC, the International University of Communications (IUC), which was accredited for master's level work and degrees. The IUC graduated several classes and then was forced to discontinue for lack of funds; it was ahead of its time. As the twenty-first century dawns, there is still nowhere in the world an equivalent of the IUC.

The following is from the 1970 prospectus of the International University of Communications, which was based in part on several public addresses, "Educational/Public Broadcasting: Universal, Unique, University," to the seventh annual College Conference of the International Radio and Television Society, April 19, 1968, New York City; "Perspective and Prospects for Educational Broadcasting," to the Institute of Electrical and Electronics Engineers International Conference on Communications, June 13, 1968, Philadelphia; and "Communications and the Urban Crisis: Doing Our Own Thing," to the American Management Association's Fourth Annual Conference on Education and Training, August 13, 1968, New York City.

One month after the presidential election of 1968, a Task Force on Communications Policy, appointed by President Lyndon B. Johnson, submitted its final report. The report, which established the significance of communications internationally and advocated educational innovation that would train communications experts, was considered too challenging to the status quo by many observers and was quietly interred by the new president, Richard M. Nixon. Among the Task Force's recommendations[1] were the following:

A truly global communications system could help knit the family of nations into a living community, based on mutual understanding, and universal diffusion of knowledge and skills. . . . Improved communications are essential to a growing world economy. They are vital to the progress of advanced and developing nations alike. . . . Above all, they offer the citizen everywhere the opportunity to acquire the knowledge and insight essential to the mature exercise of his responsibilities. . . . Within each nation, and among nations, the wise use of telecommunications is a key to success in building and reinforcing the sense of community, which is the foundation of social peace. . . . Formulation and implementation of effective telecommunications policy . . . is at present seriously handicapped by a shortage of qualified personnel. . . . The difficulty . . . is the absence of settings in which the necessarily multidisciplinary programs are being offered. . . . [B]road-gauged policy training and . . . interdisciplinary policy research could be met by the establishment of . . . a university setting. . . . [W]e believe that an institute . . . for communication policy training and research should be developed.

What was needed was an institutional model that could directly help society use media to achieve its goals and at the same time train experts to apply communications to all areas of human endeavor. By the beginning of the twenty-first century every community will need dozens and perhaps hundreds of communications channels to serve the wants and needs of its citizens. Where are these channels going to come from? Broadcast? Microwave? Cable? Fiber optics? The laser beam with a three-dimensional holograph? Satellite direct to home receiver? Some as yet untapped resource from outer space? How many new communications technologies are still in the heads of youngsters in schools or on college campuses, whose imaginations will never get beyond the restrictions of the four-walled classroom? Where will we get the personnel who understand not only our socio-political-economic needs but know how to use media to meet them? Will we achieve a national or universal visual and aural literacy sufficient to permit people not only to cope with a media-dominated world, but also to provide a base for the positive use of media for human progress?

To do all this will require educational change. Traditional approaches to achieving such change do not work; many observers of the educational scene believe that they are not intended to work. The air is filled periodically with promises of educational change that plummet quickly to the ground at the end of heavy chains held by the promisers. As noted earlier in this book, the U.S. Office of Education [*in 1980 it became the Department of Education*] is so wedded to established educational organizations, practices and leadership that its best intentions are limited—by design or necessity—principally to the appearance of change. Educational change cannot take place from within as long as it is controlled internally by those who do not wish it to change. Also, it cannot be superimposed from without upon existing institutions because such change becomes, at best, cosmetic and is washed away in a short time by those who continue to control education. Most experimental programs are usually pretenses, assuaging consciences and assuring accolades, but with results that are only temporary or inconclusive within any structure that retains its same identity and control. This has been the pattern of Ford Foundation grants, including its Comprehensive School Improvement Program, which provided $30 million from 1960 to 1970 to reform American education by having colleges and universities help elementary and secondary schools with the development of educational techniques such as flexible schedules, open classrooms, application of technology, alternative students groupings and team teaching. The Ford Foundation admitted that this program was a "failure in strategy" and that "seldom did the University function as a force for improvement of educational quality in the elementary and secondary schools."

Do those organizations that provide funds for educational development really believe that change will be achieved when the responsibility for change is put into the hands of those who are opposed to it? Foundations often have been accused of carefully limiting their programs to the appearance of change.[2] The answer is to recreate education, not try to change it. To build, not to patch. To begin at the bottom, on a structure of integrity, rather than adding on to a structure of hypocrisy. Occasionally, with individual institutions such as Hampshire College in Massachusetts, new approaches to education have come into being. Yet, they, too, ultimately succumb to the familiarity and ease of tradition.

We need a concrete communications institution model that will serve society and change education at the same time, both through actual practice and through inspirational example. Such an institution should (1) help professionals and would-be professionals in all fields learn how to use all forms of communications to directly solve critical social, economic, health, educational, environmental and other problems through (2) an educational process that makes the individual learner the most important factor. This can be done through the elimination of traditional concepts of courses, classes, curricula, credits, grades, lectures and examinations; through combining research and practical field projects; through one-to-one tutorial guidance; and through individualized learning resources as described in the multi-media resource center description in chapter four, "An Open University and School."

Such an institution must, first and foremost, understand and serve human needs, emphasizing flexible interdisciplinary learning oriented towards the social-political-economic environmental requirements on local, national, regional, and international levels, and encompassing all the arts and sciences on a professional, nontechnical basis. It must be, in fact and in effect, an International University of Communications.

Modern technology has achieved the means for instant communication among people and societies far in advance of our ability to use these means to help solve problems facing a world convulsed by unprecedented population growth, political upheaval, social revolution, and rapidly increasing individual aspirations. Too often, the potentials of new communication techniques have been grasped only by those who seek to use those potentials for narrow and self-seeking aims. Too often, as well, the form of "instant" communications has been confused with its purpose. Many communicators have been content to formulate or dramatize a problem without going on to fashion solutions made possible by the intelligent use of available resources. They mistakenly equate "instant" or "blanket" coverage of events with total communications.

Yet, the very ease with which modern communications can disseminate or withhold information, palliate anxiety, obscure disquiet, or create alarm contributes to the urgency of the problems we face. Widespread concern about a problem builds up pressure for its solution. Failure to communicate knowledge leads to the possibility of hasty adoption of measures that worsen the problem rather than solve it. The meshing of modern and traditional methods of communication into a system for solving social, political, and economic problems by rational and efficient means has become a critical necessity for human progress.

International agencies, national governments, socio-political organizations, management and industry, labor unions, state and local governments, citizens groups, professional associations, educational systems and institutions, science, law, religion, medicine, safety, and other professions and services are increasingly and critically dependent on effective guidance in understanding and using communications. The major areas of concern, therefore, of the International University of Communications (IUC) include international communications, urban and rural communications, national communications policy, educational communications, environmental communications, communications economics, communications law, information networks, health communications and, importantly, person-to-person communications. Its orientation is humanistic rather than technical. It brings together people and organizations of diverse international and national views and interests for individual and mutually dependent studies, research, resources, and services. IUC is directed toward independent thought and criticism. It not only reflects the current needs of society, but also anticipates and solves future problems.

Learning at the IUC is supplemented by research which explores the implications for communications for public and private planning and development. All research studies are independent, objective, and unclassified. Services are provided for implementation of learning and research, including workshops, seminars, consulting, conference planning, and communications production and dissemination. The IUC does not duplicate what is already being done in higher education. Where schools and departments today produce thousands of technicians proficient in the use of media for distribution, the IUC produces policy-making professionals who can step into management-level analyses of problems and who can implement solutions through the use of communications in all professional, government, societal, and industry areas.

The IUC process emphasizes peer learning, with "participants" (rather than students) and "tutors" (rather than professors) providing interchange on common-goal levels. Participants experience consecutive phases of active learning, research, and project application, rather than passive administrative formulae such as courses and credits. The staff's function is to aid each participant in every way possible to achieve his or her goals. This is the antithesis of traditional higher education practice, which sets up an adversary situation between student and professor, with the student challenged to overcome certain arbitrary roadblocks, many or most unrelated to learning, before receiving imperious acknowledgment that he or she has completed a quantitative requirement such as credits or grade average that is alleged to be equivalent to being educated. The staff of the IUC functions as tutors and as research and resource guides, working directly with the participants in planning, guidance and evaluation capacities in the major areas of concern noted above, and in all media areas, including television, radio, print, film, computers, the performing, graphic and plastic arts, space and light communications, architecture, and person-to-person communications. The staff serves the same function for subject areas such as political science, economics, sociology-anthropology, law, business and industry, labor, health and biological sciences, physical sciences, philosophy, ethics, and psychology, encompassing all the geographical and political regions of the world.

Each participant orients his or her work around one or more projects: for example, how to use communications to solve housing problems in a specific inner city; how to use communications to solve health problems in a particular rural area. In developing the background and ability to go into the field and solve the problem(s), the participant first identifies one or more critical needs in his or her major field of interest and then intensely studies applicable media and subject areas. During this first phase, the participant learns—and demonstrates knowledge of—theory and information on the problem. This is shown not through the traditional memorization examination, but through something more pertinent to real life, such as a position paper, and through evaluative discussions with other participants, tutors, staff professionals in the field, and educators from other institutions. During this phase the participant has the opportunity to attend group discussion seminars on various topics with peers and experts.

Following this phase, the participant works with a research tutor to develop a practical, applied, unclassified, objective plan to solve the particular problem posed in the project. Individual guided studies (such as reports, surveys, readings, mini-projects) demonstrate the participant's progress. Finally, the participant works with resource and service tutors to implement the research plan in the field. The participant may be attending the IUC under the sponsorship of a government office, social service agency, citizen organization, business or industry, profession, or some other group that has charged him or her with finding an answer to a particular problem. In such cases, the project implementation is therefore a practical on-the-job endeavor. Where participants are not under such sponsorship, the IUC arranges for a working situation with an appropriate group or organization operating in the participant's project area, thus providing not only a direct problem-solving contribution to a part of society and a practical learning situation for the participant, but in many cases a trial-intern period for the participant with a potential employing organization. The participant's application phase of the project is evaluated by the same combination of persons listed earlier as evaluators of the initial learning phase.

The professional orientation of the projects and the participation of working adults from many fields suggest that, at least at first, the IUC should function on the graduate level. For those who desire degrees or whose sponsoring organizations place value on them, Master of Arts in Communications degrees may be awarded upon completion of the program, with certification by an evaluation board that the major project (and minor project, if required) has been successfully implemented. Participants are not required to possess a bachelor's degree for admittance; some of the most significant contributions to society have been made by people who were school or college dropouts or who were denied any opportunity for a formal education because of economic, geographical, social, or physical problems not under their control. Formal education and life experience in combination are considered. Most important for participant enrollment, however, are (1) one or more anticipated projects oriented toward the solution of specific critical human problems (the prospective enrollee who wishes to study communications in general is referred to one of the many other universities that offer such study), (2) motivation to complete the projects in accordance with the IUC process and goals, and (3) ability to carry out the projects.

The two major requirements for tutors are (1) expert knowledge of and experience in one or more communications or subject fields and (2) the ability to work with other people on a one-to-one basis. Degrees and traditional teaching experience are not requisite. Because tutors are not on a full-time basis, but work on an ad-hoc basis with individual participants who need their special expertise, tutors are sought who are prominent in their particular fields.

The ideal participants are those persons who wish to be communications philosophers-managers as differentiated from technicians, not as a goal in itself, but as a means to more effective problem-solving in non-communications as well as communications fields. The ideal tutors are those scholars and practitioners who view communications as critical facets of modern life, rather than as theoretical subject matter to be limited to theoretical discussion, or as vocational skills to serve entertainment purposes. At least half of the participants and a substantial portion of the tutors should be from countries other than the United States. At the same time, the IUC would seek to develop satellite-linked branches throughout the world, providing a structure for the international exchange of ideas, experiences, attitudes, and feelings. Participants and tutors would be able to work at a branch anyplace in the world, as their project needs and services require.

Separate schools within the IUC develop and coordinate projects in specified areas. Included are the Schools of Urban Communications, Rural Communications, Educational Communications, Governmental Communications, Environmental Communications, Health Communications, and others reflecting the major areas of societal need and concern. Participants who complete the sequence of designing, implementing, and evaluating communications projects are ready to assume managerial and leadership positions in communications and are uniquely qualified for policy-making roles in government, industry, social service, the arts, and education. The International University of Communications can be the single most important factor in providing a cadre of people throughout the world capable of using media effectively to create humanistic progress.[3]

## NOTES

1. Excerpts from the final report of the President's Task Force On Communications Policy (December 7, 1968).

A truly global communications system could help knit the family of nations into a living community, based on mutual understanding, and the universal diffusion of knowledge and skills. But if men will otherwise, it could also perpetuate mistrust, and deepen the divisions among nations and people.

Improved communications are essential to a growing world economy. They are vital to the progress of advanced and developing nations alike. New services promise to revolutionize customary patterns of business and finance, learning, entertainment and leisure, and the processing, storage and retrieval of information. Above all, they offer the citizen everywhere the opportunity to acquire the knowledge and the insight essential to the mature exercise of his responsibilities.

Within each nation, and among nations, the wise use of telecommunications is a key to success in building and reinforcing the sense of community which is the foundation of social peace: a sense of community based on freedom, and on tolerance of diversity; a community which encourages and appreciates the unpredictable richness of human imagination; but a community nevertheless, faithful to its own rules of civility and order.

We do believe that the social and psychological effects of mass communication define one of the most important of all fields of research, both for public and for private groups, in the years before us, and we recommend that they become an active focus for sustained effort.

First, we deem it to be an accepted goal of national policy that the United States remain a leader among the nations in communications science and technology, and in communications service.

Second, we take it as self-evident that telecommunications policy should seek to maintain and develop an environment always sensitive to consumer needs. It should be an environment hospitable to productive innovation in facilities, services and management.

Third, the realm of telecommunications should be viewed as a system, extending from public and private research, at one end of the spectrum, to the provision of private and common carrier communications service, at home and abroad, at the other. Our study has taught us the necessity to keep the whole of this system, and its interconnections, steadily in view. We have found that none of its problems can be examined in isolation, and therefore that piecemeal or segmented treatment of any one of them can be misleading.

Fourth, we have assumed that special consideration should be given to the needs of developing nations. Modern telecommunications systems can be a valuable—indeed, nearly indispensable—catalyst of their economic, social and political progress.

We stand at the threshold of an immensely promising era in applying new technology. To achieve the full potential benefits of the new technology, however, operational experiments will often be needed to explore the feasibility and flexibility of full-scale systems.

Our studies indicate that improved telecommunications generally promise important contributions to the less developed world. Educational television and satellite communications are particular examples.

We propose the exploration of realistic programs of regional and international cooperation in this area, with international support, where appropriate, for such efforts.

Our studies suggest constructive possibilities for the use of television to help overcome some of the problems of urban ghetto dwellers. Isolated rural people such as inhabitants of Indian reservations could benefit from similar undertakings.

Some areas of the telecommunications system do not or need not affect the integrity of the switched public message telephone network. Here the goal of policy should be the removal of unnecessary restraints to promote innovation and to encourage greater responsiveness to consumer needs.

In our study we were repeatedly struck by the paucity of data relating to the economic characteristics and performance of the telecommunications industry. The field of telecommunications has thus far not generated anything like the amount of serious policy research that its importance justifies. Effective policy making, both by business and by government, could profit from the sustained study and critical analysis of well-informed scholarship. We therefore urge government, foundation, and business support for increased inter-disciplinary research and training in telecommunications policy.

To ensure that government is exposed to a steady flow of independent critical and creative ideas, we believe that an institute, and preferably more than one institute, for communication policy training and research should be developed outside the government. Such institutes should undertake the advanced interdisciplinary training of communications experts—economists, lawyers, engineers, management experts, social scientists and others—to deal with problems on communications policy which transcend the confines of any single discipline.

Formulation and implementation of effective telecommunications policy, moreover, is at present seriously handicapped by a shortage of qualified personnel. Our universities have not trained engineers, systems analysts, economists or lawyers equipped to grasp the interrelationships among technological developments, systems engineering requirements, the regulatory framework and economic and social policy goals; nor are opportunities afforded for officials in policy positions to obtain such skills at mid-career levels.

The difficulty at present, however, is not the students' need for support but the absence of settings in which the necessarily multi-disciplinary programs are being offered. Nor is the problem entirely one of individuals' training. We have been struck in our studies by the lack of interdisciplinary research into questions of communications policy. Yet, this is a field in which the benefits to be gained from cooperation among lawyers, engineers, and economists are clearly substantial.

Broad-gauged policy training and . . . interdisciplinary policy research could be met by the establishment of . . . a university setting, which would have as their objective the provision of advanced training at the graduate and mid-career levels in the interdisciplinary skills required to produce capable and qualified communications systems analysts and policy makers.

2. Following conferences with officers of several leading foundations in an effort to obtain support for the International University of Communications, IUC Board Member Robert Lewis Shayon concluded that foundations are only willing to put their money into "low risk, high insurance" projects, thereby making certain, though in some instances perhaps unintentionally, that real, meaningful change does not take place and that the appearance of innovation occurs only within the confines of the status quo. Shayon's judgments are borne out by Waldemar S. Nielsen's book, *The Foundations*, which describes the large private philanthropic foundations as a "sick and malfunctioning institution" that represents the attitudes and practices of the "country's ruling class." Nielsen's study concludes that foundations principally support existing operations preserving the status quo. "They do passive things," Nielsen wrote. "Foundations paint themselves in more heroic, groundbreaking innovative terms than they are."

3. The idea for an International University of Communications was first publicly advocated and described by the author in the mid-1960s. In 1969 he developed the Master Plan for the IUC and was one of the founding officers who chartered it in the District of Columbia that same year. Its Founding and Advisory Boards reflected a wide variety of backgrounds, experiences and socio-political attitudes. All of its members, however, were dedicated to the need for the humanistic use of communications, and to a learner-oriented applied concept of higher education. Board members included such persons as architect-philosopher Buckminster Fuller, educator Harold Taylor, former president of the National Conference of Christians and Jews Everett Clinchy, Common Cause president Jack Conway, University of North Carolina President William Friday, University of Denver Chancellor Maurice Mitchell, oil industry executive Benjamin Heath, Secretary of the Democratic National Committee Dorothy Bush, former National Education Association president and Assistant Secretary of Labor and Director of the U.S. Women's Bureau Elizabeth Duncan Koontz, Australian Labor Party Senator Douglas McClelland, Westinghouse Broadcasting chairman and president Donald McGannon, President of NHK (the Japan Broadcasting Company) Yoshinori Maeda, Actors Equity Association President Frederick O'Neal, Saturday Review critic Robert Lewis Shayon, Director-General of Radio Nederland L. F. Tijmstra, English television writer and president of World Wide Pictures Lord Willis, civil rights leader Whitney Young, Jr., and others of singular status.

By late 1972 the IUC was in operation, with a dozen or so enrollees, and with the volunteer efforts of a number of believing and dedicated people in and out of the Washington, D.C. area who gave of their time and talents as administrators, tutors, and staff members. The establishment of the IUC seemed to have a salutary effect on education. Following the circulation of the IUC Master Plan, plans of various schools of communication, proposals to foundations, educational organizations and institutions, industry and government offices, and communications studies reports began to reflect the IUC's philosophies and techniques. Projects similar to those advocated by the IUC began to emerge. It appeared that the time was ripe for IUC's approach. For example, after the IUC presented its Master Plan and other proposals to the U.S. Office of Education and the Ford Foundation, those two organizations issued the "Newman Report," an innovative document calling for significant change in American education which proposed many of the same processes, methods, and techniques practiced by the IUC.

In 1975 the IUC awarded its first Master's degrees, having become the first innovative graduate institution in the District of Columbia to be granted initial authority to award the degree. The IUC applied for permanent licensure. Following a thorough examination of participants, tutors, structure, philosophy, and impact on the community, the D.C. Board of Education licensing committee found the IUC's standards and accomplishments, although quite different from the usual academic requirements and resources, of superior quality. However, the Committee decided that the IUC did not have "enough money in the bank" and ordered its degree-granting authority to be held in suspension. Participants and graduates testified to the value of the program, not only to themselves, but for also providing heretofore unavailable opportunities for minorities, women and others deprived of equal educational opportunities in the past; private citizens noted the special contributions of the IUC in helping to solve problems in business, government, education, and socio-political situations, including the inner-city; administrators and tutors, including a number of highly prominent persons, signed affidavits volunteering their services without compensation for the ensuing two-year period. The D.C. Board of Education, nevertheless, decided that money was the principal consideration and that the IUC's contributions to individuals, education, and society were irrelevant. The Committee noted, in fact, that the IUC's purposes and practices were considered no differently than if the IUC "were turning out plumbers or hairdressers."

The IUC's experience is a graphic illustration of the thesis in this book that the educational establishment is reluctant to countenance any changes that go beyond appearance alone, changes that actually challenge education's lack of commitment to directly assist the society in which it exists.

# CHAPTER 13

# Involvement

The premise of this book and the tragedy of the last quarter of the twentieth century is that the promise of America's counter-cultural revolution of the 1960s and early 1970s is still waiting to be realized. The problems in communication and education that were on the brink of solution, galvanized and pricked by the innovations of alternative political, social, and economic commitments and practices, are still to be solved. Even a cursory glance at the excerpts from the 1968 report of the President's Task Force on Communications Policy is proof enough; it could have been written yesterday. (It should be noted that although this final chapter was written in 2000, some of the material in it comes from addresses made 35 years ago: "Modern Technology and Educational Involvement," to the Delaware Educational Television Association annual meeting, March 22, 1965, Wilmington, Delaware; "Media and Responsibility," to the University of North Carolina Instructional Television Conference, April 5, 1965, Chapel Hill, North Carolina; and "That Man May Survive," to the Institute on Man and Science, July 1965, Renssellaerville, New York.)

Does this mean, then, given the wasted opportunities of a remarkable period in American history, the counter-culture revolution, that the old adage, the more things change, the more they stay the same, is relentlessly true? The author hopes not. If that were true, then it would be acceptable for all peoples to adopt the "cool" attitude that pervades the people of the under-40 generation of the 1990s weaned and educated in the Reagan me-me-me philosophy: a deliberate withdrawal from their responsibilities as human beings in a world growing ever smaller; from participation in the running of their own communities; and a constant justification for sitting on their fat apathies and letting those with self-serving special political, social, and economic interests run their—and our—immediate and future worlds.

The successes of the Hitlers, Mussolinis, Stalins and other tyrants of the recent past illustrate the ability of an initially small group of ideologues to achieve power when the majority chooses apathy over participation. (In 1999, co-author Michael C. Keith and I tried to warn the American public of the real dangers of such apathy, in a book entitled *Waves of Rancor: Tuning in the Radical Right*. This book, which was chosen by President Bill Clinton for his 1999 summer reading list, shows how the extreme right—in large part emulating and praising Hitler and Nazism—not only is using the media to foment hate and violence, but is planning a Racial Holy War against anyone not a white Aryan Christian or who disagrees with its beliefs. The apathy of most Americans toward the radical right's preparations for genocide could well result in their own families becoming the victims, joining those killed in the Oklahoma City federal building bombing and in numerous other continuing bombings, shootings, and beatings of people of color, Jews, homosexuals and others by those influenced by the rhetoric of extremist groups. The impact of the media and the dangers of media illiteracy and apathy have never been clearer.)

Because of the twentieth-century revolutions in transportation, energy and communications—even considering only IBMs, atomic weapons, and spy satellites —we are not and can no longer be strangers to each other. We are all of us, all over the world, dependent upon each other for mutual survival and growth. Peace and freedom cannot be isolated, as romanticized idealism, from the pragmatic needs of the world. There is no alternative. There is no place to hide.

The key word is involvement. It has become a favorite of psychologists, journalists, commentators, and commencement speakers. We have been living, we are told, in the uninvolved generation, the "me" generation, the generation that runs from responsibility. A classic example of noninvolvement is described in the book *Thirty-eight Witnesses*, the account of the 1960s murder of a woman in Queens, New York, while thirty-eight people watched, not wanting to become involved. Few of us have ever watched someone being murdered, so perhaps we feel we have never had to become involved, except when it required no real commitment and assuaged our consciences, like taking a Thanksgiving basket to the poor, or donating old clothes and toys to the PTA Christmas campaign, or giving to our favorite charity. Becoming involved in getting our local PTA involved in a campaign to change the school system so that disadvantaged children can get the kind of education that would enable them to get their own clothes and toys and food is exceedingly more difficult for us to do.

Getting involved in changing the media and education is analogous. A survey once asked television viewers what they thought of the programs they watched. Eleven times as many said "terrible" as said "great"—about 22% to 2%. Inasmuch as programming is conditioned to audience response, how come this substantial number of citizens has not succeeded in changing the quality of television programming? Could they have limited their involvement to a survey, even though further commitment would have served their own beliefs and interests? How many letters have *you* written thus far this year to sponsors and stations, criticizing programs you don't like, praising programs you do like, and requesting policies and programming you believe are necessary to raise the standards of advertising, entertainment and public service?

It is more and more difficult to escape involvement in some matter of critical importance to society because it is more and more difficult to isolate ourselves from the world in which we live. Many of us try to pretend that we are not affected by the problems that others face. We live in the suburbs or on a comfortable mountain-top or on broad, rolling farmland or in the protective high-rise of a luxury city apartment. We send our children to private schools and don't use public transportation to get to work. What have poverty and pollution and war and miseducation to do with us? The diseases being spread from rotten water or air do not stop at our doorway. The poison from the chemicals put into animals and plants that we eventually eat is not filtered out in our shopping bag. The bigotry that comes from ignorance is not restricted to other communities. Where will *we* run if the bomb is dropped?

Our fear of involvement sometimes not only causes us to forget our interdependence with the rest of humanity, but also to forget that overwhelming numbers of other people do become involved and do make a difference. When tens of thousands participated in sit-ins and marches in the South in the early 1960s in the face of both government and citizen violence, they laid their lives on the line for human rights. When a million people marched on The Capitol and the White House in 1972 (and hundreds of thousands on numerous occasions before that) in protest of America's actions in Southeast Asia, it was a personal as well as group statement in the cause of peace, despite censure, beatings, and jailing. When an unprecedented number of young men and women exiled themselves from their country in the late 1960s and early 1970s rather than participate in or support what they considered an unjust and evil war, it was a remarkable display of personal courage. When college students stood for their individual and collective freedoms of speech and assembly in the face of clubs, tear gas and bullets from police and national guardsmen, they committed themselves to a principle. Whether we agree or disagree with any or all of these groups and individuals' beliefs and goals, their involvement affected us all and in many instances made possible the choices we have now. We are involved, whether we like it or not.

We are no longer stockaded frontier settlements, protecting and developing in our own limited image. Communications, transportation, and energy have bound us irrevocably to all other peoples and groups. Educators should no longer have any doubt, as they prepare to teach their students, that the universality of knowledge and understanding that was always necessary but largely unattainable is now possible, and without it our modern fortress is as vulnerable as if it were the log and mud pioneer stockade of our forebears. We have come to a time of indivisibility of values. We cannot have values unto ourselves except as we make them available to all humankind. We cannot offer quality education in one classroom somewhere and not share it with every other classroom in every part of the city, the state, the region, the nation and, indeed, the world.

In his inaugural address in the 1970s as President of Yale University, Dr. Kingman Brewster said that "the next decade of our trusteeship must cope with three revolutions: the explosion of knowledge; the burgeoning population; and the uncanny development of automated machines and mechanized intelligence." He said that "knowledge is our special concern. We cannot afford the restraint of knowledge for the enhancement of power or prestige of its possessors." And he stated: "If modern technology fulfills its promise, we are on the threshold of a revolution in the storing and in the transmission of knowledge which should match the revolutionary increase in population and in information." Dr. Brewster was not able to apply these concepts to Yale during his tenure there. But then, if he had, it would no longer be Yale! It is illustrative of the problems still facing us that Yale has, nevertheless, made more progress than most institutions with such deeply rotted (the term was meant to be deeply-rooted, but the Freudian typographical error is more explicit) traditions that hold dearly to the education of the past and serve as a bulwark against the education of the future.

The world has changed and is continuing to change. The media are our most powerful means for progress. The Internet has made instant worldwide human communications not only possible, but increasingly available to all. But we let content go unborn, we let it be emasculated, we let it be strangled and destroyed. It is not enough to say that the media may be doing a better job of education than has ever been done before. It is not enough to say that we are receiving, through the media, materials of a quality heretofore unknown to the masses of people. We should be able to say that, through our individual involvement, we are making sure that the media are affecting the humanistic goals of our changing world in a positive, pragmatic way. The media potentials for the improvement of society and education are not someplace in the next decade. They are here now.

President John F. Kennedy expressed our desire and need with a simplicity that provides its own eloquence. He said: "[L]et us think of education as a means of developing our greatest abilities, because in each of us there is a private hope and dream which, fulfilled, can be translated into benefit for everyone and greater strength for our nation."

Education, as it is largely constituted today, has killed many of those hopes and dreams and imprisoned the minds and imaginations of children from kindergarten through graduate school. A new vision for education is not a mirage, but a reality made possible by communications. We cannot go back. Neither can we stand still, because current educational practice, if allowed to continue, may well stifle whatever creativity and independence still remain within us.

A new world—perhaps in every decade ever new—has provided us not only with a challenge, but with responsibility, duty and opportunity. The question is not "Can we become involved?" because we can. The question is, "Will we?" My answer is, "How can we not?" What is yours?

# Index

## About the Author

ROBERT L. HILLIARD is Professor of Media Arts at Emerson College, Boston. His work, writing, and speeches in several federal government media and education positions in Washington D.C. between 1964 and 1980 provide the bases for this book. Among his more than 20 books is *Waves of Rancor: Turning in the Radical Right*, with co-author Michael Keith, which was selected last year for President Clinton's annual reading list.